MICROSOFT®
VISUAL BASIC®
GAME PROGRAMMING
FOR TEENS

SECOND EDITION

JONATHAN S. HARBOUR

THOMSON
™
COURSE TECHNOLOGY

Professional ■ Technical ■ Reference

ISBN-10: 1-59863-390-2
ISBN-13: 978-1-59863-390-0
Library of Congress Catalog Card Number: 2007920205
Printed in the United States of America
08 09 10 11 12 TW 10 9 8 7 6 5 4 3 2 1

Publisher and General Manager, Thomson Course Technology PTR:
Stacy L. Hiquet

Associate Director of Marketing:
Sarah O'Donnell

Manager of Editorial Services:
Heather Talbot

Marketing Manager:
Jordan Casey

Senior Acquisitions Editor:
Emi Smith

Project Editor/Copy Editor:
Cathleen D. Small

Technical Reviewer:
Clayton Crooks

PTR Editorial Services Coordinator:
Erin Johnson

Interior Layout Tech:
ICC Macmillan Inc.

Cover Designer:
Mike Tanamachi

CD-ROM Producer:
Brandon Penticuff

Indexer:
Sharon Shock

Proofreader:
Sandi Wilson

THOMSON
_____ ✳ _____ ™
COURSE TECHNOLOGY
Professional ■ Technical ■ Reference

Thomson Course Technology PTR,
a division of Thomson Learning Inc.
25 Thomson Place
Boston, MA 02210
http://www.courseptr.com

For Kourtney

ACKNOWLEDGMENTS

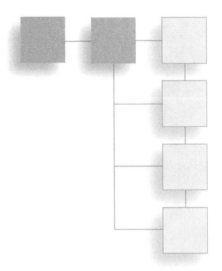

I owe many thanks to everyone at Thomson Course Technology PTR and the freelance editors who do such great work. Thank you, Cathleen Small, for your wonderful editing (as always!). Thank you, Clayton Crooks, for your technical review of the manuscript. I believe you will find this a solid book due to all of their efforts.

Thanks to my wonderful wife, Jennifer, and our rambunctious little ones, for being there. When the first edition was published, we had only two, Jeremiah and Kayleigh, but we've added two more in the meantime, Kaitlyn and Kourtney! Some day when you read this, you guys will know that you have filled every aspect of my life with joy.

I am grateful to Reiner Prokein for allowing me to use the extraordinary artwork from his website, Reiner's Tilesets: www.reinerstileset.de. I would not have even *attempted* to create the RPG in this book without Reiner's incredible artwork. Thank you for providing your high-quality tiles and sprites for beginners to use while learning game programming.

Thanks are due to Robin B. for his excellent level editor, Mappy (www.tilemap. co.uk). In addition, a big thank you goes out to Daniel Sczepansky at Cosmigo for Pro Motion (www.cosmigo.com), the powerful sprite animation software featured in this book.

ABOUT THE AUTHOR

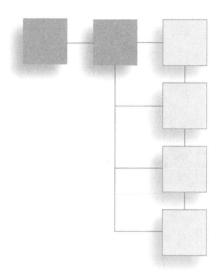

Jonathan S. Harbour is an Associate Professor of Game Development at the University of Advancing Technology in Tempe, Arizona. His current game project, *Starflight: The Lost Colony* (www.starflightgame.com), will be released in late 2007. He lives in Arizona with his wife, Jennifer, and four children: Jeremiah, Kayleigh, Kaitlyn, and Kourtney. He can be reached at www.jharbour.com.

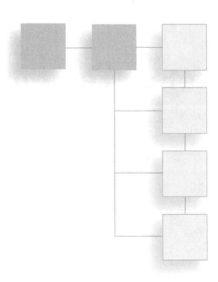

CONTENTS

INTRODUCTION

Greetings and salutations! This book will teach you how to create your own role-playing game (RPG) using Visual Basic .NET and the awesome Managed DirectX library. I will teach you step by step how to construct each part of the game using DirectX components, such as Direct3D, DirectSound, and DirectInput. If you think role-playing games are fun to play, wait until you start working on your very own RPG! Constructing an RPG is far more interesting than playing one because you are in complete control over the RPG world, and you can let your imagination loose to create adventures for others to enjoy. However, it is *not easy!*

Are you intrigued by what you've seen so far of the RPG in this book, regardless of the language? I have ported the source code to Visual C#, so if you prefer C# over Basic, we've got you covered. The C# code is *not* provided on the CD-ROM, however (due to time constraints). You may download the C# version of the code from the Thomson Course PTR website, www.courseptr.com, or from the author's site, www.jharbour.com/?page_id=5.

Visual Basic .NET and Managed DirectX

Before you can get to the point where you are able to design an adventure and build an RPG with Visual Basic .NET, you will need to learn the language and you will have to get up to speed on DirectX. My goal with this book is to teach you just what you need to know in order to make this happen. You will learn what you need to know to construct an RPG. You might choose to use a product such as RPG Maker, rather than writing your own RPG with Visual Basic .NET. That is certainly a good alternative, but wouldn't it be more interesting to have complete control over how the game works? Certainly you can create many complete RPGs of your own design with RPG Maker in the time it takes to build just one RPG from scratch by doing all of your own programming. But in the end, you will have learned a promising skill—game programming! In addition, you will have complete creative control over how the game operates.

Pacing and Experience

This book reads like a hobby book, with no pressure and limited goals, because the primary purpose of this book is to help you to have fun learning about game programming. Typing in long source code listings out of a book is not fun, so I don't ask you to do that in every single chapter in this book. Instead, you will learn to write short programs to demonstrate the major topics in each chapter, and over time you will get the hang of it. There is no memorization required here, because I'm a firm believer that repetition—practice—is the best way to learn, not theory and memorization. The Celtic Crusader game is built from one chapter to the next, with new features and gameplay elements added in each new chapter. You will learn to create this game completely from scratch in a *very* short amount of time.

Prerequisites

The goal of this book is to teach you how to create an RPG. You will benefit from a basic knowledge of Visual Basic in advance, because beyond Chapter 2 I don't spend any time explaining the Visual Basic language. Programming an RPG is a serious challenge without even considering the impact of going over DirectX at the same time. In addition, the small size of this book prevents me from doing anything other than focusing on that primary goal. If you are not at least *somewhat* familiar with Visual Basic .NET, then you may have to study harder than someone who has been learning it for a while already. We'll cover all the basics of the language in Chapter 2, and you can refer back to that chapter anytime you have a question about some of the code we're going over. Celtic Crusader is a large game, and it's *very hard* to program your own RPG! But I'll try to explain it one step at a time.

Which Version of Visual Basic?

This book supports Visual Basic 2005. Although the project files are slightly different, the code is absolutely the same for Visual Basic .NET 2003 as well. If you have 2003, you will still be able to run all of the code in the book, but you will have to create the projects on your own.

I recommend that you download the free version of Visual Basic 2005, called the Express Edition. You can find it at http://msdn2.microsoft.com/en-us/express/aa718406.aspx (or simply Google for "Visual Basic 2005 Express download," since Microsoft's website is an experiment in chaos theory).

I can't confirm at this point whether the source code in this book will compile under Visual Basic 2008 because 2008 hasn't been released yet (at the time of this writing), but I'm sure Microsoft will not wreck backward-compatibility with the new version, and you should be able to use 2008. Obviously, for best results and to keep in sync with the screenshots shown in the book, I recommend Visual Basic 2005 Express.

Managed DirectX

This book uses the Managed DirectX library. What is Managed DirectX, you ask? It is a .NET library that makes it possible for you to write DirectX code in Visual Basic or Visual C#. Normally, to write DirectX SDK code, you have to use Visual C++. You do not need to install the whole DirectX SDK in order to write Managed DirectX code (in fact it's not even included on the CD-ROM because it is not needed). You will need to have at least the DirectX 9.0 runtime installed. If you play a lot of PC games, I'm sure it is already installed on your computer.

Contacting the Author

I maintain a website at www.jharbour.com, which has information about this book that you may find useful (see the section titled "Authored Books" for a link to this book). This site also features an active online forum where you can pose questions and keep up to date with the latest discussions about Visual Basic and Managed DirectX with other programmers. If you have any problems working through this book, stop by the site to chat.

Conventions Used in This Book

The following styles are used in this book to highlight portions of text that are important. You will find Note, Tip, and Caution boxes here and there throughout the book.

Note

This is what a note looks like. Notes are additional information related to the text.

Tip

This is what a tip looks like. Tips give you pointers in the current tutorial being covered.

Caution

This is what a caution looks like. Cautions provide you with guidance and what to do or not to do in a given situation.

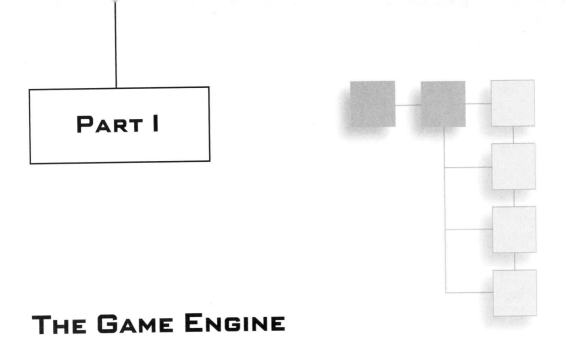

PART I

THE GAME ENGINE

Welcome to the first part of the book, covering the core techniques needed to build a game engine that will be used to create the Celtic Crusader game.

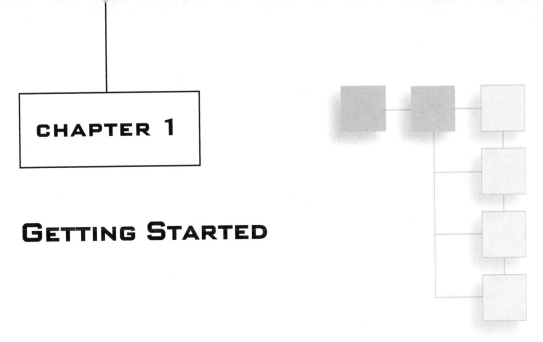

CHAPTER 1

GETTING STARTED

Welcome to the first chapter of *Visual Basic Game Programming for Teens, Second Edition*. This chapter gives you a little overview of what to expect in future chapters and helps set the pace at which we will delve into Visual Basic and Managed DirectX. The goal of the book is to take you step by step through the development of a complete game called Celtic Crusader. First, we'll learn the core techniques needed to build a 2D game engine suitable for the game. Then we'll design the game, create the game world, and begin populating it with monsters, people, places, and so on. But in order to accomplish all of that, we have to start with the basics. Here is a breakdown of the major topics in this chapter:

- What is game programming really all about?

- Creativity, talent, and hard work

- Taking a look at Celtic Crusader

What Is Game Programming Really All About?

Visual Basic .NET is a good tool to use for writing games because the language is easy to learn and it supports DirectX, the industry-standard game development library for Windows. This book treats Visual Basic .NET like a professional game development language, powered by DirectX 9.0, completely ignoring the form-based application development features that make Visual Basic so popular in the business world.

I spent quite a few years doing Visual Basic programming work for a variety of companies, and I enjoy using it, but I must admit that for every line of application code I have ever written, I was dreaming about code I could be writing for any number of games. Now, as a professor at UAT, I *live* this stuff every day, and let me tell you, it's *still* a blast! I've been working with C++ mostly for the last few years, using DirectX, OpenGL, Allegro, and other libraries, so I have a good perspective on where and how Visual Basic .NET fits into things. As a game development tool, it fares just as well as the others when using Managed DirectX.

So what is Managed DirectX? We'll get into DirectX more in the next chapter, but I can at least give you a quick rundown. DirectX is an application programming interface (API) for creating programs that can tap into the hardware of your Windows PC. DirectX gives you full control over the video card, sound system, keyboard, mouse, joysticks, and networking. *Managed* DirectX refers to the version of DirectX made available in the .NET Framework, and it is like a "wrapper" around the DirectX API functions (written in C++), making them conform to and work within the .NET Framework. This makes it possible to write DirectX code using Visual Basic and C#, which otherwise could not use the DirectX API.

The code you learn to write in this book is very similar to the code in the XNA Game Studio—you know, that awesome game development system Microsoft created for making Windows and Xbox 360 games using C# and DirectX! XNA is a neat tool that allows "smaller" independent developers (like yourself, perhaps?) to release games for Xbox 360, and best of all, it's free! The knowledge you will gain with Managed DirectX here is transferable to XNA Game Studio. The C# language is quite different from Visual Basic, but the .NET code all looks very similar. Still, if you want to get into XNA after finishing with this book, I advise you to read a beginner's book on C# programming first so you'll be able to use either language. (The more languages you know as a game programmer, the better!)

However, you have to keep something in mind: This is a small book, and our goal is to create a role-playing game (RPG) within these pages. This isn't a DirectX programming book, per se. If you feel that you are completely lost within the next few chapters, my advice is to pick up a Visual Basic primer to get up to speed, and then return to this book. Nothing in here is confusing, but a lot of information is presented at a fast pace, so you don't want to get left behind. If you are totally new to Visual Basic, then the next chapter will at least give you an overview of the language, with enough information to help you to understand the Celtic Crusader game.

Get Your Feet Wet First, Ask Questions Later

For every great game idea that someone has, a thousand more ideas are waiting to be thought up by a creative person. One thing I want you to do while reading this book is learn to think outside the box. I realize that is a cliché that you have heard many times, but it is an important concept because it helps you visualize the point very clearly. Most people, and most programmers for that matter, are unable to think beyond the experience of their collected memories. A very rare person is able to think about something absolutely, completely foreign, the likes of which has never been thought of before. The phrase "thinking outside the box" can mean many things, depending on the context, but when I'm talking about writing a game, I mean you should think of ideas that are *above and beyond* what has already been done. The greatest game ideas have *not* all been taken already!

For every *Doom* there are a dozen more trend-setting game ideas waiting to be invented. Don't be discouraged, believing that the best ideas have been discovered already. That is what many gamers believed before real-time strategy games *took over* the game industry a few years ago. What's the next great game genre? It hasn't been *invented* yet. That is your job!

Tip

Before you can let your creativity flow, you need a foundation in the basics of programming, so you aren't always bogged down, not knowing how to make your imagination come to life on the screen.

Do you really think John Carmack, John Romero, and Adrian Carmack based *Doom* on their memories of *Pac-Man* back in 1993? It's entirely possible that *Doom* is older than you are (or at least older than you were before you could play games). Many of the current generation don't understand what all the hoopla over *Doom* is about because games were so different back then. In 1993, I was playing Sid Meier's *Civilization* on my PC, *Super Mario World* on my Super NES (which you might recognize as *Super Mario Advance 2* on the GBA, which is *already* obsolete), and *Dragon Crystal* on my Game Gear. The fact is, most people did *not* play games back then, unlike today, when almost everyone *does* play games! A game like *Doom* was unbelievable at the time, which is why people are still sharing fond memories about it today; that is why *Doom 3* was created, and that is why David Kushner wrote the book *Masters of Doom*. *Doom* was so dramatically different from all the other games at the time that a whole new genre was created: the first-person shooter (FPS). FPS games dominate the world of games today, unlike any other genre.

Do you want to create a game like *Doom* using Visual Basic .NET and Managed DirectX? That goal is *absolutely* possible. The Visual Basic compiler creates intermediate language code that looks exactly the same regardless of whether you're using VB or C#, and then that "IL" code is compiled to an object file and linked, manifested, and so on until out comes an executable file. That compiled Visual Basic game code *could* deliver a gaming experience like *Doom*. Why stop there? How about *Quake*? The first two *Quake* games were not extremely advanced beyond *Doom*. Oh, sure, they were fully 3D, but it would be no problem whatsoever for your modern 3D video card to handle it without breaking a sweat *without* any optimization. Today, we need to optimize our 3D games because of the high-quality graphics they can render. But you could *brute force* your way through a game like *Quake* without any optimization because modern video cards are so powerful. However, there's no reason why you could not just build a game engine using Managed DirectX and use it to create a game like *World of Warcraft.*

I'm serious. You could *definitely* create a smaller, less ambitious version of *WoW* using Visual Basic and Managed DirectX. The graphics quality would be comparable if you had the artwork and 3D models available. The 3D game world (the terrain, buildings, water, sky, and so on) could be rendered. The most challenging aspect of the game is the server, and in the case of *WoW*, there is not a single server, or even a bunch of servers; there are *racks* and *racks* chock full of server clusters at several geographical locations around the *world*. So, while it is technically feasible to play *WoW* with your friend from Australia, the odds are that bandwidth would be a challenge. Depending on where you live, *WoW* lists the servers in your region, and those servers are probably not available to players in other regions. The reasoning has to do with latency, or lag, due to the number of jumps required to send a packet of data around the world. In a game like *WoW*, you need a fast Internet connection with very few latency problems in order for the gaming experience to be realistic.

I'm sure you've experienced the "slideshow effect," where the server becomes overburdened and cannot keep up, so players do not receive server updates for several seconds until the server can catch up. This primarily happens when a number of players are connecting with high latency, causing the connections to lag. In sufficient numbers this causes the game to stutter or go into "slideshow mode." (The phrase comes from the frequent exclamation by gamers to the effect of, "Hey, look at the PowerPoint presentation filled with screenshots of *WoW!*") Although Blizzard makes millions of dollars in player fees every month, the company *spends* millions on Internet bandwidth to make the game even possible.

So, what kind of hardware do you need to play a game built using Visual Basic and Managed DirectX? Basically, we're talking about the same kind of gaming hardware needed to play just about any game currently on store shelves. Consider the typical NHRA dragster. It can make one pass down the quarter mile before the engine needs to be rebuilt. It can do it in about *four seconds,* but only once. On the other hand, your average family sedan or minivan will take about 20 seconds to reach the 1,320-foot mark. But what about ease of use, multipurpose functionality, fuel mileage, and so on? You can't exactly strap a child's car seat to a dragster to go to a doctor's appointment. Although you could potentially get there a lot faster, the darned car can barely turn left or right, let alone navigate in traffic. So, what if we use a more realistic racecar as an example—*NASCAR.* Here, we have a little more versatility, and the *power potential* is still stratospheric. But there are no headlights, taillights, or any modern conveniences such as air conditioning or *mufflers.* Do you know how loud a car sounds without mufflers? You don't even need a racing engine to deafen yourself. At any rate, a typical *NASCAR* vehicle is insanely fast, but very inflexible and error-prone, unable to withstand the abuses of stop-and-go city traffic.

The same might be said of C++; it is incredibly fast and powerful, but very fragile. I write a lot of C++ code. I have about 15 years of experience with the language. And even after all that, I still get stuck for hours at a time trying to figure out a syntax error in my C++ programs. This happens all the time! It's part of the understanding one must have with this language—show it the proper respect, understand its power, and try not to get frustrated. Little by little you make progress, wrapping the lowest-level features of a game in a layer of protective classes, then another layer, and so on until you have a well-behaved program that is error free. *Windows* itself—yes, the operating system—was written in C++.

Here's one that will blow your mind: Visual Basic .NET was written in C++. Weird, isn't it? I'm talking about the compiler, the editor, and so on. I've written about another game programming tool for beginners called *DarkBASIC Professional*, developed by The Game Creators (www.thegamecreators.com), and *this tool* (along with its DirectX game engine) was also created in C++.

As if that is not enough, I have another example that will wreak havoc on whatever sensibilities you still have. It's *Twilight Zone* time. *Visual C++* was written in C++. . . .

Ah, back to the land of sanity, I see? This self-sustaining oddity sometimes reminds me of an M.C. Escher painting. It's almost as if Escher could see into the future, because so much of his work looks like 3D computer graphics. Visit his online gallery at www.mcescher.com when you need a break from writing code.

I believe you can create a *Quake III*–style game engine using Visual Basic with Managed DirectX with a modern video card, and that was not possible with the previous version of Visual Basic, so I guess that can be called progress. But writing a high-quality first-person shooter is about a lot more than just cranking out polygons. You have to write the code to load a BSP level, to load a MD2-animated 3D model file, to add dynamic lighting to the scene, to load and play sound effects and music, and that's just the technical side. You also have to consider the game's *design*, because a game that just looks cool is not all that great without a good story, and that's where the designer comes in. *Quake II* didn't have much of a design behind it, and actually it seems to me that id Software sort of tacked on the story after the game was nearly finished. But we're talking about id Software here, not "*<insert your name>* Game Studio."

Let Your Creativity Fly

The important thing to realize, though, is that thinking outside the box and coming up with something unprecedented is just the first step toward creating a new game. You must have the technical know-how to pull it off. In the field of video games, that means you must be a skilled programmer. If you are just getting started, then this book is perfect because Visual Basic allows you to practice some of your game ideas without getting too bogged down with a difficult programming language (such as C++). These languages have a tendency to suck away all of your time and leave your mind numb and unable to think creatively. Writing solid code has a tendency to do that to a person, which is why it is a huge help when you start with a not-too-difficult language, such as Visual Basic.

Tip

You don't need to be a C++ programmer to write a killer game! All it takes is good artwork, a good story, and well-written code. You don't need to write *fancy* code with complex algorithms, you simply must follow through and *complete the game*. That is really what it's all about.

Creativity, Talent, and Hard Work

I have seen some super high-quality games written with DarkBASIC. After you have finished with this book, I encourage you to consider *DarkBASIC Pro Game Programming, Second Edition* (Thomson Course Technology PTR, 2006). Once you have mastered the BASIC language and written a few games with it, maybe then you will have some experience with which to support a study of C++. I've ported some games from Visual Basic to C++/DirectX, and then to DarkBASIC. (Isn't that weird?) In fact, the tile scroller engine developed in this book was featured in that DarkBASIC book; see Chapter 15, "2D Game Worlds: Level Editing and Tile-Based Scrolling." And for the C++ code, see Chapter 11, "Tile-Based Scrolling Backgrounds" in *Beginning Game Programming, Second Edition* (Thomson Course Technology PTR, 2006). Source code is *very similar* among languages when you understand the *concepts* behind it. The tile-based scrolling code you'll learn to create in this book formed the foundation of several games created in other languages.

What you want to strive for as a budding game programmer is an understanding of the *concepts*, and the best way to do that is to write games using your favorite language. Believe it or not, I got started in programming with Microsoft BASIC, which came with most of the old computers at the dawn of the PC industry (on such systems as Apple II, Commodore PET, and IBM PC).

I have to say that technical programming language skills are about equal in importance to your creativity. I've known some very talented programmers who don't have an ounce of creativity in their bones, so they are not able to do anything unique and interesting without someone else giving them the ideas first. It's okay to be a person like that—really, really good at programming but not very creative—because you can always borrow ideas from other games and things like movies, and leave the ideas to a game designer or another person who needs your technical skills. It doesn't matter if you have the technical or creative bent, because you really need to learn everything you can.

The Sky Is the Limit

Did you know that you can write your own games for the Game Boy Advance? I'm talking about the GBA, the GBA SP, *and* the DS. Imagine seeing your own games running on the GBA. Would that be the coolest thing ever, or what? That's something you definitely *can* do once you have learned enough and mastered a few programming languages, as I have suggested in the previous few paragraphs. All console programming, such as that for the GBA, is done in C++. For more information on GBA programming, you can download my free e-book, *Programming the Game Boy Advance*, from my website at www.jharbour.com. This e-book is intermediate to advanced, assuming that you already know how to program in C++.

Did you know that you can also write your own games for the Xbox? Microsoft provides XNA Game Studio for free, and it uses Visual C# 2005 Express as the compiler. For a small annual fee, you can upload your XNA programs to a special "developer's" location on Xbox Live Arcade, and then download the game to your Xbox 360 and see *your own code* running on a real 360.

You don't need to limit your creative juices to just what you *think* is possible. In fact, don't limit yourself at all, and don't assume that you *can't* do anything, even if you have tried and failed. If you can imagine something, no matter how out of this world it might seem, then it's possible to build it. That is what human imagination is all about. What Jules Verne imagined back in the late 1890s— ideas that were so crazy that everyone laughed at them—suddenly became a reality fewer than 70 years later. Imagine that—people riding around in horse carriages, on dirt or cobblestone roads, and some crazy writer suggests that people will walk on the moon. What a lunatic, right? If you lived in 1890, you probably would have thought he was crazy! It's easy for us to make fun of people when we later know better (something called *hindsight*), just as it is easy to criticize a small flaw in a complex automobile or computer. (It's *easy* to critique; it's *hard* to create. Why do you think there are so many weblogs? Non-creative people tend to criticize what they are not able to create on their own.)

Jules Verne described the rocket ship that would blast off the Earth with an explosion of mighty power that would lift the huge rocket off the ground and propel the men into space so they could land on the moon. Doesn't that sound familiar? If you have ever watched a video of the Apollo 11 mission, it is uncanny how Jules Verne described the launch 70 years before that time. Even today, boosters are launched into orbit using the same basic technology, although the rockets are a lot more powerful and more efficient than they were during the Apollo program (so much so that private companies are springing up with plans to usher in space tourism in the near future).

Learn the Trade

The most technically skilled programmers are often those who copy the most creatively talented people in the world. From that perspective, people are still copying the work of John Carmack (of id Software), who continues to crank out unbelievable game engines. The vast majority of game developers are trying to keep up or succumb to Carmack's genius and end up paying to use his latest game engine. Carmack is one of the few who possesses both unmatched technical skill and incredible creative talent. Although he was born with the talent, he learned the technical skill purely from hard work, putting in an unbelievable number of hours at his keyboard, experimenting, tweaking, and trying new things, day after day, month after month, year after year. . . and he is still going at it.

If your whole purpose is just to have some fun while learning how to write your own game, and you have no real desire to become a master of it, that is perfectly okay! I am one of those people. I just love writing games for the enjoyment of myself and others, and I don't really care whether my latest game is any good. If you are approaching game development from the standpoint of a hobby, the whole point is to have fun. If you want to get serious, attend a game-development college, and then get a job as a professional game developer, you probably take the subject a little more seriously. There are benefits to just treating this subject as a hobby: no deadlines or pressure, and the freedom to do whatever you want. Have you always wanted to create your very own role-playing game (or another type of game), and you've decided to learn how to do it on your own? That's great! In fact, that is largely the direction this book takes. If your goal is to do this for a living, then I wish you the very best; this book may be your first stepping stone on the path toward that dream.

When I suggest you think outside the box, therefore, I'm advising that you try not to succumb to the "been there, done that" mentality of creating yet another mod (using a game engine like *Battlefield 1942*), or another *Tetris* clone, or another version of *Breakout*. These terrific learning experiences are very common because these latter two types of games are easy to make and demonstrate important concepts in 2D game programming. A game engine mod, on the other hand, is an entirely different issue; most mods require little or no programming.

They are merely conversions with new 3D models and game levels to match a new theme (as is the case with *Desert Combat* (a *Battlefield 1942* mod) and *Counter-Strike* (a *Half-Life* mod). Try to come up with some completely original game ideas and develop them; no matter how simple a game concept is, if it's a brand-new idea, then it will probably be interesting! Of course, the fun factor is entirely up to you, the game's designer and programmer.

Note

For a good example of an indie game developed by a team of volunteers, check out *Starflight: The Lost Colony* at www.starflightgame.com.

Taking a Look at Celtic Crusader

This book uses a single game project to teach the subject and give an overall picture of how the topics in each chapter are put to use in a real game. The alternatives are to forego a sample game altogether or to just use simple mini games (which are not much more than graphics demos, really) in each chapter to explain how a new subject you have learned can be put to use. Small demos and mini games provide good examples of individual subjects, but an entire game will give you a grasp of the big picture. This game is developed entirely in 2D, using Direct3D surfaces and textures. Figure 1.1 shows the game as it will look when you are finished with it in this book's last chapter.

Building a Role-Playing Game

I chose to create a complete RPG for this book because no other subject digs deeper into the depths of game programming than a real RPG with all of the functionality you expect from this genre. Since I come from the old school of gaming, I am still fond of classics such as *Ultima VII: The Black Gate*. My second choice was a game based on *Star Trek*, but there are the obvious copyright problems when using a TV show as the basis for a game. If you really love some subject such as *Star Trek*, then I encourage you to go ahead and write a game about that subject and then give it away to your friends. The learning experience is enhanced when you are working on a game about a subject that you really enjoy and that has a lot of texture, with a huge background story surrounding it.

The RPG you create as an overall learning experience is called Celtic Crusader and takes place in the ancient land of mythical England. While the ancient Celtic civilization has a lot of history and myth, the background story is not very

Figure 1.1
Celtic Crusader is a game you create from scratch in this book.

important here. The goal is to write a complete game while learning important new skills with each new chapter.

The Story

The premise of the story is basically this: Norwegian Vikings have been invading England and Ireland for centuries, conquering and then being driven off in rebellions. The story in Celtic Crusader does not include just fantasy creatures as you might find in some RPGs, such as vampires, skeletons (see Figure 1.2), werewolves, giant snakes, giant spiders, dragons (see Figure 1.3), and the like.

Note

The images shown here for the Celtic Crusader game were created by Reiner Prokein, who makes them freely available to hobby game programmers with no strings attached. You may browse Reiner's sprites and tiles at www.reinerstileset.de.

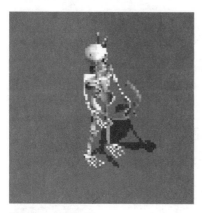

Figure 1.2
A skeleton archer.

Figure 1.3
A dragon.

While fantasy characters are a lot of fun to kill in most RPGs, and Celtic Crusader has a lot of creatures to fight (such as the skeleton knight shown in Figure 1.4), this game also features some human characters that your player will encounter.

Good Guys versus Bad Guys

I am taking this game in a slightly different direction and following a real-world scenario, as you might find in the *Ultima* and *Legend of Zelda* series. There are a lot of human characters in Celtic Crusader (as you learn in the next few chapters), and the player can choose from several character classes. See Figures 1.5 and 1.6.

Figure 1.4
A skeleton knight.

Figure 1.5
A Viking knight.

Figure 1.6
A Viking archer.

Figure 1.7
This white mage is a good NPC (we hope!).

Figure 1.8
This mighty warrior is a good NPC.

Good *non-player characters (NPCs)* also help the player (or whom the player must help) to successfully complete the game's primary quest or subquests. See Figures 1.7 and 1.8.

Adventure Game or Dungeon Hack?

Two types of classic RPGs exist in my opinion: adventure games and dungeon hacks. The typical dungeon hack is made up of a town where you can equip your character (purchase weapons, armor, and so on) using the treasure you find in the dungeon, which is usually made up of many levels and driving deep into the Earth, and is often portrayed as a gold mine that became infested with evil creatures.

While you are killing bad guys, your experience is going up and you are finding gold. As your experience goes up, your skills go up as well, and this is reflected by your character's level. A level-20 warrior, for instance, can dispatch level-5 skeleton archers with the back of his hand, so to speak, while a level-18 fire dragon poses a serious threat! This type of game is typically very simple in concept, lacking any serious storyline or plot—hence the term *dungeon hack*. *Diablo* and *Dungeon Siege* epitomize this type of game, and this is the goal for Celtic Crusader.

The other type of RPG, the adventure game, usually takes place on the surface rather than in a deep mine and involves an often deep storyline with multiple subquests to challenge the player. This game allows the player's character to gain experience, weapons, and special items, such as armor, amulets, magic rings, and so on. Although the main quest of an adventure RPG might be very, very difficult, the subquests allow the player's character to reach a level sufficient to beat the game's main quest. The subquests offer plenty of opportunity for a creative game designer to insert fascinating stories and interactions with NPCs like the one in Figure 1.9. *Ultima VII* is a good example of this type of game.

I must admit, the latter is my choice type of RPG between the two, because in an adventure RPG, you can create multiple towns across the countryside and allow the player to explore a vast world. The dungeon hack is a lot of fun, I'll admit, and both types of RPG have merit. I've chosen the dungeon hack type of game for the example version of Celtic Crusader, but the game world can easily accommodate a large adventure game.

Figure 1.9
An interesting female NPC who is strangely lacking any armor or weapons. Perhaps an unadorned spellcaster?

Describing the Player's Character

The most robust RPGs usually allow the player to create a custom character to play, although in recent years this has taken a backseat to hack-and-slash games like *Baldur's Gate* (which is okay because it introduces another type of gamer to the great fun had with an RPG and gives the type of person who would not normally play an RPG a glimpse into a bigger world). You can usually choose from five character types:

- Warrior class

- Paladin class

■ Thief class

■ Scout class

■ Wizard class

This is just a glimpse at a larger game that you have an opportunity to create in this book! Of course, you can tweak and modify the game to suit your own imagination, and you will have the technical know-how after reading this book to do just that. We'll be going over the game engine for Celtic Crusader step by step and we will develop the game in each new chapter, but the complete game with quests and goals is up to you!

Summary

This chapter introduced you to the main concepts you'll be learning about in the rest of the book from a high-level point of view. In the upcoming chapters, you will learn how to take the first step toward writing games with Visual Basic by creating your first Visual Basic .NET project and delving into the Managed DirectX library. This chapter was short on details but long on ideas, presenting a glimpse of the Celtic Crusader game, an RPG that you create while following along with this book. The next two chapters will get you going with Visual Basic and DirectX very quickly.

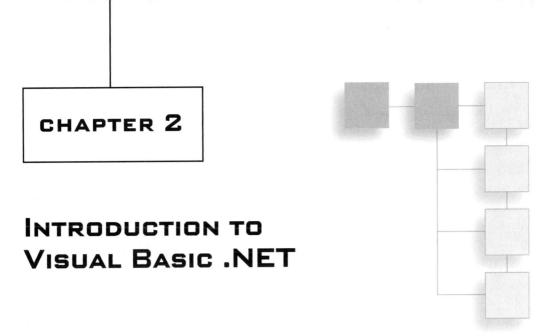

CHAPTER 2

INTRODUCTION TO VISUAL BASIC .NET

This chapter is a basic overview of Visual Basic .NET, a little theory here, a little source code there, and a lot of new stuff throughout. Visual Basic .NET is an exciting language, and it's absolutely a blast to use! As I'm sure you will find out soon enough, the learning curve for Visual Basic is really short. You'll be up to speed and able to write your own programs from scratch in no time. I'll help you through the tough spots and introduce you to key topics and those parts of the language that you need to get things done. The rest is up to you! Software development is all about creativity, so put on your creative hat and stretch your fingers. Here's what we're doing:

- What is Visual Basic .NET?
- Writing your first Visual Basic .NET program
- Variables of all types
- Branching/conditional statements
- Subroutines and functions
- Mathematical operators
- Relational operators
- Looping statements
- Arrays
- Structures
- Object-oriented programming

What Is Visual Basic?

Visual Basic is a graphical programming language and the top of the class in Rapid Application Development (RAD) tools for Windows. In fact, Visual Basic is the most popular Windows development tool in the world, with millions of users. The key to the success of Visual Basic is a fantastic and easy-to-learn language that powers a drag-and-drop visual user interface design tool. Visual Basic .NET shares this Windows Form engine with other .NET languages, so all of the source code that you write with Visual Basic .NET is compatible with Visual C# and Visual C++. But what is a user interface? The Graphical User Interface, or GUI as it has come to be known, is a visual method of using software, primarily with a mouse. In the old days of UNIX and MS-DOS, computer users were forced to memorize strange commands and had to type them into a command-line interface. Type a command, hit Enter, and the computer spews out some information (or more commonly, it would beep with a rude error message).

Windows replaced MS-DOS, and along with it came even more complexity. Windows is not an easy operating system to program. Believe it or not, in the old days, Windows programmers had to use Microsoft C, which ran under MS-DOS! Talk about ironic. Not only was Windows difficult to program, the development tool didn't even run under Windows. As you can imagine, those were not the good old days. Most veteran Windows programmers have no fondness for the way things used to be. Visual Basic was really written to solve the problem and make Windows programming easier. The ability to drag controls onto a form and mold the controls to your liking using simple properties is a trademark feature of Visual Basic.

The .NET Framework

There are cases in which the complexity of software is just too much for a single person to grasp. System maintenance is becoming more important as software continues to evolve. Businesses depend on software for day-to-day work. The days of custom-building monumental software systems are coming to an end, because such systems are impossible to maintain. The .NET Framework brings several languages and design tools together into a seamless whole so that people can focus on gathering the requirements for a system, building prototypes, and then completing their applications. The .NET Framework makes it possible to write huge Windows programs without needing a Windows API reference book handy. That is, essentially, the layman's definition of .NET!

Definition

The *.NET Framework* is the core architecture behind Visual Basic .NET and the other .NET languages, providing common runtime, compatible code libraries, a fully integrated Windows API library, along with ASP.NET and ADO.NET.

Microsoft, as well as many other software companies, has tried in earnest to come up with a standard for code reuse, such as the Component Object Model (COM). Microsoft's COM has allowed developers to build custom user-interface controls and code component libraries that are reusable across many languages (such as Microsoft Visual Basic and Visual C++, and Borland Delphi and C++Builder, all of which support COM). The ability to write source code using Visual Basic, and then reuse that same code in Borland Delphi, is significant! These two languages are utterly alien to each other! Visual Basic was originally based on the BASIC language, while Delphi was based on Pascal. Numerous other companies support COM as well, and this has only benefited their customers.

Windows Messages and Event Procedures

The "engine" that works behind the scenes in a VB.NET program interprets the Windows messaging system, which is how Windows tells your program when something happens to the user interface. The controls are part of the form and therefore have access to all of the messages that the operating system sends the program. For example, when you click a button on a form, Windows sends your program a special message that includes a header pointing to the form and the control that triggered the message. Visual Basic receives this special message from the operating system and routes it to the form containing the specific button that was clicked.

What happens at this point? The form engine, which is part of the VB.NET runtime library (and also closely tied to the .NET Framework), checks to see whether you have created a Click event for that button. If so, the event is called; otherwise, the message is discarded. From that point, it is up to you (the programmer) to decide what happens inside that event.

As you can imagine, there are thousands of different messages streaming through the Windows operating system, which are being routed to operating system processes and running applications. Visual Basic .NET handles all the details for you by breaking down the complexity into a number of events that are called automatically in your program.

Writing Your First Visual Basic .NET Program

If you are new to Visual Basic, then we'll get started right away by writing a simple program. If you're already familiar with the language, you may skip ahead.

VB uses the concept of a "solution" to "solve programming problems." Most programs are written, after all, to process data in one way or another, and that data may not be in a suitable format that is useful. Visual Studio .NET treats a project workspace as a solution, and the workspace (or solution) file even has an extension of .sln.

Visual Studio .NET solutions can become quite complex. Not only can you have multiple Visual Basic projects in the solution, you can have multiple languages as part of the solution. Isn't that amazing? In previous versions of Visual Studio, it was possible to create ActiveX components and share them between languages— in essence, these were Component Object Model (COM) objects, which is what Visual Studio 6.0 was based upon. That is no longer an issue with Visual Studio .NET. While you can still use COM and ActiveX, these technologies are now obsolete because it is possible to use .NET languages interchangeably.

Definition

Components are pieces of programs that are written in such a way that they can be used by more than one program. This is called "code reuse" and it is a very important concept that is at the core of Microsoft's .NET strategy.

Greetings to the World

Now it's time to get down to business. Are you tired of theory already? I'm not! This stuff is fun. But theory means nothing without practice. I've watched a lot of Jackie Chan movies, but I still don't know anything about Kung Fu. If you want to master something you have got to practice and start with the basics.

Start Visual Studio .NET by selecting Start, Programs, Microsoft Visual Studio .NET, and then select the Microsoft Visual Studio .NET program from the list that pops up. The default Start Page should be the first thing that is displayed when Visual Studio .NET starts running. The Start Page shows all of the recent solutions that you have worked on (or it could be blank if this is the first time you have used it). There is a button on the Start Page called New Project that you will click in order to start a new project. If, for some reason, the Start Page does not show up by default when you run Visual Studio .NET, just click the File menu at the top of the screen and select New, Project (as shown in Figure 2.1).

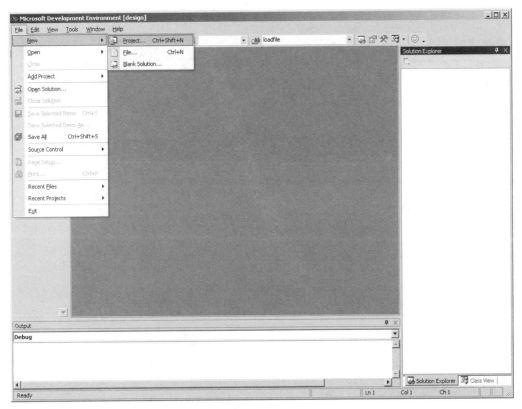

Figure 2.1
Creating a new project with Visual Basic .NET.

Using either method, the New Project dialog should appear. See Figure 2.2.

Let's dissect this New Project dialog before going any further, because it is sort of complicated. On the left side of the dialog is a list of Project Types (shown in Figure 2.3), which includes the following:

- Visual Basic Projects

- Visual C# Projects

- Visual C++ Projects

- Setup and Deployment Projects

- Other Projects

- Visual Studio Solutions

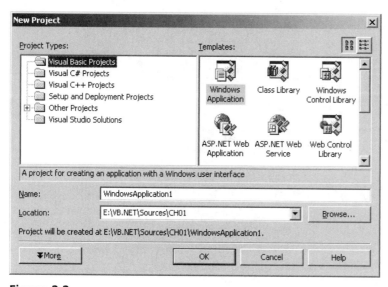

Figure 2.2
The New Project dialog.

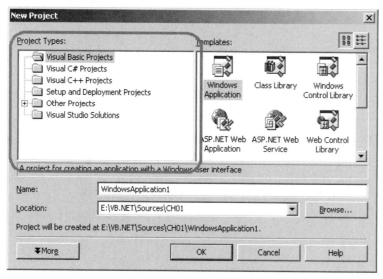

Figure 2.3
The Project Types available in the New Project dialog.

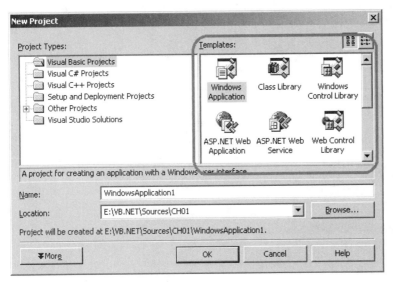

Figure 2.4
The Templates available in the New Project dialog.

The first option in the list, Visual Basic Projects, should be selected by default. On the right side of the dialog is the list of Templates for each project type (see Figure 2.4).

You will notice that each language has its own set of icons for these templates, to make it easier to differentiate between them (usually when you have a large solution with multiple languages). Here is the list of templates for Visual Basic:

- Windows Application

- Class Library

- Windows Control Library

- ASP.NET Web Application

- ASP.NET Web Service

- Web Control Library

- Console Application

- Windows Service

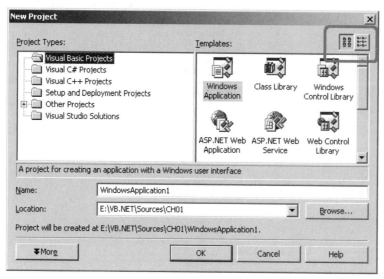

Figure 2.5
The Large Icons and Small Icons buttons.

- Empty Project

- Empty Web Project

- New Project in Existing Folder

If you look at the top-right corner of the New Project dialog, you should see two small buttons that affect the layout of the items in the template list (shown in Figure 2.5).

You can switch between Large Icons and Small Icons by pressing either of these two buttons. The Small Icons view is sometimes more convenient because you can see more items in the list than you can when large icons are displayed. Regardless of the view you settle on, for this program you will want to select Console Application. See Figure 2.6.

Did you notice how the project name changed when you selected the Console Application template? The name was changed to ConsoleApplication1. Click on the Name field now and change the name of the program to Greeting, as shown in Figure 2.7.

The next thing that you might want to do is select where the new project files will be stored on your hard drive. Select the folder by typing it into the Location field (as shown in Figure 2.8) or locate an existing folder using the Browse button.

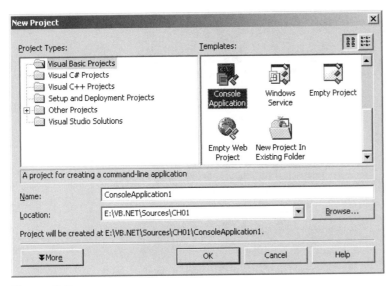

Figure 2.6
The Console Application project type.

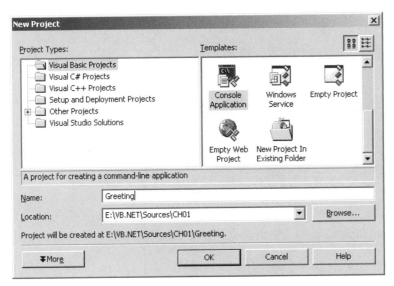

Figure 2.7
Changing the name of the new program.

Pay no attention to the folder name in the screenshot, because that is just the location where I stored the project. You can store the project anywhere you like, although it makes sense to organize your projects under a main folder. In this case, I stored my projects in E:\VB.NET\Sources. You will likely see this path in later sample programs as well.

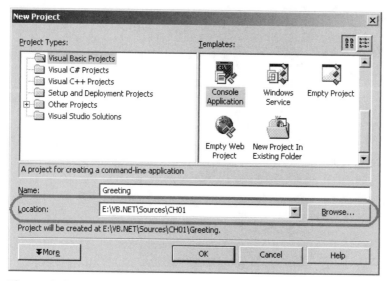

Figure 2.8
Setting the target folder for the project.

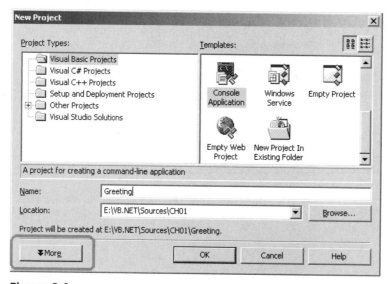

Figure 2.9
The More button provides additional options in the New Project dialog.

You are now ready to create the new project by pressing the OK button. But first, take a look at the More button at the bottom-left corner of the dialog (see Figure 2.9).

When you press the More button, the dialog grows to display a hidden field and checkbox, as shown in Figure 2.10.

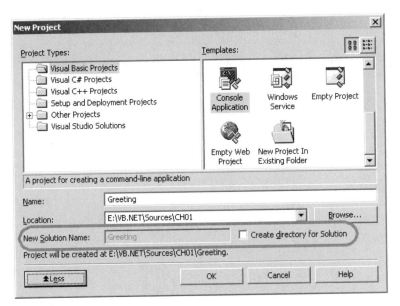

Figure 2.10
Additional options for the project.

Since this is an option that is not often used, it can be hidden away with the More/Less button. Visual Studio .NET is replete with features like this, where you can show or hide relevant information to suit your tastes. In this case, you can have Visual Studio create a new folder for you when the project is created.

Code Editor Window

When you click OK to close the New Project dialog, Visual Studio creates a new solution and a new project for you, as shown in Figure 2.11.

Because this is a console application, there's no form or controls available in this program. What this means is that when you compile the program, you can actually run it from a Command Prompt. When you run the program from within Visual Studio, a new Command Prompt window automatically appears.

Now let's add some code to make this program actually do something useful. This program needs to display a line of text and then wait for the user to press Enter to continue. Add the following two lines of code inside Sub Main:

```
Console.WriteLine("Welcome to Visual Basic .NET!")
Console.ReadLine()
```

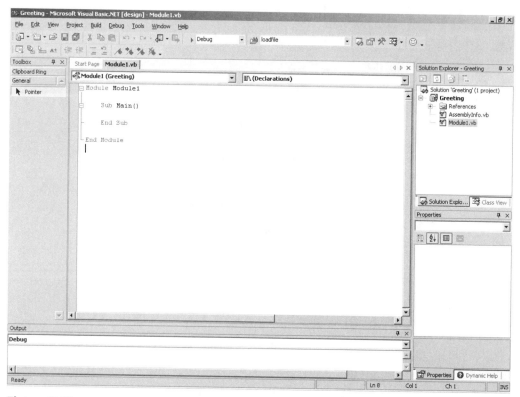

Figure 2.11
The new Console Application project is ready for your source code.

It should be pretty obvious that the first line displays the message "Welcome to Visual Basic .NET!", but what about the second line? ReadLine is a function that reads a line of characters from the keyboard and is ended with the Enter key.

Hint

You can start a program running in Visual Basic .NET by pressing the F5 key.

So this basically means that you can type in a line of characters, and ReadLine will grab them out of the console. You can actually see what was typed in because ReadLine returns the characters as a string. In order to receive the string, you need to copy the value returned by ReadLine into a string variable.

Variables must be declared before they are used in Visual Basic .NET. To declare a new variable, you must use the Dim keyword, which is short for "dimension," referring to the process of reserving memory for the new variable. The actual process no longer even remotely resembles the BASIC language, on which Visual Basic was originally based, but Dim has been around for so long now that it would not be a Visual Basic program without it. As I mentioned a moment ago, ReadLine returns a string. So this program needs a string variable. Declare the variable like this:

```
Dim name As String
```

How about that? You can create any variable you need using Dim. Here is the rest of the source code for the Greeting program. Type the lines in bold between the two existing lines of the program.

```
Console.WriteLine("Welcome to Visual Basic .NET!")
Console.Write("Please type your name: ")
Dim name As String
name = Console.ReadLine()
Console.WriteLine("Hello, {0}!", name)
Console.WriteLine()
Console.WriteLine("Press Enter to quit...")
Console.ReadLine()
```

After you have made the changes to the source code, the program should look like Figure 2.12. (The new lines have been highlighted in the code editor window.)

After you type in the new code, save the project by clicking File, Save All. You can also save the project by clicking the Save All icon on the toolbar. After saving the project, go ahead and run the program by pressing F5. Figure 2.13 shows the output of the Greeting program.

There is one line of this program that displays the characters typed into the console (the user's name), and it looks kind of funny:

```
Console.WriteLine("Hello, {0}!", name)
```

It's probably obvious to you what this line of code does from looking at the output, but how does it work? The curly braces surround a number that refers to the variable that follows. This is a feature of the WriteLine subroutine. WriteLine allows you to display the contents of variables in whatever order you want. Just separate each variable by a comma and then refer to them as {0}, {1}, {2}, and so on. I'll cover WriteLine in more detail later, so don't worry if you don't understand it at this point.

Congratulations, you have successfully run your first Visual Basic .NET program! This program might be simple, but it helped to show you some key features of the

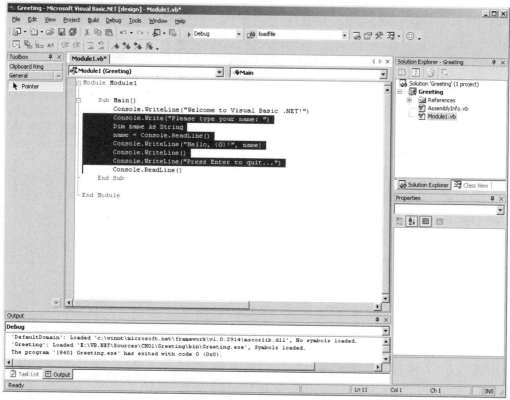

Figure 2.12
The new Greeting program in the Visual Basic .NET editor.

language and gave you some experience working with the Visual Basic editor. You can now close the Greeting program by selecting File, Close Solution.

Variables of All Types

Here's a simple question: What is a variable? A variable is something that can change, with the connotation that it can change unexpectedly. For example, weather forecasters often speak of variable winds and variable temperatures— meaning that the wind and temperature could change without warning. In the context of computers, however, variables only change when told and cannot do anything on their own.

In the old days when programmers used machine language and assembly language, they would create variables by grabbing a chunk of memory and then storing a number in the newly acquired spot. This was called *memory allocation*,

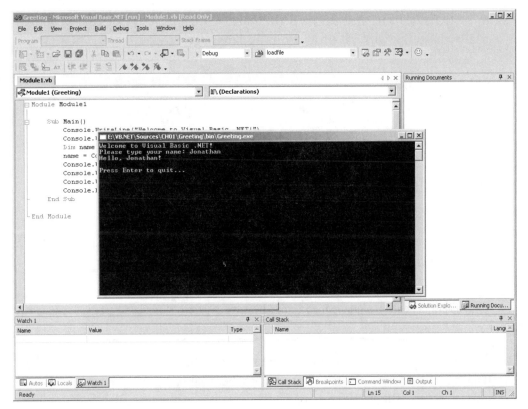

Figure 2.13
The new Greeting program reads user input and displays the contents of the string variable.

which is a valid term in software today. Reserving a space in the computer's memory was a manual process, which required the programmer to keep track of exactly where that space was located by creating a pointer—which is where variables came from.

In order to make the task easier, programmers developed assembly languages that permitted the use of mnemonic words to replace the specific addresses of memory in which information is stored. Rather than keep track of the address in memory of a pointer, which in turn points to another address in memory where actual data is located, a mnemonic was used as the pointer. Mnemonics are easier to remember than physical addresses in memory; therefore, this greatly eased the job of writing programs.

Over time, these mnemonic words came to be known as variables. So, when you hear the word "variable," just remember that it is just a pointer to a location in memory in which some data is stored. VB.NET keeps track of the type of data stored in that location and does all the hard work for you, but this process is essentially the same with all programming languages.

Using Variables

The `Dim` command is used to create new variables. The syntax of `Dim` looks like this:

`Dim Variable_Name As Data_Type`

Here's an example of a real `Dim` statement:

`Dim Counter As Integer`

This statement creates an `Integer` variable, which is capable of holding a number that has no decimal point.

Definition

A *variable* is an entity in a program, identified by name, that can store data based on its data type (such as Integer or String).

In addition to the `Dim` statement, there are two other ways to declare variables. The `Public` command causes a variable to be visible to other modules in the program, whereas the `Private` command prevents other modules from seeing a variable (and is the default when using `Dim`).

A data type is the attribute of a variable, which determines what kind of data it represents. There are 12 intrinsic data types in VB.NET, as shown in Table 2.1. I have rounded off the values in order to make them easier to comprehend. In my experience, the extreme range of a data type should not be an issue; just declare variables that are certain to be large enough to hold the value.

Definition

A *data type* represents the type of data stored in a variable. The data type tells VB how to handle the data.

When deciding what data types to use in a program, consider the number of bytes for each variable and select the most efficient data types. However, you must take care not to limit the variables too much, even if you think they will never exceed the data type range. This is not a license to write buggy code; it is simply a reminder than you can always make a program stable later on, but you can't always make it faster once you have written most of the code. Selecting the appropriate data types early on is important.

Table 2.1 Variable Data Types

Data Type	Bytes	Range
Byte	1	0 to 255
Boolean	2	True or False
Char	2	0 to 65535 (Unicode)
Short	2	−32,768 to 32,767
Integer	4	~ +/−2,147,483,647
Single	4	~ +/−3.4028235E38
Object	4	Any value
Date	8	Jan 1, 0001 to Dec 31, 9999
Double	8	~ +/−1.79769313486231E308
Long	8	~ +/−9,223,372,036,854,775,807
Decimal	16	~ +/−79,228 × 10^{24}
String	2 × length	2 billion characters

Most of the time, I use *Integers*, *Doubles*, and *Strings*, which keeps the code simple and gives programs plenty of room to breathe.

What's So Special about Strings?

The String data type is the most frequently used type in VB and deserves special recognition. Without strings, VB.NET would be hobbled by difficult string-handling functions. The String data type is versatile in that it can contain up to two billion characters. Although it is definitely a possibility, I have never personally seen a two-gigabyte text file! Humorous as that may sound, a string could conceivably grow to that size, although I suspect that Windows would run out of memory before the string was filled to capacity. Most strings rarely exceed a few hundred characters. The String data type requires two bytes for each character (because VB.NET strings use Unicode to store characters). To create a new String, simply use the Dim statement (or the affiliated Public or Private statements):

```
Dim FirstName As String
```

Simple string handling can be accomplished by setting a string equal to a value or another variable. There are two ways to combine strings: using the plus sign (+)

and using the ampersand sign (&). Prior versions of Visual Basic required the ampersand when combining strings, but VB.NET can use either.

```
Dim String1 As String = "This is String1"
Dim String2 As String = " and this is String2."
Dim String3 As String
String3 = String1 & String2
Console.WriteLine("String3 = {0}", String3);
```

The result of this snippet of code looks like this:

```
This is String1 and this is String2.
```

Branching/Conditional Statements

Branching statements are built into programming languages so that programmers can add logic to a program. Without branching (also known as *conditional*) statements, the program would only be able to forward the input directly to the output, without any processing. Although this may be something that you want the program to do (such as to display a text file on the screen or print a document), it is far more likely that you will need to actually do something with input data. Branching statements allow you to create complex program logic.

The If...Then Statement

The most common branching statement used in programming languages is the If...Then statement, which is often called the If...Then...Else statement. Here is the general syntax of the de-facto logic statement as it is used in Visual Basic:

```
If "condition is true" Then
    "perform commands based on true result"
Else
    "perform commands based on false result"
End If
```

Figure 2.14 is an example of an If...Then...Else statement and shows how input is tested for a true or false condition, whereupon program execution continues down the chosen path.

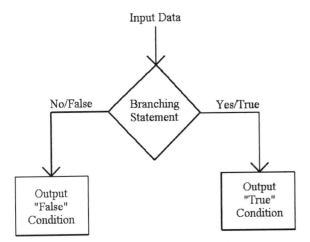

Figure 2.14
Illustration of a branching statement showing how program logic works.

Single-Line If...Then Statements

There is another format you can use with this branching statement, in which the `Else` and `End If` parts are not needed. Rather, you can code an `If...Then...Else` statement on a single line. Although this format is supported by Visual Basic, it is generally considered bad form, due to the lack of a closing statement—this is often a source of bugs in a program and difficult to track down. However, this form does save three lines of code. The real benefit to using this form is when you have to test many conditions in a row and you want to keep the code listing short. Of course, such situations beg for an alternate design altogether.

```
If "condition" Then "true statement"Else "false statement"
```

Using If...Then

How about a real example? Okay, here is how you might code the branching statement for a payroll program that calculates overtime pay.

```
If HoursWorked > 40 Then
    PayRate = 1.5
Else
    PayRate = 1.0
End If
```

The Select...Case Statement

There are times when the If...Then statement is just too unwieldy, particularly when a large number of conditions must be tested. In such circumstances, the Select...Case statement is a good alternative. In fact, you may feel free to use this branching statement instead of If...Then at any time; it's entirely up to you. Some prefer Select...Case because it is easier to add new cases to the condition in the future. I use it anytime there are more than two conditions to be tested. Here is the general format of the Select...Case statement:

```
Select Case "evaluation"
    Case value-1 [To value-2][, value-3]
        "perform condition-1 statements"
    Case value-1 [To value-2][, value-3]
        "perform condition-2 statements"
    Case value-1 [To value-2][, value-3]
        "perform condition-n statements"
    Case Else
        "perform alternate statements"
End Select
```

The Select...Case branching statement is versatile in that it is easy to add new cases (as you can see). It is also easier to read than in an If...Then statement when dealing with a lot of cases. To demonstrate how Select...Case works, let's rewrite the previous If...Then code as a Select...Case.

```
Select Case HoursWorked
    Case Is > 40
        Console.WriteLine("You worked over time.")
    Case Is = 40
        Console.WriteLine ("You worked regular time.")
    Case Else
        Console.WriteLine ("You worked part time.")
End Select
```

If you type that Select...Case statement into VB.NET, you will notice that the editor adds the word Is before each condition. For example, if you type Case > 40, the editor will fill in Case Is > 40. This is simply the syntax required in Select...Case statements for Boolean evaluations. If you need only compare a range of values or a single value, the Is isn't needed. For example:

```
Select Case Mileage
    Case Is < 10
```

```
        Console.WriteLine ("The mileage is terrible.")
    Case 11, 12, 13, 14, 15
        Console.WriteLine ("The mileage is poor.")
    Case 16, 17, 18 To 20
        Console.WriteLine ("The mileage is average.")
    Case 21 To 30
        Console.WriteLine ("The mileage is good.")
    Case 31 To 50
        Console.WriteLine ("The mileage is great.")
    Case Is > 50
        Console.WriteLine ("The mileage is amazing!")
End Select
```

Subroutines and Functions

Subroutines are important for breaking up a large program into smaller, more manageable pieces, leading to better code reuse and legibility. Subroutines are also important for creating program logic. Quite often, the conditional statements in a branching statement point to a subroutine to keep the branching statement short. If each case in a branching statement includes a page of source code, it's easy to lose track of each case! Therefore, subroutines are essential parts of a programming language.

This won't be a comprehensive discussion of subroutines, because every chapter from this point forward will use subroutines. You will have ample opportunity to learn all that is possible with subroutines, including how to pass multiple parameters (or as many parameters as you like), passing by value or by reference, and optional parameters. Rest assured, these advanced topics will be covered. At this point, it's more important to grasp the functional use of subroutines and how they apply to branching in a program. I will introduce you to additional features as they are needed, rather than all at once.

Using Subs and Functions

Visual Basic supports two types of subroutines: Sub and Function. A Sub is a subroutine that doesn't need to return a value (which is the case with a Function). Here is the basic syntax for a Sub:

```
[Public/Private] Sub SubName([Parameters])
End Sub
```

Here is an example of a Sub that does not have a parameter:

```
Private Sub PrintHello()
    Console.WriteLine("Hello!")
End Sub
```

Here is an example of a Sub that includes a String parameter:

```
Private Sub PrintHello(Name As String)
    Console.WriteLine("Hello, " & Name & "!")
End Sub
```

Hint

Note that the ampersand character, &, is used to tie strings together, not the plus character, +. The plus character is used to copy numbers, whereas the ampersand is used to copy characters.

Returning Values from Functions

A Function is similar to a Sub, but a Function is able to return a value. Here is the basic syntax for a Function:

```
[Public/Private] Function FunctionName([Parameters]) As DataType
End Function
```

Here is an example of a Function that does not have a parameter:

```
Private Function One() As Integer
      return 1
End Function
```

Strange as it may appear, this is a legal function! Do you see how the value is returned using the return statement? Here is another example of a Function, only this time with a parameter:

```
Private Function TimesTen(Num As Integer) As Integer
      return Num * 10
End Function
```

The TimesTen function is a little more interesting because you can have it return a value that is based on a parameter! The possibilities are utterly endless on what you can do with the power of subroutines. The return value of a function is determined by the data type of the function, which can be any data type that you use when creating variables, as well as custom data types that you create. Functions can also return an Object, which means that it can return any data type or even a user interface control (odd as that may sound).

Mathematical Operators

Visual Basic provides a good assortment of mathematical operators that you can use in your programs. These operators are built into the language. Using number conversion functions, such as `CLng` (for converting to a `Long`) and `CDbl` (for converting to a `Double`), you can apply mathematical operations to a variety of variables in a program. (Remember, a `Long` integer is a whole number, while a `Double` precision floating point has a decimal point.)

Visual Basic performs number conversion on the fly, based on the result of the operation. Technically, these are holdovers from Visual Basic 6.0 and made available using the Microsoft.VisualBasic namespace, but they are so convenient, and VB.NET provides no decent equivalents, that they have been essentially adopted as an official feature of VB.NET by professionals. At the most basic level are the mathematical operations for completing addition, subtraction, multiplication, division, modulus, and exponents.

Addition and Subtraction

The plus sign and minus sign are used to add and subtract numbers. This includes variable assignment and formulas used in branching statements. Addition is commonly used to increment the value of a counter variable. For example:

```
Dim N As Integer = 0
N = N + 10
```

Note the use of an initializer for the variable, N. Although Visual Basic automatically sets numbers to zero upon initialization, it is sometimes convenient to include the explicit initializer. The second line, N = N + 10, is called a formula, because the variable is *receiving* the value of an addition operation. You could just as easily use a function to return a number that is assigned to the variable. For example:

```
Private Function Twelve() As Integer
    return 12
End Function
```

```
Dim N As Integer = 0
N = 10 + Twelve()
```

Visual Basic .NET provides another way to add a number to a variable, called a *shortcut operator,* which looks like this: += and -=. Here is an example:

```
Dim N As Integer = 0
N += 10
```

Multiplication and Division

Multiplication was invented to make adding and subtracting easier, because it allows you to add or subtract many numbers quite easily. Like most programming languages, Visual Basic uses the asterisk (*) for multiplication. Here is an example:

```
Dim A As Integer = 9
Dim B As Integer = 6
Console.WriteLine("{0} times {1} = {2}", A, B, A * B)
```

Here is what the Console message looks like:

```
9 times 6 = 54
```

As you might have guessed, there is also a shortcut operator for multiplication, and I'll wager that you can guess what it looks like! If you guessed *=, then you are right!

```
Dim A As Integer = 12
A *= 12
```

How about a real-world example? The circumference of a circle is two times the radius times pi, or $C = 2\pi r$. Expressed in Visual Basic source code, here is how you can calculate it (note: the last line is a comment showing the result you should get by running this mini program):

```
Dim Radius As Integer = 10
Dim Circumference As Decimal
Circumference = 2 * System.Math.PI * Radius
Rem the answer is 62.8318530717959
```

Here is an example of integer division:

```
Dim A As Integer = 12
Dim B As Integer = 4
```

Table 2.2 Division Characters

Char	Name	Description
/	Forward slash	Floating-point division (decimal remainder)
\	Backslash	Integer division (no remainder)

```
Dim C As Integer
C = A \ B
```

There are two ways to divide numbers in Visual Basic. First, standard division uses the forward slash character (/). This is below the question mark on a U.S. keyboard. Second, the backslash character (\), which is above the Enter key on a U.S. keyboard, is designed to return just an integer as an answer, dropping any remainder. Be sure to learn the difference between these characters, because the latter one doesn't work for floating-point numbers (such as Decimal, Single, and Double). Use Table 2.2 as a reference.

Here is another example of a division operation, this time using a floating-point number:

```
Dim A As Decimal = 973.65
Dim B As Decimal = 18.50
Dim C As Decimal
C = A / B
```

Trick

If you have a hard time remembering which division character to use, consider this analogy. The backslash is a downward slope that's quick and easy (using integers), whereas the forward slash is a hill that's difficult to climb (using decimals). You can also think of integers as a "downgrade" in precision, while thinking of floats as an "upgrade" in precision.

Modulus

After talking so much about remainders in floating-point and integer division, it is fitting that the next operator is the modulus, or Mod, operator. This works similarly to the other math operators, except there is no shortcut for modulus, because you must use the word *Mod*. Here is an example:

```
Dim A As Integer = 10
Dim B As Integer = 3
```

```
Dim C As Integer
C = A Mod B
```

The result of the last statement is that C = 1. Can you figure out why? When you divide 10 by 3, the answer is 3, but there is a remainder of 1. Mod ignores the answer and returns the remainder. Although this might not seem very useful to you at present, Mod is an extremely powerful math operator that can solve some uniquely difficult problems. One classic example is determining whether a number is an integer or float by looking at the remainder. You can perform that check using the following condition:

```
If A Mod B = 0 Then
```

Here is a complete example:

```
If A Mod 2 = 0 Then
    Console.WriteLine("The variable is a whole number")
Else
    Console.WriteLine ("The variable is a floating-point number")
End If
```

Note

We'll use the modulus operator to make sprite animation possible in Chapter 4, "Sprites: The Key to 2D Games."

Relational Operators

The human mind is capable of seeing the differences and relationships between individual things and groups of things, such as cars in a car lot. By simply driving past a car lot, you are probably able to tell at a glance what types of cars are being offered for sale, such as pickup trucks, compact cars, vans, and sport-utility vehicles.

Computer programs are not blessed with the ability to instantly come to a conclusion with limited information. Rather, computers must evaluate differences at a highly detailed and specific level. For instance, a human might look at two cars and claim that they are absolutely identical. But a computer might examine the same two cars and find that they are made of different components, built in different years, and even point out flaws in the paint. As a result, computers are able to examine things with great precision, something humans are incapable of doing.

Table 2.3 Data Type Conversion Functions

Name	Description
CBool	Convert passed value to a Boolean
CByte	Convert passed value to a Byte
CChar	Convert passed value to a Char
CDate	Convert passed value to a Date
CDbl	Convert passed value to a Double
CDec	Convert passed value to a Decimal
CInt	Convert passed value to an Integer
CLng	Convert passed value to a Long
CObj	Convert passed value to an Object
CShort	Convert passed value to a Short
CSng	Convert passed value to a Single
CStr	Convert passed value to a String

Relational operators deal with how values compare to each other, or rather, how they relate to each other. Relational operators are usually found within formulas that result in a Boolean (true or false) value, and are based on simple rules, such as equal, not equal, greater than, and less than. The way that objects relate to each other is determined by their data types. Variables of the same data type can relate directly without any conversion needed. But variables of different data types require some form of conversion before they can be compared using a relational operator.

Visual Basic usually converts data types automatically, but there are times when the conversion just doesn't work. The important thing to remember is that Visual Basic may interpret a formula incorrectly when working with different data types; therefore you may want to use an explicit conversion function, as listed in Table 2.3.

The actual operators used to perform relational comparisons are covered next, with a description of how to use each one. Table 2.4 provides a quick reference.

Here is an example of a test for an equal condition:

```
If (A = B) Then
    Console.WriteLine("True")
```

Table 2.4 Relational Operators

Operator	Description
=	Equal to
<>	Not equal to
<	Less than
>	Greater than
<=	Less than or equal to
>=	Greater than or equal to

```
Else
    Console.WriteLine ("False")
End If
```

Looping Statements

Looping is a way of repeating something to accomplish a task (such as summarizing or averaging some values) or to process a long list of information. For example, it requires a loop to load a text file and display it in a TextBox, because the program must load each byte of the text file in order. Another example of a repeating process is drawing a picture on the screen, one pixel at a time, as each pixel in the picture file (which might be saved as a JPG, GIF, BMP, or other format) is copied to the screen.

Looping is the process of repeating or iterating through a series, from a starting point to a fixed ending point, or upon the completion of a condition. Suppose you have a list of names, as follows:

- Bob

- Jane

- Mary

- Steve

If you need to print out all this information, you could display each name separately, like this:

```
Console.WriteLine("Bob is #1")
Console.WriteLine ("Jane is #2")
```

```
Console.WriteLine ("Mary is #3")
Console.WriteLine ("Steve is #4")
```

That might work for small lists, but what about lists with hundreds, thousands, or millions of entries? Computer databases could easily have millions of records, after all, and there's no way you can process each one individually. Obviously, a looping command is needed! How might you iterate through a series of sequential numbers? First, you start with a variable that is set to one. Each time through the loop, you add one to the variable. At the end of the loop, the variable will equal some number. Here is the basic concept:

1. Start with a value.

2. Add one to the value.

3. Repeat until a condition is met.

The condition that needs to be met might be a Boolean formula, such as (Num > 100) or (A = B). The condition might also be that the counter variable has reached a certain number. This is what computer science calls a For Loop, odd as that may sound. The reason it is called For Loop is because something happens "for every pass through the loop."

For Loop

The Visual Basic For Loop looks like this:

```
For variable = start To finish
    repeating commands
Next variable
```

Do Loops

The Do Loop is another form of looping command built into Visual Basic. Whereas For Loops are adept at handling number sequences, Do Loops excel when it comes to relational looping, in which a process will repeatedly loop until some Boolean condition is satisfied. There are four variations of the Do Loop.

The first form of the Do Loop is the Do While...Loop. This version causes the enclosed commands to repeat as long as the condition is true. You can para-phrase it like this: "While the condition is true, continue repeating the com-mands." Because of this wording format, it's possible that the repeating commands might never execute if the condition is false from the start. Here is the format for this version of the Do Loop:

```
Do While condition
    repeating commands
Loop
```

The Do While...Loop command is more versatile than the For Loop because you can have multiple conditions applied to the loop through every iteration. For example:

```
Do While EndOfFile = False
    'process the file
Loop
```

The Do...Loop While command is the reverse of the Do While...Loop command. The format of the condition and the way this loop handles repetition are similar, but there is one difference.

Here is the format of the command:

```
Do
    repeating commands
Loop While condition
```

The third type of Do Loop is the Do Until...Loop command. This one is also similar to the other Do Loops, but this format differs from the Do While...Loop in that it continues to repeat *until* the condition is met, rather than *while* the condition is met. It is the negative version of the Do Loop that continues as long as the condition is false. Here is the general format of the Do Until...Loop command:

```
Do Until condition
    repeating commands
Loop
```

The fourth version of the Do Loop is Do...Loop Until. This is the late conditional form of the Do Until...Loop, in which the condition is checked at the end of the loop rather than at the beginning. Therefore, this loop is guaranteed to process the repeating commands at least once.

```
Do
    repeating commands
Loop Until condition
```

Here is an example:

```
Do
    'process the file
Loop Until FileOpen = False
```

Arrays

Looping commands really start to make sense when dealing with long lists of information, as the preceding section demonstrated. But what happens when you don't have a ListBox control handy to use as a container for the information? The answer is an *array*, which is a variable that has many elements. Suppose you have a variable called Age, declared as an Integer, which holds your age. What if you would like to keep track of the age of everyone in your family or your class? You could create many Age variables, as follows:

```
Dim Age1 As Integer
Dim Age2 As Integer
Dim Age3 As Integer
Dim Age4 As Integer
```

That is an inefficient way to handle all of the data, and there is an additional problem that arises when you add another variable to the list, such as Age8. When you do that, you have to go back and modify the program so that Age8 is used properly. Obviously, there must be a better way.

The answer is an array. This is how you would declare the Age array:

```
Dim Ages(8) As Integer
```

Doesn't that look a lot more efficient? Not only can you iterate through an array with a looping command, you can also add new elements to an array at will, and if your program is written properly, you won't have to rewrite anything to add more elements.

Let's devise a hypothetical situation to help illustrate. There are eight people in your class, and you want to write a program that displays all of their ages using only a few lines of code, because you are in a hurry to get it finished. First, you need to declare an array of names to go along with the Age array:

```
Dim Names(4) As String
```

You need to fill the array with some data. For the sake of simplicity, let's do it the hard way. Here is how you might load the Names and Ages arrays:

```
Names(0) = "Thomas"
Ages(0) = 32
Names(1) = "James"
Ages(1) = 20
Names(2) = "Percy"
Ages(2) = 24
Names(3) = "Gordon"
Ages(3) = 38
```

Now that the arrays have been filled with sample data, let's write a loop to quickly display the arrays:

```
Dim n As Integer
For n = 0 To 3
    Console.WriteLine("{0} is {1} years old.", Names(n), Ages(n))
Next
```

Structures

The preceding section demonstrated how to combine two arrays of related information in a display. That method did work, but it was inefficient. For one thing, what if the names and ages need to be sorted? Sorting one of the arrays would mess up the sequence of the other array. What happens if you need to keep track of several more pieces of information about each person in this hypothetical situation, such as height and weight? Things could become messy in a hurry with four arrays to deal with.

Tip

Pay close attention to this section because we'll be using structures extensively in the Celtic Crusader game!

A structure combines several variables into a group, which is then handled as a single entity. The real power of a structure, then, is the ability to create an array of that structure, rather than multiple arrays for each variable. Sound interesting? It is that, and extremely useful as well. Here is the general format of a structure:

```
Structure struct_name
    variable1 As data_type
    variable2 As data_type
```

```
      variable3 As data_type
End Structure
```

Let's create a real structure based on the `Names` and `Ages` arrays created in the previous section. Here is how you might design the structure in order to incorporate the previous two arrays:

```
Structure Students
      Dim Name As String
      Dim Age As Integer
End Structure
```

As you can see, it looks very similar to the individual array declarations for `Names` and `Ages`, but I have made the variable names singular. One important point to note is that once inside a structure, variables are referred to as *methods*.

Once you have created the structure, you can declare an array variable of the structure like this:

```
Dim people(8) As Students
```

Filling a structure array differs a little from filling a simple variable array. How do you get to those variables (oops, I mean methods) after you have created the structure array? Well, for starters, take a look at the variable itself, called `people`. There you will find the clue to accessing the methods within. As with built-in objects in Visual Basic .NET, such as `System.Math`. Visual Basic provides the IntelliSense drop-down list any time you type in the name of an object followed by a period.

If you have Visual Basic .NET open, go ahead and create a new Console Application project, and type in the preceding structure definition so you can try this out. Now, move the cursor to the blank line under `Sub Main()` and type in:

`people(0).`

That's it, just `people(0)` followed by a period. Because you declared `people` to be a structure array, you should see the drop-down list showing the two methods in that structure. But wait, what are those other items in the drop-down list? `Equals`, `GetHashCode`, `GetType`, and `ToString` don't belong in there! After all, the structure just has two methods, `Name` and `Age`. Don't worry about those extra methods. They are just standard methods built in that Visual Basic .NET adds to the structure definition for advanced use.

Okay, now you at least have an idea of how to access the methods inside a structure. So, let's fill in the names and ages in this structure array to see how it works:

```
people(0).Name = "Thomas"
people(0).Age = 32
people(1).Name = "James"
people(1).Age = 20
people(2).Name = "Percy"
people(2).Age = 24
people(3).Name = "Gordon"
people(3).Age = 38
```

See how the structure name (people) now references the array index (0 to 7) instead of the method names? It makes more sense to do it this way, and it's more logical. Now you can add more methods to the structure and reference them like you did with Name and Age. Let's print out the array so you can see how that looks with a looping command.

```
Dim n As Integer
For n = 0 To 7
    Console.WriteLine("{0} is {1} years old.", _
        people(n).Name, people(n).Age)
Next
```

Object-Oriented Programming

Object-oriented programming (OOP) is a large-scale concept, which is more of a methodology than a specific way of writing programs. Applicable to many different languages, including Visual Basic .NET, OOP has been around for many years, but Visual Basic only received the full treatment with the .NET version. If this is your first exposure to OOP (or to programming, for that matter), it may not be clear how useful it is to be able to reuse source code on later projects or even share source code between projects currently in development. Try to think in the abstract: How can I write this program in such a way that when I'm finished, I can use parts of it again in another project? That way of thinking is a step in the right direction. To accomplish something like that, you need to break down a problem into manageable pieces, and then write the source code for those individual pieces separately, linking them together at the end to form a whole program.

If you are new to programming, you can learn how to write OOP code correctly from the start and avoid having to change your way of thinking later. Software evolves; it changes every year. Visual Basic .NET and all of the languages that make up Visual Studio .NET are radically different from Visual Basic 6.0. Although those new features are more complicated, they are in tune with OOP and help to solve programming problems more efficiently.

Encapsulation

Encapsulation is the process of pulling all the data, and source code that manipulates that data, inside a self-contained entity (which is easier to refer to as just an object). By keeping all the data inside the object, as well as all the sub-routines and functions that work with the data, you prevent others from using the data incorrectly. In addition, encapsulation enables you to design the format of the data, as well as the processes, so that everything follows the object model—if properly designed, it's a blueprint for the system.

Suppose you have an apple tree in your backyard. You are a kindly neighbor; therefore, you offer free apples to anyone who comes by for a visit. Soon, however, your neighbors begin to help themselves to the apples without even bothering to knock on the door and say hello. They have ignored you completely and helped themselves to the goodies.

To prevent this, what you really need to do is add a layer of control between your neighbors and your apple tree—for instance, a fence with a locked gate. But ideally, you need to pass out the apples yourself. So you do just that; every time a neighbor stops by for an apple, you select a ripe and healthy apple and present it to your neighbor. The neighbor thanks you and goes on his way. You have interfered with the neighbor's ability to gain direct access to the source of the apples, but in doing so, you made sure the neighbor received only good apples, because you threw out any bad apples beforehand.

This analogy aptly describes encapsulation of data. You want other processes in the program to have access to certain information, but you want to make sure that those processes don't do something incorrect with the information, possibly causing a bug in the program. Does encapsulation limit or slow down a program? Not really. It takes the outside process just as much time to grab the information stored in a variable as it takes for your own custom process to provide the information to that outside process.

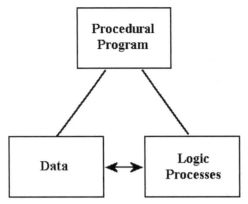

Figure 2.15
Procedural programs expose data and logic processes.

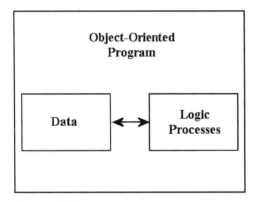

Figure 2.16
Object-oriented programs hide data and logic processes.

Let me give you an example to help clarify the matter. Figure 2.15 shows an example of a procedural program that has full access to both the data and the logic processes, which are both exposed in the source code. Figure 2.16, on the other hand, shows an example of an object-oriented program, which *encapsulates* the data and logic processes within the source code, preventing outside processes from interfering.

Inheritance

Inheritance is another key component of an OOP program. Inheritance is the ability of one object to borrow things from another object. Inheritance is a play on words; it is more like cloning than receiving money from a departed loved

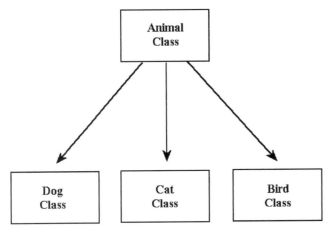

Figure 2.17
The Dog, Cat, and Bird classes all inherit data and logic processes from the Animal class.

one. I suspect reproduction and cloning sounded too biological, so the word inheritance was used instead. Regardless, the concept is that one object receives the attributes of another object. When the new object is used, it has a copy of the older object inside itself, which is very similar to the way genetics works. The parent passes down genes to offspring. See Figure 2.17.

Polymorphism

Polymorphism is the last of the three concepts that comprise an OOP program. Polymorphism as a word means "many shapes" and refers to the ability for the traits inside an object to change in response to different inputs or outputs. Polymorphism is probably not as important to the overall OOP scheme as encapsulation and inheritance are, but it does play an important role in aiding the other two with multipurpose attributes that can accommodate many different situations.

Polymorphism is arguably the least important of the three major traits of an object-oriented program, but it does provide a powerful and useful set of features that are difficult to do without once you have gotten used to them.

Properties

Without getting into too much detail at this point, I'd like to show you how to start using OOP. The true power of OOP comes from using Classes, which are covered shortly. A *property* is a special type of subroutine that behaves like a variable, so you can assign values to a property or read the value of a property as if it were a variable. But properties are definitely not variables! In practice, properties can be a very powerful form of encapsulation, allowing you to hide variables and processes behind a simple interface. You may not be able to overload a property, but you scarcely need to, because properties are already so simple to use. Now, here is what a real property looks like:

```
Dim decCirc As Decimal
Property Circumference() As Decimal
    Get
        Return decCirc
    End Get
    Set(ByVal value As Decimal)
        decCirc = value
    End Set
End Property
```

Note the use of the statements Get and Set. This is what allows a property to act like a simple variable when it is actually a subroutine. Then, in your program, you can set the Circumference property like this:

```
Circumference = 100.0
```

Or you can retrieve the value of the Circumference property like so:

```
Dim circ as decimal = Circumference()
```

Classes

Classes are the key ingredients of object-oriented programming and provide a basis for creating objects. An object is a self-contained, functional component in a program, which accomplishes a single task, regardless of whether that task is simple or complex. A well-designed OOP program will utilize many different and versatile objects that work together to accomplish the goals of the program. The real power of this is that over time a programmer (or programming team) will be able to use these objects in more than one project.

A professional programming shop will have an assortment of such objects collected over time in a *class library*. The class library may be comprised of many smaller libraries of classes (as shown in Figure 2.18).

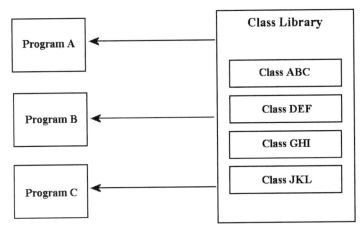

Figure 2.18
Class libraries provide commonly-used source code routines as self-contained classes that become objects when used in a program.

The Format of a Class

Classes can contain any information that you want and can generally be declared Friend or Public. Private classes can also be created, but their scope must fall within another class. Friend classes are visible only within the current namespace (in previous versions of Visual Basic that would have been *current project* scope). Generally, classes are created so that they can be used and reused in more than one application; therefore, classes are almost universally declared with Public scope. For all practical purposes, here is a sample class definition (with a single member variable) as you will see it most often:

```
Public Class MyClassName
    Private intVariable As Integer

    Sub New()
        intVariable = 0
    End Sub

    Property Variable() As Integer
        Get
            Return intVariable
        End Get
        Set(ByVal Value As Integer)
            intVariable = Value
        End Set
    End Property
End Class
```

Class Variables

The first thing you will notice in the sample MyClassName class is the member variable called intVariable. Member variables can be declared with Public, Private, or Protected scope. You are already familiar with the first two; what, then, does Protected mean? Protected member variables are sort of in between Public and Private, accessible to descendant classes but not outside the class. Private member variables, on the other hand, are *not* visible to other classes (not even descendants). Public variables are visible all the time.

Class Constructor

The next thing you will notice in the sample MyClassName class is a constructor called Sub New(). Odd as it may appear, this is how constructors are created in VB.NET, by overloading the New operator. Remember, when you create a new object, you use New, right? Well, New is just an operator, like +, -, >, <, or =. VB.NET overloads the New operator to act as the constructor for the class. In case you are not familiar with the term, a *constructor* is a subroutine (method) that runs when the class is first instantiated (which means *created*).

Class Properties and Methods

The most common type of subroutine you will use in a class is a property, although you can add any Sub or Function that you want to a class, and it then becomes a member method of the class. I am a big fan of properties, and I am pleased that properties now play such a big role in Visual Basic's OOP capabilities. You are free to use a property to do more than just provide access to a private variable. Anytime you need to return a value, for example, it is convenient to use a property, because properties are referenced just like variables in a class (and it's often difficult to tell the difference).

Summary

If you were a newcomer to Visual Basic .NET, I sincerely hope this chapter provided a good introduction to the language. You learned the basics of variables and data types, subroutines and functions, conditional statements, structures, classes, and many more key concepts. Since teaching VB.NET is not a goal of this book, we will not spend any more time on the features of the language itself, but rather on game programming concepts. You may want to refer back to this chapter anytime you run across code later that you don't understand.

If you would like to study the concepts presented in this chapter in more detail, I have provided a number of example programs on the CD-ROM for you to examine while learning VB.NET. The concepts represented by these programs were not explicitly covered in this chapter but I think you will find them to be of educational value.

- A Breakout-style game called Blocks

- A random chance game called Dice War

- A digital clock program

- A guessing game

- A math tutoring program

- A version of the infamous Tic-Tac-Toe game

- A simple typing tutor program

So, without further ado, let's move ahead to the next chapter and get started with DirectX!

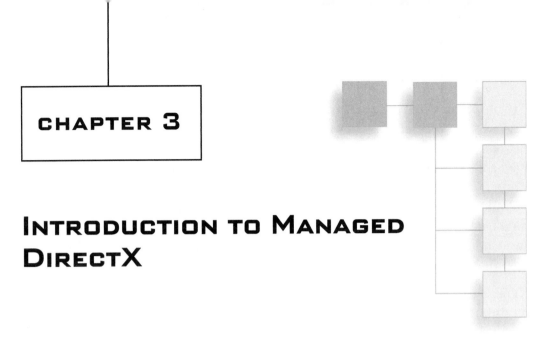

CHAPTER 3

INTRODUCTION TO MANAGED DIRECTX

This chapter takes you through the process of writing source code that loads a bitmap file and draws it on the screen using Direct3D. You will learn all about Direct3D surfaces and textures in this chapter. You need to learn about several DirectX components, which appear in this chapter, because they are used throughout the book. You might be surprised to learn that Direct3D is used to draw bitmaps on the screen. This seems odd because Direct3D is used to create advanced 3D games, such as *Star Wars: Empire at War* and *Battlefield 2.* But we can use Direct3D to render graphics in 2D as well (games such as *Age of Mythology*). Before you get started working on a role-playing game, you need to start with the basics. First, we need to fire up DirectX, initialize Direct3D, and then render something. This chapter shows you how to do just that.

- Adding a reference to the DirectX library
- Testing the DirectX library
- Creating the primary device
- Loading and rendering a bitmap

Getting Started with DirectX

If you are new to Visual Basic .NET, then I hope you spent some time going through the previous chapter learning the basics of the language. Granted, that was a *crazy* crash course in Visual Basic programming! But it should have given you a good head start—or a review if you haven't touched Visual Basic in a long time. You may be surprised by the fact that we won't be doing much with Windows Forms in Visual Basic. I'm going to show you how to take over a form and hand it to Direct3D, at which point it will be used as a rendering surface. But we won't be adding controls to a form. This is game programming! We aren't creating database applications here!

If my enthusiasm for game programming has not been obvious enough yet, I will continue to tell you how much fun it is to write your own games. I love Visual Basic! I got started with VB 5.0 and spent many years programming with VB 6.0, both professionally and casually. I was very happy when Microsoft created the DirectX type library for Visual Basic when DirectX 8.0 was released. I covered that subject many years ago in *Visual Basic Game Programming with DirectX*, which was a huge book. I spent a lot of time working on a networked game called Stellar War that was very challenging to write in VB. (You can see a screenshot at www.jharbour.com/?page_id=4).

But the problem is, most gamers appreciate artwork and gameplay—not *cool* techno-geeky stuff like Windows Sockets. I've learned over time that *cool code* does not interest people—they want *gameplay*. So, we're focusing all of our attention here on the creation of an RPG engine and focusing on a single game called Celtic Crusader. It's a fun subject! RPGs are fun to play—if they manage the balance between micro-management and playability. *Gameplay* and *fun factor* are all that matter. We will not even touch a subject that isn't directly related to a feature in the game! So, let's dive into DirectX. I'm eager to show you how easy it is to get Direct3D up and running with a little code.

Let's start by creating a new Visual Basic project and learn how to configure it to work with DirectX. This is surprisingly easy compared to, say, doing the same in Visual C++. I write Direct3D and OpenGL programs from scratch all the time, and let me tell you, doing this in Visual Basic or C# is a *breeze*! Now, don't get me wrong, I *like* writing games in C++, and I *enjoy* using libraries such as Allegro, DirectX, and OpenGL. But it is *really* easy to do this in Visual Basic! Just to get Direct3D initialized and to load and draw a bitmap image on the screen requires about 300 lines of code in Visual C++. Of course, you can copy and paste code

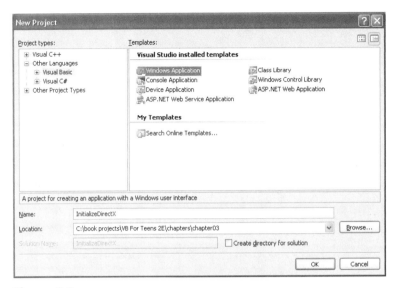

Figure 3.1
Creating a new Windows Application project in Visual Basic.

from another project, so you don't have to write all the code from scratch each time, but it's still a lot of code to wade through before you can even get started working on a game. The great thing about Managed DirectX and Visual Basic or C# is just how *easy* it is to get something running quickly.

Start up Visual Studio 2005. Open the File menu and choose New, Project. This brings up the New Project dialog box shown in Figure 3.1.

Always choose Windows Application for the project type when working on a game in Visual Basic. When you choose this template, Visual Basic will create a new project and add a default form to the project for you, as shown in Figure 3.2.

This is the usual starting point for a program in Visual Basic, which is exactly what you need at this point: a blank canvas with which to work. Visual Basic programmers normally use forms and Toolbox controls to build an application, such as a business database that tracks customers. That you are using Visual Basic to write games is kind of odd, as it was never designed as a game development tool. With its simple language, GUI editor, and built-in compiler, Visual Basic is easy to learn and use, which is why it has become such a popular choice for game programmers. I tend to use C++ more often, but it has taken me *years* to master that difficult language.

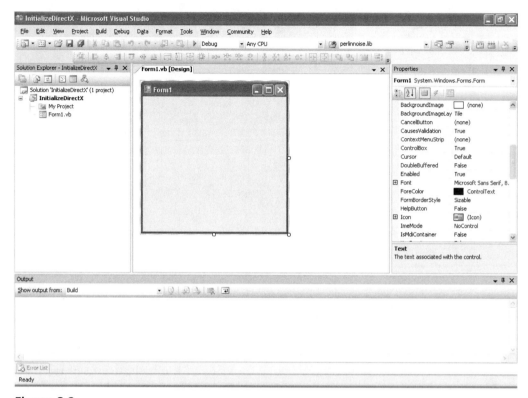

Figure 3.2
The default form in your new Windows Application project.

If you press F5 right now, the program will quickly compile and run, showing a useless blank window called Form1. The Visual Basic form makes it easy to initialize a DirectX program, because the form has all the properties of a standard window (something that you have to create the hard way in C++). I want you to gain some familiarity with the three most common menus that we'll be using: the Project menu, the Build menu, and the Debug menu. The Project menu is used to add new controls, classes, modules, and references to your project. This is where we will go to add the DirectX library to our project. The Build menu is used to compile your project. The Debug menu is used to run the program.

You can skip the Build step by just pressing F5 to run the program, and Visual Basic will figure out whether it needs to recompile the program on its own. But you can also just perform a build yourself by pressing the F7 key. Go ahead and try that now. You should see some messages appear in the Output window at the bottom of Visual Basic that looks like Figure 3.3. What you want to look for is the last line, which tells you whether the build succeeded or failed. Often, when

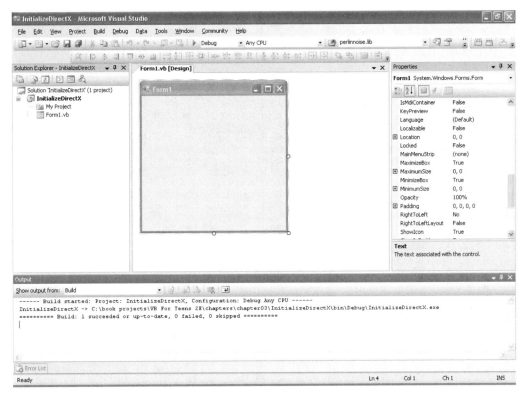

Figure 3.3
The default form in your new Windows Application project.

compiling a game, the compiler could print out a list of 100 or more errors! When this happens, don't freak out, because it's usually just one or two "real errors" causing all of the rest in a sort of chain reaction. Most of the errors usually clear up when you fix the first few errors in your code.

Referencing the DirectX Library

Now we're going to add the DirectX library to our new project so that VB.NET will be able to recognize the DirectX code you are about to write. To add DirectX support to your Visual Basic program, you will need to add a *reference* to DirectX, which is not automatically added as a default library for new projects. Open the Project menu and select Add Reference, or right-click the project name in the Solution Explorer and choose the same option that pops up in the context menu. The Add Reference dialog box is shown in Figure 3.4.

Scroll down the list until you come to the Microsoft group of libraries, and you will soon see DirectX as part of the list. There are many components of DirectX

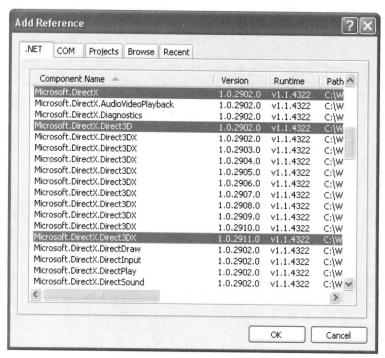

Figure 3.4
The Add Reference dialog box is used to add the DirectX library to your project.

shown, along with various versions of each component (for backwards compatibility). In my example here, you can see about a dozen references to Direct3DX in the list. (Direct3DX is an extension or "helper" library for Direct3D.) Just look for the latest version of any component and select it. You can use the Ctrl key while selecting items in the list to select more than one. All we need at this point are the following references:

- Microsoft.DirectX

- Microsoft.Direct3D

- Microsoft.Direct3DX

Testing the DirectX Reference

Now that the DirectX library has been added to the project, you should be able to view the DirectX objects using IntelliSense while writing source code. Take a peek

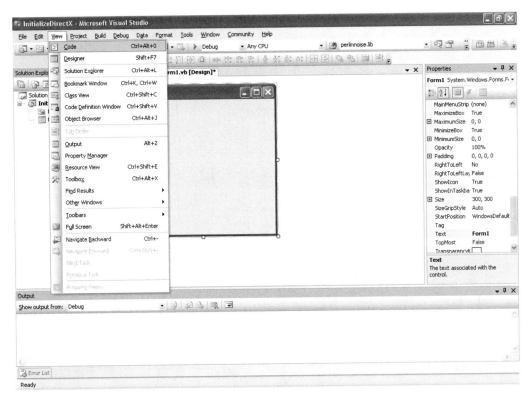

Figure 3.5
Switching to the source code editor view using the View menu.

to see whether DirectX is visible to your Visual Basic program. Double-click the form to open up the source code editor window (alternatively, you may use the View menu and select Code to open the code editor, as shown in Figure 3.5).

If you opened the code window using the View menu rather than by double-clicking the form, then the Form_Load subroutine is not automatically created for you. I wanted you to be aware of the option in the View menu, but it's much easier to just double-click the form to open the code window, especially the first time in a new project, since it adds Form_Load for you.

However, let's not let VB do everything for us! You can create the Form_Load event using the two drop-down lists above the code editor. The first list is called the Class Name list, while the second one is called the Method Name list. The Class Name drop-down list on the top-left of the code editor window normally shows General in the list. Open the list and choose Form1 Events, as shown in Figure 3.6.

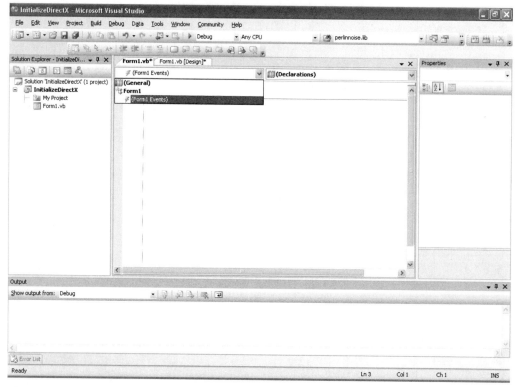

Figure 3.6
The Class Name drop-down list.

When you choose Form1 Events in the Class Name list, then the Method Name list is populated with the methods (also known as *subroutines* or *functions*) in the class you chose. In this instance, we want to see the list of subroutines for Form1. As you can see by opening the list in Figure 3.7, there are hundreds of subroutines for Form1! Select the Load method as I have done in this figure. Presto, you have added the Form_Load method to your program.

So, what is Form_Load all about? Form_Load is a subroutine that runs when the program first starts up. To be more precise, it runs when the form is loaded, which is not exactly when the program starts up, but rather when Visual Basic creates the form and makes it visible.

Ready to Write Some Code?

Now let's start writing some code. You are probably already familiar with IntelliSense. This is a feature Microsoft invented to make programming easier

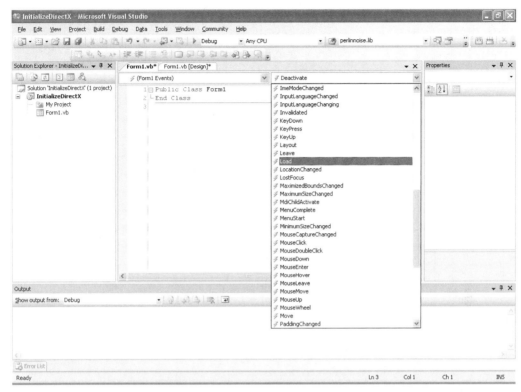

Figure 3.7
The Method Name drop-down list.

(especially for beginners). When you start typing code, the editor watches what you type and tries to help you by listing things you might be interested to know about the objects you're referring to in your code. For an experienced programmer, IntelliSense can sometimes get in the way, but for a beginning to intermediate programmer it is a wonderful feature. The alternative is to look up things in a reference book or on a website!

Now, let's write that code. Position the cursor *before* Form_Load, just after the class definition (the first line of code in the program), and type the following to see whether the DirectX reference is working:

```
Dim device as
```

As soon as you hit space after typing "as," IntelliSense will show you a list of objects visible to your program. It's quite a list, too! These are the .NET Framework components you can use in your program. You can continue typing your code, and IntelliSense will sort of work around your code, updating itself whenever your code refers to a new object.

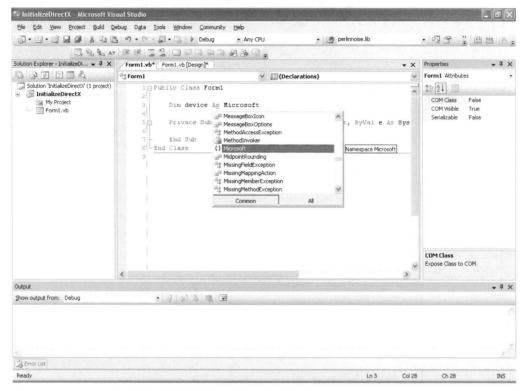

Figure 3.8
Taking a peek at the namespaces and components listed by IntelliSense.

For example, type "Microsoft" next and watch how IntelliSense will jump to the Microsoft namespace in the list, shown in Figure 3.8. This really makes programming much simpler, wouldn't you agree?

After typing Microsoft, then type a period (.) and watch how IntelliSense changes. Now we're browsing *inside* the Microsoft namespace, looking at all of the components available within that namespace, shown in Figure 3.9.

At this point, you can use the down arrow key to move the selection down the list to DirectX, and then press the Enter key to select it. This will add the word "DirectX" to your code. You can also use the mouse to select an item from the list, but experienced programmers rarely take their fingers off the keyboard because it tends to break their train of thought to reach for the mouse. Mainly, this is true because we aren't finished yet with this line of code!

After the DirectX entry, type a period (.) again. Now we're *drilling down* into the framework of DirectX. The next item is Direct3D. But that's not the last item

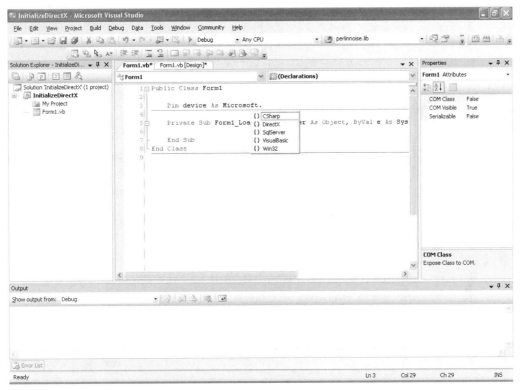

Figure 3.9
The list of components found inside the Microsoft namespace.

either! We have one more to go, and it's called "Device." The final line of code should look like this:

```
Dim device As Microsoft.DirectX.Direct3D.Device
```

If you find yourself using a namespace more than once in a program and you want to cut down on the amount of typing you have to do to drill down to a specific component, there's a way to add a namespace to the program as an automatic scope so that IntelliSense drills down for you to the level at which you want to code. You can do this by adding an `Imports` statement to the top of the code. We'll use Microsoft.DirectX a lot, so it would be helpful to add this to the program. Add the following line to the top of the program (even above Public Class Form1):

```
Imports Microsoft.DirectX
```

Now while you are writing code, IntelliSense will automatically add the components inside Microsoft.DirectX to the global list of items. Since we've drilled down into DirectX, you will see Direct3D show up as a global component in the IntelliSense list. This can be a timesaver, but it can also lead to confusion. Just be aware of this feature and use it whenever it seems appropriate.

Creating the Primary Device

We now have a *device* variable, which represents the video card and is used to initialize Direct3D. Initializing the device takes a little more than just creating a variable for it. The device has to be configured so Direct3D knows how you plan to use it. This is where you set things like the screen resolution, color depth, windowed or full-screen mode. If you're writing a 3D game, you also have to set up the 3D rendering options as well.

First, let's resize the form to 800 × 600. This is a good resolution to use at this point because on most monitors it is only about half the size of the screen. This code is just manipulating the form's properties at this point.

```
Me.Size = New Size(800, 600)
Me.Text = "DirectX Initialization Demo"
Me.SetStyle(ControlStyles.AllPaintingInWmPaint Or ControlStyles.Opaque, True)
```

We do not want to run in full-screen mode yet. When working on a game in Direct3D, you want to use windowed mode so that you can see error messages that pop up. For instance, if you're loading a texture and the image file is missing, you will want to display an error message and then terminate the program. We'll use Messagebox.Show to display pop-up messages, and this doesn't work very well in full-screen mode. Although there's a setting in Direct3D that will make a message box appear over the full-screen display, it is not the preferred way to work.

Next, we need to tell Direct3D how we want it to operate when rendering graphics. We do this using *presentation parameters*: a structure that contains properties that determine how Direct3D will render graphics after the device has been created. Among other things, the presentation parameters tell Direct3D how big the window is.

```
REM set up the presentation parameters
Dim params As New Direct3D.PresentParameters
params.Windowed = True
params.SwapEffect = Direct3D.SwapEffect.Discard
params.AutoDepthStencilFormat = Direct3D.DepthFormat.D16
params.EnableAutoDepthStencil = True
```

```
params.BackBufferCount = 1
params.BackBufferWidth = 800
params.BackBufferHeight = 600
```

Next, we'll do a little bit of checking to see whether the video card is capable of handling the Direct3D device we intend to create.

```
rem check video card capabilities
Dim adapterNumber As Integer = Direct3D.Manager.Adapters.Default.Adapter
Dim flags As Direct3D.CreateFlags
flags = Direct3D.CreateFlags.HardwareVertexProcessing
flags += Direct3D.CreateFlags.PureDevice

Dim caps As Direct3D.Caps
caps = Direct3D.Manager.GetDeviceCaps(adapterNumber, _
        Direct3D.DeviceType.Hardware)
If caps.DeviceCaps.SupportsHardwareTransformAndLight = False Or _
    caps.DeviceCaps.SupportsPureDevice = False Then

    MessageBox.Show("Your video card is obsolete.", _
        "Hardware Problem")
    End
End If
```

That code will just perform a simple test to see whether the video card is capable of hardware transform and lighting (T&L), which is very old 3D technology at this point, so it will complain if someone tries to run the program on an ancient PC without a 3D card (which is preferable to just letting the program crash).

Next, we can actually create the new device:

```
rem create the Direct3D device
device = New Direct3D.Device(adapterNumber, _
    Direct3D.DeviceType.Hardware, Me, flags, params)
```

Lastly, we need to add another subroutine to the program. This new subroutine is called OnPaint, and it handles the refresh of the screen. If you run the program before adding OnPaint, the window will appear, but the surface of the window will be garbled with the image of the background. The OnPaint event is run by VB whenever the screen needs to be refreshed. In the case of our little program, that happens primarily when the program starts up. But it is also called whenever the window is minimized or overlapped by another window and needs to redraw itself.

Figure 3.10
The DirectX Initialization Demo program.

```
Protected Overrides Sub OnPaint(ByVal e As PaintEventArgs)
    device.Clear(Direct3D.ClearFlags.Target + _
        Direct3D.ClearFlags.ZBuffer, Color.Blue, 1.0, 0)
    device.BeginScene()
    device.EndScene()
    device.Present()
    Me.Invalidate()
End Sub
```

That's all there is to it! When you run the program by pressing F5, you should see the blue-colored window shown in Figure 3.10. This program is important because it represents that you now have the ability to initialize Direct3D in a Visual Basic program. At this point, the program is waiting for graphics—3D primitives and models as well as 2D bitmaps and sprites—to render. Direct3D is doing a lot of work here to just render a blue screen without any real content. It is even double buffering the screen, fully expecting to have worlds to render!

Tip

A *double buffer*–also called *back buffer*–is a duplicate of the screen, stored in memory, where you send all graphics output to. By working with this scratchpad in memory, and then drawing the whole double buffer to the screen all at once, you greatly improve the quality of the game, reducing flicker and screen refresh problems.

What can you do after DirectX has been initialized? The sky's the limit, really. This is the point where you start drawing graphics on the screen, and it is the starting point for your game. For this first program, we just cleared the screen with a color and then displayed the window. The next program will show you how to load a bitmap file and render it on the screen using Direct3D, which is an important next step toward building a game!

Loading and Rendering a Bitmap

The ability to load a bitmap file is at the core of a game and is an absolutely essential, make-or-break, mission-critical thing that just has to work or the game might as well be running on Pioneer 11 out beyond the orbit of Pluto. (Yeah, maybe it runs, but you won't see anything.)

By the way, did you know that NASA now has a project in the works called Interstellar Probe? You can read about it at http://interstellar.jpl.nasa.gov. You know, sometimes I get the feeling that programming a game is more of a challenge than programming a NASA spacecraft.

The New LoadBitmap Project

The InitializeDirectX program was a good starting point as far as showing you how to write the initialization code for Direct3D, but it didn't do much. Let's take it a little further by writing some new code that loads a bitmap file and displays the image on the screen. This chapter does not fully go into the use of bitmaps, as that is reserved for a future chapter. However, I will show you how to load a bitmap and then copy it to the back buffer, which is then displayed on the screen. The output of the program is shown in Figure 3.11.

I recommend starting with a new, blank project for this program, rather than modifying the last program, because you will benefit from the practice. Create a new project in Visual Basic; go into Project, Add Reference and add the references again to Microsoft.DirectX, Microsoft.Direct3D, and Microsoft.Direct3DX. You can then open the code window for Form1 and get started on the program with the following source code.

Variables

Let me go over it from a top-down fashion, explaining the code as if you are reading it, because that is easier to follow. First you have the program comment,

Figure 3.11
The LoadBitmap program demonstrates how to use Direct3D surfaces.

constants, and variable definitions. The SCREENW and SCREENH constants define the resolution of the game's window. The Direct3D.Device variable is used for rendering, while the Direct3D.Surface variable will hold the bitmap image.

```
Imports Microsoft.DirectX
Imports Microsoft.DirectX.Direct3D

Public Class Form1

    REM define some useful constants
    Const SCREENW As Integer = 800
    Const SCREENH As Integer = 600

    Dim BLACK As Integer = RGB(0, 0, 0)

    REM Direct3D device variable
    Dim device As Direct3D.Device

    REM create image from a Direct3D surface
    Dim image As Direct3D.Surface
```

This code is quite an improvement over the last program that you worked on just a few minutes ago, so you're making good progress already! First, I have declared some constants at the top. These are values that you can easily change at the top of the program, affecting things like the resolution (with more constants to be added in future programs). I've also created a color constant so it's easier to change the background clearing color. Next, you see two groups of variables: the Direct3D device and a Direct3D surface for use as an image. The surface variable is something new that you haven't seen before, and we use another one in the OnPaint event to get a reference to the back buffer. Direct3D.Surface is a class, just like Microsoft.DirectX. Classes are an *object-oriented programming (OOP)* concept, which you were briefly introduced to in the previous chapter.

Program Startup

Let's look at the Form1_Load subroutine next. This is the subroutine that runs when the form is first displayed by Visual Basic. This is basically just the code we've gone over previously in the chapter, but combined into a single listing.

```
REM resize the form
Me.Size = New Size(SCREENW, SCREENH)
Me.Text = "Bitmap Loading Demo"
Me.SetStyle(ControlStyles.AllPaintingInWmPaint Or _
    ControlStyles.Opaque, True)

REM get the desktop display mode
Dim adapterNumber As Integer = Manager.Adapters.Default.Adapter
Dim mode As DisplayMode
mode = Manager.Adapters.Default.CurrentDisplayMode

REM set up the presentation parameters
Dim params As New PresentParameters
params.Windowed = True
params.SwapEffect = SwapEffect.Copy
params.AutoDepthStencilFormat = DepthFormat.D16
params.EnableAutoDepthStencil = True
params.MultiSample = MultiSampleType.None
params.BackBufferCount = 1
params.BackBufferWidth = SCREENW
params.BackBufferHeight = SCREENH

REM check video card capabilities
Dim flags As CreateFlags
flags = CreateFlags.HardwareVertexProcessing
flags += CreateFlags.PureDevice
```

```
REM create the Direct3D device
device = New Device(adapterNumber, DeviceType.Hardware, _
    Me, flags, params)

REM load the bitmap file
image = device.CreateOffscreenPlainSurface(SCREENW, SCREENH, _
    Format.A8R8G8B8, Pool.Default)
SurfaceLoader.FromFile(image, "sky.bmp", Filter.None, BLACK)
```

Some new code in Form_Load requires some explanation. The first group of code changes the size of the form to 800 × 600, the desired resolution we're using for this program. The bit of code is similar to the Direct3D initialization we used in the previous program, InitializeDirectX. In the near future when we begin working on the Celtic Crusader game, I'll help you package some of this code into reusable subroutines so we don't have to write them over and over again.

Toward the bottom, after the device is created, we have the code to create a Direct3D surface and then load a bitmap file into that surface. SurfaceLoader is a class found within Direct3D, but we don't need to use the Microsoft.Direct3D qualifier because that was included at the top of the program as an import statement. This code can also be put into a reusable subroutine. I would like to be able to write a subroutine that accepts a single parameter—the filename of a bitmap file—and have it load the bitmap into the surface. We'll do something like that later on as well.

When you take a look at the code that actually loads a bitmap file, it's rather simple because you can use the SurfaceLoader class, which has a subroutine called FromFile that handles bitmap file loading for us. The only drawback is that you have to create the surface in memory first before loading the bitmap, because the subroutine doesn't create the memory for you. That complicates things! Fortunately, we have a helper routine in the Direct3D device class called CreateOffscreenPlainSurface that fulfills this need.

Drawing the Surface Image

Okay, the hard part is done and there's just some minor code left to be written to get this program finished. The last bit of code includes the OnPaint event (which is run anytime the form window changes) that displays the image after it has been loaded.

One thing that requires some explanation here is the StretchRectangle subroutine. This is used to copy one surface onto another surface, and it is quite useful. It allows you to specify the exact rectangle to copy from, as well as the exact rectangle to copy to within the destination surface. We could use this subroutine to draw animated sprites! I have actually done just that in Visual C++ when using a Direct3D surface to handle sprite animation. In the C++ library, the function is called StretchRect, but in Visual Basic the subroutine name is StretchRectangle. This is the workhorse for Direct3D surfaces, and we will use it extensively to create the tile-based scroller engine for Celtic Crusader. At this early stage, let's just *use* StretchRectangle without being concerned about how it works or how we can use those rectangle parameters to do advanced 2D rendering—we'll save that subject for later!

```
Protected Overrides Sub OnPaint(ByVal e As PaintEventArgs)
    REM begin rendering
    device.BeginScene()

    REM clear the back buffer
    device.Clear(ClearFlags.Target + ClearFlags.ZBuffer, Color.Green, 1.0, 0)

    REM specify the drawing rectangles for the image
    Dim source_rect As New System.Drawing.Rectangle(0, 0, SCREENW, SCREENH)
    Dim dest_rect As New System.Drawing.Rectangle(0, 0, SCREENW, SCREENH)

    REM get reference to the back buffer
    Dim backbuffer As Direct3D.Surface
    backbuffer = device.GetBackBuffer(0, 0, BackBufferType.Mono)

    REM draw the image
    device.StretchRectangle(image, source_rect, backbuffer, dest_rect, 0)

    REM stop rendering
    device.EndScene()

    REM copy back buffer to the screen
    device.Present()
End Sub
```

The Form1_KeyDown event is a normal Form subroutine that you can use to detect key presses. We'll learn about DirectInput too, but at this point we just want a simple way to detect when the Escape key is pressed in order to end the program. This is better than requiring the user to click the window's Close (X) button. Before ending the program, we dispose of the Direct3D device and the surface to free up memory. It's always a good idea to free up resources your game used before ending the program, but VB will usually take care of cleanup when you forget to do so.

```
Private Sub Form1_KeyDown(ByVal sender As Object, _
    ByVal e As System.Windows.Forms.KeyEventArgs) Handles Me.KeyDown
    REM check key code for ESC key
    If e.KeyCode = Keys.Escape Then
        REM destroy the Direct3D device
        device.Dispose()

        REM destroy the image
        image.Dispose()

        REM end the program
        End
    End If
End Sub
```

Video Card Adapter Information

Before concluding this chapter, I want to share with you an interesting program I wrote. It is called AdapterInformation and it is shown in Figure 3.12. I'm not going to go over the source code here because it's off topic and not particularly important. I just think this is interesting, and I suspect that you will too. What this program does is poll the adapter information from Direct3D to find out the details of the video card in your PC.

In the screenshot shown here, you can see that the video card in my PC is a NVIDIA GeForce Go 6400. This is a very good video card for a small 12-inch laptop! I've played *World of Warcraft* on this during meetings (with the sound turned off, of course!). The video card has an advertised 256 MB of DDR2 memory, but this program is reporting 270 MB. Perhaps those 14 additional megabytes are reserved for the frame buffer and 256 MB are actually just texture memory.

You can also see the chipset version number, the driver file, and the driver version. Although my driver is more than a year old, I haven't been able to upgrade it because NVIDIA doesn't offer GeForce Go 6000-series drivers directly, only through the original equipment manufacturer, and no driver is available from the manufacturer either, so I'm stuck with an old NVIDIA driver—but it works great so I don't mind. Feel free to open up the project on the CD-ROM to examine the code and run it on your own system.

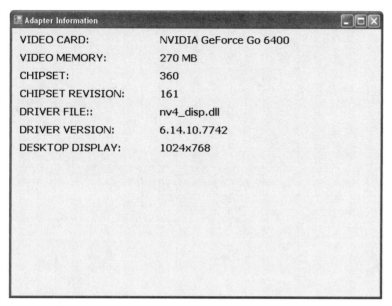

Figure 3.12
The AdapterInformation program displays detailed information about the video card.

Level Up

Congratulations, you have gained a level of experience with VB.NET! This chapter was very important to your understanding of how to interface with DirectX from Visual Basic. You learned some critical concepts, such as how to create and initialize the Direct3D device, how to create a surface in memory, and how to load a bitmap file. You are only at level two so far, and you have a long way to go before you'll be writing your own games from scratch. The next few chapters will help you level up your skills and get you moving in the right direction.

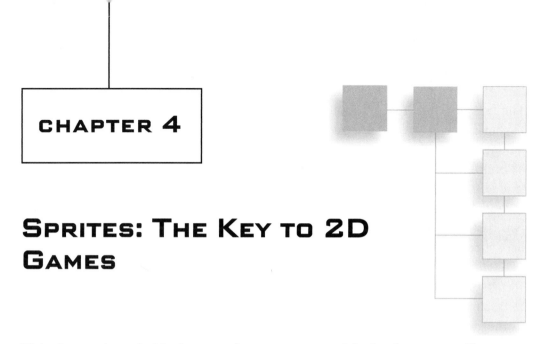

CHAPTER 4

SPRITES: THE KEY TO 2D GAMES

This chapter is probably the most important part of the book, so you will want to consume this material more thoroughly than any other subject. We have a lot of ground to cover here, and we'll be going through it thoroughly because this is the foundation of Celtic Crusader. You will leave this chapter with a solid grasp of sprite programming knowledge and with the ability to load a sprite sheet and draw a sprite with animation. Because we want a sprite to draw transparently over any background image in a game, you'll first learn how Direct3D uses an alpha channel in a bitmap image to render an image with transparency. This chapter moves along at a pretty good clip, so you don't want to skip a single paragraph, or you might miss some important detail. Here is what you will find in this chapter:

- Introduction to sprites

- Learning how Direct3D draws sprites

- Loading a texture

- Using the Direct3D sprite handler

- Creating support classes

- Sprite animation theory

- Adding animation support to the sprite class

Introduction to Sprites

The first question that often arises when the discussion of sprites comes up is, "What is a sprite?" To answer this question simply, a *sprite* is a small, transparent, animated image that moves on the screen. You might have trees or rocks or buildings in your game that don't move at all, but because those objects are loaded from a bitmap file when the game starts running, and drawn in the game separately from the background, it is reasonable to call them sprites. There are two basic types of sprites. One type of sprite is the "normal" sprite that I just described, which I refer to as a *dynamic sprite*. This type of sprite is often called a *2D Actor* in game design theory. The other type of sprite might be called a *static sprite*; it is the sort that doesn't move around on the screen. A static sprite is used for scenery or objects that the player uses (such as items that might be picked up in the game world). This type of sprite is often called a *2D Prop*.

I'm going to treat any game entity that is loaded and drawn separately from the background as a sprite. So, I might have a whole house, which normally would be considered part of the background, as a sprite. I use that concept in the sample program later in this chapter.

One of the problems that may confuse someone new to DirectX is just how to handle sprites when there is only one way to render graphics: using Direct3D. Direct3D is a high-performance 3D rendering library that powers most of the games created today for the Windows platform. But how suited is Direct3D for handling 2D sprites? You learned in previous chapters that Direct3D lets you use surfaces to draw images on the screen. But what about drawing sprites, which must be transparent and animated?

Figure 4.1 shows an example sprite of an Orc warrior. The sprite is really just the detailed pixels that you see at the center of the image, showing the Orc warrior holding a mace and shield. The sprite itself only takes up about half of the actual size of the sprite because the computer only sees sprites in the shape of a rectangle. It is physically impossible to even store a sprite without the rectangular boundary because bitmap images are themselves rectangular. The real problem with a sprite is what to do about all the transparent pixels that should *not* be shown when the image is displayed on the screen (or rather, on the back buffer surface).

The amateur game programmer will try to draw a sprite using two loops that go through each pixel of the sprite's bitmap image, drawing only the solid pixels. Here is the pseudocode for how one might do this:

Transparent Pixels

Sprite Boundary

Figure 4.1
The sprite boundary is a rectangle that encloses the sprite with transparent pixels.

```
For Y = 1 To Sprite_Height
  For X = 1 to Sprite_Width
    If Pixel At X,Y Is Solid Then
      Draw Pixel At X,Y
    End If
  Next X
Next Y
```

This pseudocode algorithm goes through each pixel of the sprite image, checking for solid pixels, which are then drawn while transparent pixels are ignored. This draws a transparent sprite, but it runs so slowly that the game probably won't be playable (even on a top-of-the-line PC).

And yet, this is the *only* way to draw a transparent sprite! By one method or another, some process must check the pixels that are solid and render them. The key here is understanding how Direct3D works, because this very critical and time-consuming algorithm is quite old and has been built into the silicon of video cards for many years now. The process of copying a transparent image from one surface to another has been provided by video cards since Windows 3.11 first started supporting the concept of a "video accelerator." The process is called *bit block transfer* or just *blit* for short. Because this important process is handled by an extremely optimized and custom video chip, you don't need to worry about writing your own *blitter* for a game any longer. (Even the Nintendo Game Boy Advance has a hardware blitter.)

How Does Direct3D Draw Sprites?

Direct3D doesn't use the term *blit* to describe the process of drawing a texture onto a polygon or a surface, because that does not use a bit-block transfer. Rather, it uses an algorithm called *texturing*, from which we get the name for textures. The video card uses a process called *alpha blending* to draw textures with a translucent effect (which means you can see through them like a window) or with full transparency. Fifty-percent translucency means that half of the light rays are blocked by the texture, and you can only see about half of the image. Zero-percent translucency is called *opaque*, meaning that *none* of the image is visible (it is completely blacked out), and in 3D terms this mean that no light passes through an opaque texture. The opposite is 100-percent translucency, which lets *all* light pass through, which means that the texture is totally *transparent*. Figure 4.2 illustrates the difference between a fully opaque sprite and a transparent sprite. (Notice how the shadow is also visible on the background.)

When an image needs to be drawn with transparency in Direct3D, a texture is used where a certain pixel color on the texture image is considered the "transparent" color, and the process of alpha blending causes that particular pixel color to be completely blended with the background. At the same time, no other pixels in the texture are affected by alpha blending, and the result is a transparent sprite. In addition to transparency support, you can also draw a Direct3D texture with a global translucency effect so that the solid pixels become translucent. This is a

Figure 4.2
The sprite on the right is drawn without the transparent pixels.

very cool effect that you might use, for example, for a ghost or wraith creature in your game. This process is called *color key transparency*, and it is obsolete.

The professional way to handle transparency today is with an alpha channel embedded inside the bitmap image. For this to work, you must use a bitmap file format that supports an alpha channel. Unfortunately and mysteriously, the Windows Bitmap format does not support an alpha channel, so when using a Windows bitmap, you have to use the older color key transparency. The first edition of this book used this technique, but we're upgrading this time around to full alpha channel support, and our new file format of choice is Portable Network Graphics, or PNG, which DirectX can also handle.

Direct3D Sprites

The key to drawing transparent sprites with Direct3D, as you might have guessed at this point, is through the use of a texture. Now, if you are at all familiar with 3D graphics, then I'm sure you have heard the word *texture* used many times before. It is second only in popularity to the ubiquitous polygon in 3D lore (which is also obsolete, as the new term of choice is "face"). Textures are used to paint the surface of a face (i.e. *polygon*) in 3D space. If you have ever painted before, then you may think of how a wall feels after a fresh coat of paint has dried on it, and you probably remember how the wall's texture feels beneath your fingers. The texture of paint also affects how the surface looks and feels when it is cured.

But in the 3D realm, *texture* is a misused term that describes the application of a bitmap to a face. In effect, a texture in the context of 3D graphics is nothing more than a bitmap image; on the other hand, the word *texture* brings up quite a different meaning when you ponder it outside the context of computer graphics. So, it's more of a term that describes *how* an image is applied to a face rather than *what* that image is. Textures are *textured*; bitmaps are *blitted*. This is why you can't use a Direct3D surface object to draw a sprite, because this object does not support transparency. Instead, you have to use a Direct3D texture object.

A Direct3D texture is similar to a Direct3D surface. While a surface represents the image that is visible on the screen (and is only addressed in 2D terms), a texture exists in 3D when it is applied to a face. Advanced texture handling provides for special effects, and Direct3D can apply many effects to a texture, such as bump mapping, normal mapping, and *pixel shader* programs (mini programs that run inside the GPU to affect how a texture looks).

Loading a Texture

The key to loading a bitmap file into a surface revolves around a subroutine in the Direct3DX library. (Remember, that is the Direct3D extension, a set of subroutines and classes that help Direct3D.) In the previous chapter, we used an object called SurfaceLoader (located in the `Microsoft.DirectX.Direct3D` namespace). SurfaceLoader fills a surface with the bitmap image loaded from the specified file. You may also recall that we have to create the surface in memory first, before loading the bitmap image.

Direct3D textures are a little bit easier to work with than surfaces, in my opinion. You should have no problem understanding how to use textures once you've had a chance to play around with some example code. To load a texture, you can use another helper object called `TextureLoader`, which has a function called `FromFile` that you can use to load a file.

Note

I have not fully explained the word *function*. A *function* in Visual Basic is a subroutine (Sub) that returns a value, while a Sub does not return a value. But in the C++ language, *every* subroutine is called a function, regardless of whether it returns a value. Since DirectX was built in C++, it's often helpful to refer to DirectX subroutines as *functions*. To further complicate matters, a function located inside an object-oriented *class* is called a *method*. Subroutines, functions, and methods are *essentially* the same thing.

There is a bit of inconsistency with Direct3D textures. In contrast to surfaces, a texture need not be created in memory prior to calling `TextureLoader.FromFile`. This function creates the texture in memory and then loads the bitmap into the texture object, after which the texture may be used to paint a face or—in the interest of 2D games—to draw a sprite, with all of the benefits of a 3D system. Direct3D textures can be scaled or *translated* (which means moved in 3D), as well as rotated. The translation part of a 3D object allows that object to move around in the 3D world. In the context of a 2D sprite, this aspect of the sprite's textured nature gives it the ability to move around on the surface where it is drawn (more on that shortly). The ability to change the scale (or rather, *resolution*) of a texture also makes it possible to change the scale of a sprite as it is drawn.

There are a lot of variations of the `TextureLoader.FromFile` function because this function is a Direct3D utility that handles many options when creating a new texture. Fortunately, there are simple versions of the function as well as complex versions. If we just want to load a bitmap file into a texture without regard for any additional options, there are only two parameters with which we need to be concerned: the Direct3D device and the filename.

```
image = TextureLoader.FromFile(device, filename)
```

Visual Basic Pathnames

Now would be a good time to discuss pathnames in Visual Basic. A path is a complete description of a directory location. If you consider a file with an absolute path, as in the following example:

C:\Program Files\Microsoft Visual Studio 8\Common7\IDE\devenv.exe

The filename is located at the end, "devenv.exe," while the path to this filename is all of the directories specified in front of the filename. The complete "path" to a file can be described in this absolute format.

The problem is that Visual Basic compiles programs into a subdirectory under your project directory called *bin*. Inside bin, depending on whether you're building the Debug or Release version of your program, there will be a folder called bin\Debug or bin\Release. You need to put all of your game's bitmap files inside this folder in order for it to run. You would not want to store your game's files inside the main folder of the project because when it runs (inside bin\Debug, for instance) it will not know where the files are located, and the program will crash.

You can hard-code the path into your game, but this is a terrible idea because then anyone who tries to play your game will have to create the exact same directory that you did when you created the game. So, the moral of this story is: Put your artwork and other game resources inside bin\Debug while working on your game. When your game is finished and ready for release, then copy all of the files together into the same folder with the executable.

The Direct3D Sprite Handler

Direct3D has a built-in helper class called Sprite that makes it possible to draw 2D graphics on the screen without concern for the 3D rendering system. The C++ version of Direct3D.Sprite is called D3DXSprite, and is located in the DIRECT3DX library, but this is abstracted into Direct3D.Sprite for Managed DirectX (which is what we're using). Thus far, we haven't really used Direct3D.Sprite because the LoadSurface program in the previous chapter used

StretchRectangle to draw an image. Now we need to take a look at the drawing functions in Direct3D.Sprite.

The first step to using Direct3D.Sprite is to create an object variable like this:

```
Dim sprite_handler As Direct3D.Sprite
```

Note the name I chose for this object. It is no mistake that I have called it sprite_handler rather than just *sprite* or something similar. The Direct3D.Sprite object is a *global* object like the Direct3D *device*. Once created, you can use the device any number of times in your game, and then destroy it when closing. The same applies to Direct3D.Sprite. It is a sprite handler in the sense that this object draws all of our sprites, each of which comes from a texture. So, in essence, Direct3D.Sprite renders textures onto the screen to simulate a 2D game in a 3D environment.

The next step is to initialize the sprite object to ready it for use:

```
sprite_handler = New Direct3D.Sprite(device)
```

Since we have to pass the Direct3D device when creating the sprite handler, it's obvious that the device must be created in advance.

Now let's take a look at how to draw a sprite. There are two drawing functions in Direct3D.Sprite. One, simply called Draw, renders a texture using 3D vectors, so you basically have to tell it where the sprite is located using the usual X,Y position on the screen and include a Z component by setting it to zero. The Vector3 struct is easy to use, but really isn't necessary for drawing 2D sprites on the screen. There is another function that is both easier to use *and* more powerful, because there are several variations of it: I'm speaking of the Draw2D function. Since Draw2D is more suitable, we'll ignore the other one. We'll take a look at several of the *six* versions of Draw2D in order to draw tiles and sprites in various ways. But let's just look at the simplest version right now.

```
Dim center As New PointF(0, 0)
Dim angle As Single = 0.0
Dim position As New PointF(0, 0)
sprite_handler.Draw2D(ocean, center, angle, position, Color.White)
```

The Draw2D function that is easiest to use still has five parameters! But let's just look at them rather than worrying about it. The first parameter is the texture. Then there are three weird parameters followed by the last one, which is a color value. Why do we need to set a color for a texture, when it is coming from an image? This is actually a very cool parameter that lets you adjust the color value of the image dynamically. We'll use this feature to flash a character red whenever he gets hit! You could also slowly fade a color down to black to make it disappear! So, there are some very good possibilities. It's always a great thing when you can do some special effect without needing any new artwork, just using the image you already have.

The LoadTexture Program

Now let's take a look at a complete example that loads two images and draws them. The first image is an ocean image, while the second is a pirate ship that will be drawn transparently over the ocean. Figure 4.3 shows what the program looks like. This is one of the last programs I will list entirely in the book. Future examples will just list key portions of code, with the assumption that you will be able to load up the project from the CD-ROM to get the complete listing. (Both the water and the pirate ship images were created by Reiner Prokein, like *all* of the artwork featured in this book.)

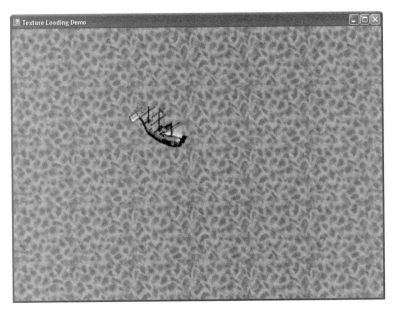

Figure 4.3
The LoadTexture program demonstrates transparent sprite rendering.

```vb
Imports System.Drawing
Imports Microsoft.DirectX
Imports Microsoft.DirectX.Direct3D

Public Class Form1
    'define some useful constants
    Const SCREENW As Integer = 800
    Const SCREENH As Integer = 600
    Dim BLACK As Integer = RGB(0, 0, 0)

    'Direct3D objects
    Dim device As Direct3D.Device
    Dim backbuffer As Direct3D.Surface
    Dim sprite_handler As Direct3D.Sprite

    'create image from a Direct3D surface
    Dim ocean As Direct3D.Texture
    Dim pirateship As Direct3D.Texture


    Private Sub Form1_Load(ByVal sender As System.Object, _
     ByVal e As System.EventArgs) Handles MyBase.Load
        'resize the form
        Me.Size = New Size(SCREENW, SCREENH)
        Me.Text = "Texture Loading Demo"
        Me.SetStyle(ControlStyles.AllPaintingInWmPaint Or ControlStyles
        .Opaque, True)

        'get the desktop display mode
        Dim adapterNumber As Integer = Manager.Adapters.Default.Adapter
        Dim mode As DisplayMode = Manager.Adapters.Default.CurrentDisplayMode

        'set up the presentation parameters
        Dim params As New PresentParameters
        params.Windowed = True
        params.SwapEffect = SwapEffect.Copy
        params.AutoDepthStencilFormat = DepthFormat.D16
        params.EnableAutoDepthStencil = True
        params.MultiSample = MultiSampleType.None
        params.BackBufferCount = 1
        params.BackBufferWidth = SCREENW
        params.BackBufferHeight = SCREENH
```

```
        'check video card capabilities
        Dim flags As CreateFlags
        flags = CreateFlags.HardwareVertexProcessing
        flags += CreateFlags.PureDevice

        'create the Direct3D device
        device = New Device(adapterNumber, DeviceType.Hardware, Me, flags, _
        params)

        'get reference to the back buffer
        backbuffer = device.GetBackBuffer(0, 0, BackBufferType.Mono)

        'create the sprite handler
        sprite_handler = New Direct3D.Sprite(device)

        'load the background as a texture
        ocean = TextureLoader.FromFile(device, "ocean.bmp")

        'load the pirate ship
        pirateship = TextureLoader.FromFile(device, "pirateship.png")
End Sub

Sub draw_ocean()
        'demonstrate Direct3D.Sprite.Draw
        Dim rotation_center As New PointF(0, 0)
        Dim rotation_angle As Single = 0.0
        Dim position As New PointF(0, 0)
        sprite_handler.Draw2D(ocean, rotation_center, rotation_angle, _
            position, Color.White)
        sprite_handler.Flush()
End Sub

Sub draw_ship()
        'demonstrate Direct3D.Sprite.Draw2D
        Dim rotation_center As New PointF(48, 48)
        Dim rotation_angle As Single = 0.0
        Dim position As New PointF(300, 200)
        sprite_handler.Draw2D(pirateship, rotation_center, rotation_angle, _
            position, Color.White)
        sprite_handler.Flush()
End Sub
```

```
Protected Overrides Sub OnPaint(ByVal e As PaintEventArgs)
    'begin rendering
    device.BeginScene()

    'clear the back buffer
    device.Clear(ClearFlags.Target + ClearFlags.ZBuffer, Color.Green, _
    1.0, 0)

    'draw the sprites
    sprite_handler.Begin(SpriteFlags.AlphaBlend)
    draw_ocean()
    draw_ship()
    sprite_handler.End()

    'stop rendering
    device.EndScene()

    'copy back buffer to the screen
    device.Present()
End Sub

Private Sub Form1_KeyDown(ByVal sender As Object, _
    ByVal e As System.Windows.Forms.KeyEventArgs) Handles Me.KeyDown
    'check key code for ESC key
    If e.KeyCode = Keys.Escape Then
        device.Dispose()
        ocean.Dispose()
        pirateship.Dispose()
        End
    End If
End Sub
End Class
```

Creating Some Helper Classes

There are a lot of properties that you have to keep track of when drawing sprites
on the screen. If you think about if for a moment, you may wonder how you keep
track of where each sprite is located on the screen and how you move it around.
As an example, suppose you have a hero character that is moved around using the
keyboard arrow keys or perhaps a joystick. How do you take a texture full of
sprites and turn that into something that moves around on the screen?

This discussion revolves around a subject called *logistics,* which is the organization of a complex task or the management of things being moved, and is often used to describe how military units are deployed or how a business acquires raw materials for use in manufacturing. Dealing with sprites requires that you take care of all the logistics yourself! You might be able to imagine using simple variables such as X and Y to track the sprite's location on the screen. What about the sprite's image size and its speed, direction, and animation variables? All of this data has to be handled, and that's just for one sprite.

A well-written game handles the logistics of sprite movement using what you might call a sprite manager. The *sprite manager* is like a colonel in the military who takes orders from the high-ranking general and carries out those orders to the lower-ranking officers who are in charge of the soldiers. Sprites may also be thought of as products on an assembly line, while a supervisor makes sure they are assembled correctly. *You* are the general (or manager), and you need a colonel (or supervisor) to handle the logistics of sprite management, so that you can focus on more important things (such as the game's design). A sprite manager is simpler than you might imagine because it is just made up of a class and a few helpful subroutines that work with the class.

A *class* is like a custom data type that you can create yourself, but classes include variables and subroutines together. This makes it much easier to handle many objects without using a bunch of global variables. I refer you back to the previous chapter if you need a refresher on this subject.

Tip

Very important! Your textures in Direct3D must have a width and height that are powers of two! For instance, 128×128, 256×256, 512×512, and 1024×1024. If you load an image into a texture that does not have standard dimensions, Direct3D will resize your texture when it is loaded, which will result in image skewing in your game. You will know this is a problem when your sprites have been set up properly, but they still do not draw correctly. I use PNG files with a resolution of 1024×1024 for most of the sprite sheets in Celtic Crusader.

Writing the Sprite Class

I recommend you modify the LoadTexture program for the following exercise. If you want to just create a new project, that's okay too. If you don't already have a new project available, go ahead and create a new Windows Forms application for Visual Basic, then add the following references using the Project, Add Reference menu: Microsoft.DirectX, Microsoft.Direct3D, Microsoft.Direct3DX.

Let's create the sprite class first and then add the code for the rest of the project. Open the Project menu and select Add Class. The new class name will be CSprite. You aren't required to start every new class name with a "C," but it does help to keep your own classes separate from system classes (such as Direct3D.Sprite). Of course, we could just create our own namespace, but I want to keep the code as simple as possible at this point. Here's the code for the CSprite class:

```
Imports Microsoft.DirectX
Imports Microsoft.DirectX.Direct3D

Public Class CSprite
    Private ref_d3d As CDirect3D
    Private image As Direct3D.Texture
    Private desc As SurfaceDescription
    Private pos As PointF
    Private rotation As Single

    'make these public for convenience
    Public FrameWidth As Integer
    Public FrameHeight As Integer
    Public Columns As Integer
    Public StartFrame As Integer
    Public EndFrame As Integer
    Public TotalFrames As Integer
    Public CurrentFrame As Integer
    Public FrameThreshold As Integer
    Public FrameCounter As Integer
    Private velocity As PointF
    Public Function GetVelocity() As PointF
        Return velocity
    End Function
    Public Sub SetVelocity(ByVal value As PointF)
        velocity = value
    End Sub
    Public Sub SetVelocity(ByVal vx As Single, ByVal vy As Single)
        velocity.X = vx
        velocity.Y = vy
    End Sub

    Public Sub Move()
        pos.X += velocity.X
        pos.Y += velocity.Y
    End Sub
```

```
Public Sub KeepInBounds(ByVal boundary As Rectangle)
    If pos.X < boundary.Left Or pos.X > boundary.Right Then
        velocity.X *= -1
        pos.X += velocity.X
    End If
    If pos.Y < boundary.Top Or pos.Y > boundary.Bottom Then
        velocity.Y *= -1
        pos.Y += velocity.Y
    End If
End Sub

Public Sub Animate()
    Me.FrameCounter += 1
    If Me.FrameCounter > Me.FrameThreshold Then

        Me.CurrentFrame += 1
        If (Me.CurrentFrame > Me.EndFrame) Then
            Me.CurrentFrame = Me.StartFrame
        End If

    End If
End Sub


Public Sub DrawFrame()
    Dim frame As New Rectangle
    frame.X = (Me.CurrentFrame Mod Me.Columns) * Me.FrameWidth
    frame.Y = (Me.CurrentFrame \ Me.Columns) * Me.FrameHeight
    frame.Width = Me.FrameWidth
    frame.Height = Me.FrameHeight

    Dim dest As New Rectangle(Me.GetX(), Me.GetY(), _
        Me.FrameWidth, Me.FrameHeight)

    Me.Draw(frame, dest)
End Sub


Sub New(ByRef d3d As CDirect3D)
    Me.ref_d3d = d3d
    Me.image = Nothing
    Me.pos = New PointF(0.0, 0.0)
    Me.rotation = 0.0
End Sub
```

```
Function GetPosition() As PointF
    Return Me.pos
End Function
Function GetX() As Integer
    Return Me.pos.X
End Function
Function GetY() As Integer
    Return Me.pos.Y
End Function
Sub SetPosition(ByRef pos As PointF)
    Me.pos = pos
End Sub
Sub SetPosition(ByVal x As Integer, ByVal y As Integer)
    Me.pos.X = CSng(x)
    Me.pos.Y = CSng(y)
End Sub

Function GetSize() As Point
    Return New Point(desc.Width, desc.Height)
End Function
Function GetWidth() As Integer
    Return desc.Width
End Function
Function GetHeight() As Integer
    Return desc.Height
End Function

Public Sub Load(ByVal filename As String)
    image = TextureLoader.FromFile(ref_d3d.GetDevice(), filename)
    desc = image.GetLevelDescription(0)
End Sub

Sub Draw()
    Dim center As New PointF(0.0, 0.0)
    ref_d3d.GetSprite().Draw2D(Me.image, center, Me.rotation, _
    Me.pos, Color.White)
End Sub

Sub Draw(ByVal srcrect As Rectangle, ByVal destrect As Rectangle)
    Dim dest_size As New SizeF(destrect.Width, destrect.Height)
```

```
            Dim position As New PointF(destrect.X, destrect.Y)
            ref_d3d.GetSprite().Draw2D(image, srcrect, dest_size, _
                position, Color.White)

    End Sub

    Protected Overrides Sub Finalize()
        MyBase.Finalize()
        image.Dispose()
    End Sub
End Class
```

We're going to add a lot more to the CSprite class before we're done with it, including support for animation. But this simple version will suffice at this point. It's always preferable, in my opinion, to build something up one step at a time rather than to construct something in its entirety all at once and then try to use it. By building something in stages, you ensure that you will have working code every step of the way.

Note

We will make *extensive* changes to CSprite in later chapters, replacing its code entirely at some point. Rather than give you the finished version of CSprite now, I'll show you how it will evolve over time to meet the needs of the game during development. This naturally illustrates how a game is actually built, because it's impossible to create perfect classes and structures prior to using them.

Writing the Direct3D Class

I'm sure you noticed a glaring problem while examining the CSprite class. It refers to a nonexistent class called CDirect3D for most of its functionality! Well, not to worry, we'll write that class right now. It will be very nice to have all of that Direct3D code wrapped up in a class so we don't have to look at the initialization code any longer. Instead, Direct3D will be fired up in only a couple lines of code. Likewise, the CSprite class will make it possible to load and draw a sprite with only a few lines of code. But, you may be wondering . . . to what end? These are all just preliminary details toward building our RPG engine, and I'm not particularly interested in this low-level code; I'd prefer to move on to the higher-level code of the game as soon as possible. So, let's see that new CDirect3D class and get on with it! Create a new class in the same manner that you did previously and type in the following code:

```
Imports Microsoft.DirectX
Imports Microsoft.DirectX.Direct3D

Public Class CDirect3D

    Private device As Direct3D.Device
    Private backbuffer As Direct3D.Surface
    Private sprite_handler As Direct3D.Sprite
    Private ref_form As System.Windows.Forms.Control

    Function GetDevice() As Direct3D.Device
        Return Me.device
    End Function

    Function GetSprite() As Direct3D.Sprite
        Return Me.sprite_handler
    End Function

    Sub New(ByRef p_form As System.Windows.Forms.Control)
        Me.ref_form = p_form
    End Sub

    Sub StartRendering()
        device.BeginScene()
        device.Clear(ClearFlags.Target + ClearFlags.ZBuffer, _
        Color.Black, 1.0, 0)
    End Sub

    Sub StopRendering()
        device.EndScene()
        device.Present()
    End Sub

    Sub StartSprites()
        sprite_handler.Begin(SpriteFlags.AlphaBlend)
    End Sub

    Sub StopSprites()
        sprite_handler.End()
    End Sub
```

```
Public Sub Init(ByVal width As Integer, ByVal height As Integer, _
ByVal windowed As Boolean)
    'get the desktop display mode
    Dim adapterNumber As Integer = Manager.Adapters.Default.Adapter
    Dim mode As DisplayMode = Manager.Adapters.Default.CurrentDisplayMode

    'set up the presentation parameters
    Dim params As New PresentParameters
    params.Windowed = windowed
    params.SwapEffect = SwapEffect.Copy
    params.AutoDepthStencilFormat = DepthFormat.D16
    params.EnableAutoDepthStencil = True
    params.MultiSample = MultiSampleType.None
    params.BackBufferCount = 1
    params.BackBufferWidth = width
    params.BackBufferHeight = height

    'check video card capabilities
    Dim flags As CreateFlags
    flags = CreateFlags.HardwareVertexProcessing
    flags += CreateFlags.PureDevice

    'create the Direct3D device
    device = New Direct3D.Device(adapterNumber, DeviceType.Hardware, _
        ref_form, flags, params)

    'get reference to the back buffer
    backbuffer = device.GetBackBuffer(0, 0, BackBufferType.Mono)

    'create the sprite handler
    sprite_handler = New Direct3D.Sprite(device)

End Sub

Protected Overrides Sub Finalize()
    MyBase.Finalize()
    sprite_handler.Dispose()
    device.Dispose()
End Sub
End Class
```

Testing the New Classes

All right, let's see how these two new classes can improve our code to get a couple of things up on the screen. The following program is called SpriteTest. If you

Figure 4.4
The TestSprite program demonstrates the CDirect3D and CSprite classes in action.

add the CDirect3D and CSprite class files to the project, and add the DirectX references as well, then you will be able to run the following code to produce the output shown in Figure 4.4. At this early stage, I recommend you open the SpriteTest program from the CD-ROM and follow along in the book as you examine the code. You will need to copy all of the code from the CD-ROM to your hard drive before opening it because the files will be read-only (and you cannot run code on the CD). The portions of code specific to the new classes are highlighted in bold.

```
Imports System.Drawing
Imports Microsoft.DirectX
Imports Microsoft.DirectX.Direct3D

Public Class Form1
    Const SCREENW As Integer = 800
    Const SCREENH As Integer = 600

    Dim d3d As CDirect3D
    Dim terrain As CSprite
    Dim tavern As CSprite

    Private Sub Form1_Load(ByVal sender As System.Object, _
ByVal e As System.EventArgs) Handles MyBase.Load
```

```
        'resize the form
        Me.Size = New Size(SCREENW, SCREENH)
        Me.Text = "Sprite Class Test Program"
        Me.SetStyle(ControlStyles.AllPaintingInWmPaint Or _
            ControlStyles.Opaque, True)

        'create Direct3D object
        d3d = New CDirect3D(Me)
        d3d.Init(SCREENW, SCREENH, True)

        'load the terrain
        terrain = New CSprite(d3d)
        terrain.Load("terrain.png")

        'load the tavern
        tavern = New CSprite(d3d)
        tavern.Load("tavern.png")
    End Sub

    Protected Overrides Sub OnPaint(ByVal e As PaintEventArgs)
        d3d.StartRendering()
        d3d.StartSprites()

        terrain.Draw(New Rectangle(0, 0, 512, 512), New Rectangle(0, 0, 800,
        600))

        tavern.SetPosition(300, 200)
        tavern.Draw()

        d3d.StopSprites()
        d3d.StopRendering()
    End Sub

    Private Sub Form1_KeyDown(ByVal sender As Object, ByVal e As _
System.Windows.Forms.KeyEventArgs) Handles Me.KeyDown
        If e.KeyCode = Keys.Escape Then
            terrain = Nothing
            tavern = Nothing
            d3d = Nothing
            Me.Close()
        End If
    End Sub

End Class
```

Wow, look at how short the program is compared to the previous one! This is where a class really demonstrates its usefulness. Once you've moved reusable code into a class, you will not have to add that code to your program again, because it will always be available from within the class itself. Regardless of all the other features of object-oriented programming, this feature alone (encapsulation), described in Chapter 2, is the most useful to us.

Now let's examine the SpriteTest program in more detail. The key portions of code in this program are the lines that create and initialize the CDirect3D and CSprite objects:

```
' create Direct3D object
d3d = New CDirect3D(Me)
d3d.Init(SCREENW, SCREENH, True)

' load the terrain
terrain = New CSprite(d3d)
terrain.Load("terrain.png")

' load the tavern
tavern = New CSprite(d3d)
tavern.Load("tavern.png")
```

When initializing the CDirect3D object, we pass a parameter to it, a reference to "Me," which is the current form (Form1). By passing Form1 to the CDirect3D class, you give the class access to the form's properties and functions. But we only really need the form in order to give Direct3D something to attach itself to when it is initialized.

Next, we do something similar with the CSprite objects, terrain, and tavern. When creating the new sprites, I passed a reference to the CDirect3D object to the sprites. This gives them the capability to be totally self-contained, because the CDirect3D class handles all rendering, including sprite drawing. Thus, by giving the sprites a reference to the CDirect3D object, the sprites have the ability to *draw themselves*, among other things. Generally speaking, you don't always want a game entity (such as a sprite) to perform its own rendering; this is usually done by the game engine, within a game loop. I know we haven't discussed these things yet, but they're coming up shortly. However, the goal right now is not to create a multipurpose game engine, but only to get sprites up on the screen as simply and easily as possible. In other words, this is as complicated as I'm willing to make these classes, and yet, they will work great for the tasks I have planned for them. You'll see!

Tip

I have been using sprite images with embedded transparency without really explaining how these sprite images were created. I'm not ignoring the subject; I'm just putting it off in order to cover the most important issues at hand right now: namely, the creation of a reusable sprite class. We'll spend more time explaining alpha channel transparency in the core game chapters. If you want a more thorough education in game artwork, I recommend you pick up the book *Game Art for Teens, Second Edition* (Thomson Course Technology PTR, 2005) by Les Pardew.

Sprite Animation

After you have written a few games, you most likely find that many of the sprites in your games have similar behaviors, to the point of predictability. For instance, if you have sprites that just move around within the boundaries of the screen and wrap from one edge to the other, you can create a subroutine to produce this sprite behavior on call. Simply use that subroutine when you update the sprite's position. If you find that a lot of your sprites are doing other predictable movements, it is really helpful to create many different behavioral subroutines to control their actions.

Here is a subroutine called MoveSprite that would be a good addition to the CSprite class. The routine keeps the sprite inside the boundary of the screen, and the sprite's movement is based entirely on a pair of velocity variables. Let's just consider this pseudo-code at this point:

```
Public Sub MoveSprite()
    SpriteX = SpriteX + VelX
    If SpriteX < 0 Or SpriteX > SCREENWIDTH - SpriteWidth
        VelX = VelX * -1
    End If
    SpriteY = SpriteY + VelY
    If SpriteY < 0 Or SpriteY > SCREENHEIGHT - SpriteHeight Then
        VelY = VelY * -1
    End If
End Sub
```

This is just one simple example of a very primitive behavior (staying within the boundary of the screen), but you can create very complex behaviors by writing subroutines that cause sprites to react to other sprites or to the player, for instance, in different ways. You might have some behavior subroutines that cause a sprite to chase the player, or run away from the player, or attack the player. The possibilities are truly limited only by your imagination, and, generally, the most intelligent games are the most fun because most players quickly figure out the patterns followed by so-called "dumb" sprites. The AnimateSprite program demonstrates sprite movement as well as animation, so you may refer to that program for an example of how the sprite movement code is used.

Animation Theory

Sprite animation goes back about three decades, when the first video game systems were being built for arcades. The earliest arcade games include classics such as *Asteroids* and used vector-based graphics rather than bitmap-based graphics. A *vector-based* graphics system uses lines connecting two points as the basis for all of the graphics on the screen. Although a rotating vector-based spaceship might not be considered a sprite by today's standards, it is basically the same thing. In fact, any game object on the screen that uses more than one small image to represent itself might be considered a *sprite.* However, to be an *animated sprite,* the image must simulate a sequence of images that are drawn while the sprite is being displayed on the screen.

Animation is a fascinating subject because it brings life to a game and makes the objects in the game seem more realistic than static objects. An important concept to grasp at this point is that *every* frame of an animation sequence must be treated as a distinct image that is pre-rendered and stored in a bitmap file; as an alternative, some animation might be created on the fly if a technique such as rotation or translucency were used. (For instance, causing a sprite to fade in and out would be done at runtime.) Although professional 2D games do not often use rotation as a means to draw a sprite with many angles or movement directions, it is still a valid technique, especially if your sprites are somewhat small and not very detailed. Rotating a sprite with Direct3D produces nice results, so we can use rotation if we want to.

Animation is accomplished through the use of a *sprite sheet.* A sprite sheet is a bitmap image containing many columns and rows of tiles, and each tile consists of a single frame of animation for that sprite. It is not uncommon for a sprite with eight directions of movement to have 64 or more frames of animation just for one activity (such as walking, attacking, or even dying).

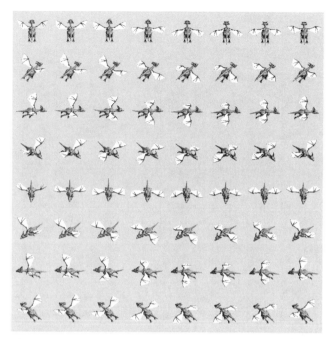

Figure 4.5
This dragon sprite has eight frames of animation for each of the eight directions that it can travel, resulting in 64 total frames of animation.

Figure 4.5 shows a dragon sprite with 64 frames of animation. The dragon can move in any of eight directions of travel, and each direction has eight frames of animation. We'll learn to load this sprite sheet as a Direct3D texture and then draw it transparently on the screen with animation later in this chapter.

Note

This dragon sprite was provided courtesy of Reiner's Tilesets and is available at www. reinerstileset.de, as well as on this book's CD-ROM. In fact, all of the artwork in this book was created by Reiner Prokein, who makes his beautiful creations available for free. In addition to the several hundred animated sprites already available, he creates new game art every month.

The trick to animating a sprite is keeping track of the current frame of animation along with the total animation frames in the animation sequence. This dragon sprite is stored in a single, large bitmap image and was actually stored in 64 individual bitmaps before I converted it to a single bitmap using Pro Motion. (Pro Motion is an excellent sprite animation editor available for download

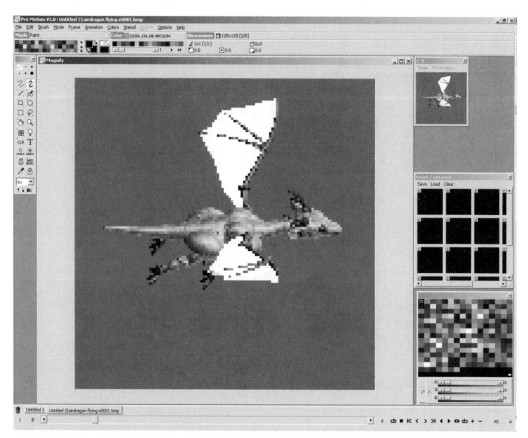

Figure 4.6
Cosmigo's Pro Motion is an excellent graphic editor with superb sprite animation tools.

at http://www.cosmigo.com/promotion.) You can see the dragon sprite loaded into Pro Motion in Figure 4.6.

You can load a sprite animation sequence as a series of individual bitmap files using one of Pro Motion's many features. From the File menu, select Animation, Load as Single Images to bring up the Load Animation as Single Images dialog box shown in Figure 4.7.

Pro Motion displays a message telling you the resolution of the sequence of bitmaps along with the number of frames that will be added, allowing you to accept or cancel the import. After loading the individual files as a single animation sequence, you can then view the sprite animation using the Animation menu. The animation window can be scaled (see Figure 4.8), and the animation's speed can be slowed down or sped up so you can see what the sprite looks like in

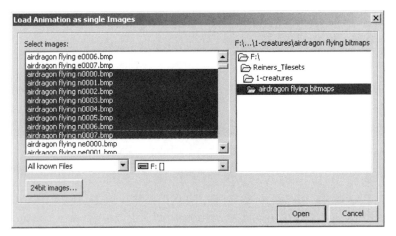

Figure 4.7
Loading a sprite animation as a series of individual bitmap files in Pro Motion.

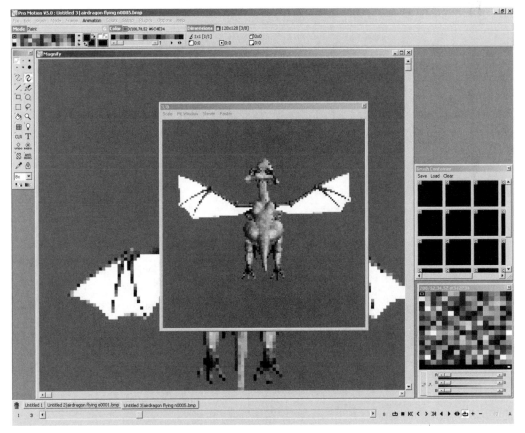

Figure 4.8
Animating the sprite using Pro Motion's animation player.

your game. In addition to these features, of course, you can edit the sprite images directly with the multi-featured pixel editing tools available in Pro Motion.

After importing a series of animation sequences and manipulating the animation and image sequence, you can then export the animation as a single, large bitmap file containing all the sprite animation frames. A single large sprite sheet is called an *AnimStrip* in Pro Motion. Figure 4.9 shows the Save Animation dialog box. You can choose the type of file to save; AnimStrip as BMP is what you want.

Although I don't have room here to fully explore the many features of this terrific sprite animation program, I encourage you to experiment and learn how to use it. Pro Motion can be your close companion while working on a sprite-based game.

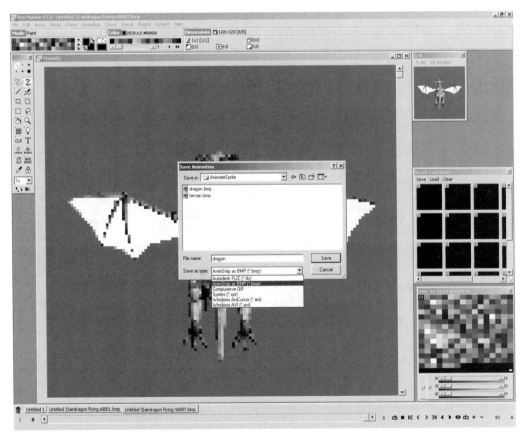

Figure 4.9
Saving a sprite animation sequence into a single bitmap file.

Tip

I have converted about two dozen animated sprites from their source images into sprite sheets for use in Celtic Crusader. You may find all of this ready-to-use artwork on the CD-ROM in the \artwork folder. There are many sprites available here for you to use when enhancing Celtic Crusader after you've finished reading this book.

Getting a Handle on Animation Sequences

After you have exported an animation sequence as a sprite sheet image, the trick is to get a handle on animating the sprite in source code. Storing all the frames of animation inside a single bitmap file makes it easier to use the animation in your program. However, it doesn't necessarily make it easier to set up; you have to deal with the animation looping around at a specific point, rather than looping through all 64 frames. Now you'll start to see where all of those odd properties and subroutines in the CSprite class will be used.

I have animated the dragon sprite by setting the StartFrame property to a specific frame depending on the user's keyboard input. That way the dragon flies around on the screen in any of the north, south, east, or west directions. Although the sprite images are available for all eight directions (including northwest, northeast, southwest, and southeast), I chose to stick to the four cardinal directions to keep the code simpler for this first example program. Here is how I handle the sprite based on user input (this code should be located in the Form1_KeyDown event):

```
Select Case (e.KeyCode)
    Case Keys.Up
        dragon.SetVelocity(0.0, -2.0)
        dragon.StartFrame = 0
        dragon.CurrentFrame = 0
        Me.Invalidate()
    Case Keys.Down
        dragon.SetVelocity(0.0, 2.0)
        dragon.StartFrame = 32
        dragon.CurrentFrame = 32
        Me.Invalidate()
    Case Keys.Left
        dragon.SetVelocity(-2.0, 0.0)
        dragon.StartFrame = 48
        dragon.CurrentFrame = 48
        Me.Invalidate()
```

```
        Case Keys.Right
            dragon.SetVelocity(2.0, 0.0)
            dragon.StartFrame = 16
            dragon.CurrentFrame = 16
            Me.Invalidate()

        Case Keys.Escape
            ground = Nothing
            dragon = Nothing
            d3d = Nothing
            Me.Close()
End Select
```

Note how this section of code handles both the movement and animation of the dragon sprite at the same time. This is usually the case, which is why these two subjects are being covered together in this chapter. The important part of this code to consider is how I set StartFrame to a specific value based on the keyboard input. When the up arrow key is pressed, then the first frame of animation is 0. For the left arrow key (which causes the dragon to move to the left), the first animation frame is 48. This corresponds with the number of frames inside the dragon.bmp file. Take a look at Figure 4.10 for a description of each row of images in this file.

For reference, here is the Animate routine from the CSprite class. Note how Animate takes into account the StartFrame and EndFrame properties. This makes it

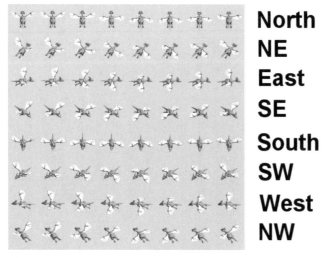

Figure 4.10
The dragon bitmap is comprised of eight rows of animation for each direction.

possible to animate portions of the sprite sheet, rather than the whole animation sequence, and it will cut down on the code in our main program. Just think, you can set the StartFrame and EndFrame properties for a sprite, and then call Animate to automatically have the CSprite class keep the animation frames looping within the range you specified. We'll use this feature to animate a portion of a sprite based on the direction it's facing.

```
Public Sub Animate()
    Me.FrameCounter += 1
    If Me.FrameCounter > Me.FrameThreshold Then
        Me.CurrentFrame += 1
        If (Me.CurrentFrame > Me.EndFrame) Then
            Me.CurrentFrame = Me.StartFrame
        End If
    End If
End Sub
```

Animation Support in CSprite

While we're looking at code like this Animate routine, let's examine the animation properties in CSprite, since we glossed over these details earlier. The animation properties were defined as follows:

```
Public FrameWidth As Integer
Public FrameHeight As Integer
Public Columns As Integer
Public StartFrame As Integer
Public EndFrame As Integer
Public TotalFrames As Integer
Public CurrentFrame As Integer
Public FrameThreshold As Integer
Public FrameCounter As Integer
```

It is obvious how the animation properties are helpful by looking at the DrawFrame subroutine, which is responsible for drawing a sprite with animation support. There is quite a bit of complex code packed into these lines of code, but they bring animation to life as a result! In fact, you might think of this little routine as the "animation engine" in our CSprite class. First, a rectangle is created and set up to grab the current frame of animation out of the sprite sheet. Notice how that frame is captured in the rectangle, using some tricky division and modulus calculations.

```
Public Sub DrawFrame()
        Dim frame As New Rectangle
        frame.X = (Me.CurrentFrame Mod Me.Columns) * Me.FrameWidth
        frame.Y = (Me.CurrentFrame \ Me.Columns) * Me.FrameHeight
        frame.Width = Me.FrameWidth
        frame.Height = Me.FrameHeight

        Dim dest As New Rectangle(Me.GetX(), Me.GetY(), _
Me.FrameWidth, Me.FrameHeight)

        Me.Draw(frame, dest)
    End Sub
```

To get the current frame, we need to find out where that frame is located inside the sprite sheet in the least amount of code possible. To get the Y position of a frame, you take the current frame and divide by the columns to get the appropriate row (and then multiply that by the frame height, or height of each tile).

To get the X position of the frame, perform that same division as before, but get the remainder (modulus result) from the division rather than the quotient, and then multiply by the sprite's width. At this point, the rest of the rectangle is set up using the sprite's width and height. The destination rectangle is configured to the sprite's current position, and then a call to the existing Draw subroutine takes care of business.

The AnimationTest Program

To demonstrate how sprite animation works, you need to write a complete program that draws a single sprite on the screen, animates it, and makes it possible to move it around. This could be autonomous, where the sprite just moves around randomly or in a fixed direction, but I wanted to demonstrate how user input can be used to direct the sprite. And in this case, since it is a dragon sprite, I thought it would be fun if you could move the dragon yourself. It looks really cool flapping its wings while you control where it goes. Figure 4.11 shows the output of the AnimationTest program.

Creating the New Project

To create the AnimationTest program, fire up VB.NET and create a new Windows Application project like usual. Add the reference to the normal three DirectX libraries that you have set as references in past projects: Microsoft.DirectX,

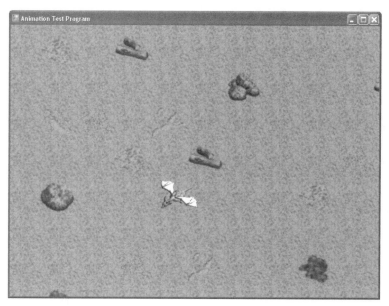

Figure 4.11
The user controls an animated dragon on the screen in the AnimationTest program.

Microsoft.DirectX.Direct3D, and Microsoft.DirectX.Direct3DX. You need the CDirect3D.vb and CSprite.vb files for this new program, so copy them over from the previous project (along with the new changes added). If you are still very new to VB.NET and you don't quite understand how to configure projects yet, feel free to open the AnimationTest project from the CD-ROM.

This program requires the terrain.bmp and dragon.bmp files from the CD-ROM.

```
Imports System.Drawing
Imports Microsoft.DirectX
Imports Microsoft.DirectX.Direct3D

Public Class Form1
    Const SCREENW As Integer = 800
    Const SCREENH As Integer = 600

    Dim d3d As CDirect3D
    Dim ground As CSprite
    Dim dragon As CSprite

    Private Sub Form1_Load(ByVal sender As System.Object, _
ByVal e As System.EventArgs) Handles MyBase.Load
```

```vb
        'resize the form
        Me.Size = New Size(SCREENW, SCREENH)
        Me.Text = "Animation Test Program"
        Me.SetStyle(ControlStyles.AllPaintingInWmPaint Or _
            ControlStyles.Opaque, True)

        'create Direct3D object
        d3d = New CDirect3D(Me)
        d3d.Init(SCREENW, SCREENH, True)

        'load the terrain
        ground = New CSprite(d3d)
        ground.Load("terrain.png")

        'load the dragon
        dragon = New CSprite(d3d)
        dragon.Load("dragon.png")
        dragon.SetPosition(300, 200)
        dragon.FrameWidth = 128
        dragon.FrameHeight = 128
        dragon.Columns = 8
        dragon.StartFrame = 0
        dragon.TotalFrames = 64
        dragon.FrameThreshold = 10
    End Sub

    Protected Overrides Sub OnPaint(ByVal e As PaintEventArgs)
        d3d.StartRendering()
        d3d.StartSprites()

        ground.Draw(New Rectangle(0, 0, 512, 512), New Rectangle(0, 0, 800, 600))

        dragon.Move()
        dragon.KeepInBounds(New Rectangle(0, 0, SCREENW - 128, SCREENH - 128))
        dragon.Animate()
        dragon.DrawFrame()

        d3d.StopSprites()
        d3d.StopRendering()
    End Sub

    Private Sub Form1_KeyDown(ByVal sender As Object, _
ByVal e As System.Windows.Forms.KeyEventArgs) Handles Me.KeyDown
```

```
    Select Case (e.KeyCode)
        Case Keys.Up
            dragon.SetVelocity(0.0, -2.0)
            dragon.StartFrame = 0
            dragon.EndFrame = 7
            Me.Invalidate()
        Case Keys.Right
            dragon.SetVelocity(2.0, 0.0)
            dragon.StartFrame = 16
            dragon.EndFrame = 23
            Me.Invalidate()
        Case Keys.Down
            dragon.SetVelocity(0.0, 2.0)
            dragon.StartFrame = 32
            dragon.EndFrame = 39
            Me.Invalidate()
        Case Keys.Left
            dragon.SetVelocity(-2.0, 0.0)
            dragon.StartFrame = 48
            dragon.EndFrame = 55
            Me.Invalidate()
        Case Keys.Escape
            ground = Nothing
            dragon = Nothing
            d3d = Nothing
            Me.Close()
    End Select
End Sub

End Class
```

Level Up

It's kind of amazing how short this final program is, considering all that is going on in this code! First of all, we're using Direct3D to render a background image and an animated sprite. The sprite is moving and animating with transparency, and we're only looking at a few dozen lines of code. This is truly remarkable! But it's a testament to the power of modular object-oriented programming. By moving most of the reusable code into a class, we've eliminated a lot of that code from the front end of the program, letting the classes do all of the real work. We're on track toward eliminating the low-level DirectX code, making it possible to focus on the high-level game code that is necessary to build an RPG engine.

The most remarkable accomplishment in this chapter is the creation of a robust sprite class. Anytime we need to give our sprites some new feature or behavior, it will be possible with this class. However, there is one subject that is even more vitally important, but that has yet to come up: the game loop. Thus far, I've been showing you code that uses Visual Basic's `OnPaint` event to do our drawing. That is about to change in the upcoming chapter.

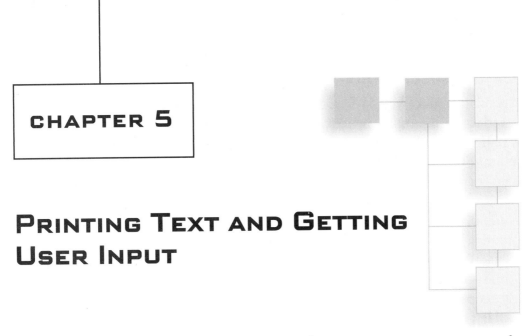

CHAPTER 5

PRINTING TEXT AND GETTING USER INPUT

In years past, programming the input devices for a game was an enormous task, requiring the programmer to write an interrupt service routine (often in assembly language) to handle multiple key presses, while mouse and joystick input required custom code depending on the make and model of input device. Today, DirectX is the dominant game development library in the world, and with it comes DirectInput, a comprehensive library for programming input devices such as a keyboard, mouse, or joystick. This chapter explores DirectInput in detail, providing all the code you need to handle the user input for a game written with Visual Basic. From a simple keyboard interface to multi-button mouse routines, this chapter will give you enough information to get your game people on the move. Here is a breakdown of the yada, yada, yada...

- Getting user input

- Programming the keyboard

- Programming the mouse

- Printing text

Getting User Input

Let me introduce you to DirectInput, the DirectX component that provides an interface to the input devices. To develop your understanding of DirectInput, you'll write a sample program to test each type of input device. The most significant benefit to using DirectInput for keyboard and mouse input in a game is that there is no need to use a VB form to detect input events (such as KeyDown, KeyPress, KeyUp). There is the additional problem of transforming mouse movement events into a graphical, full-screen DirectX program, which may be running in a completely different resolution than the Windows desktop. Obviously, if you track a click somewhere on the window in a game, and the game is actually running at a resolution of 320 × 240 pixels (just as an example), the mouse input events are unlikely to even show up! (Or more likely, such events will have to be converted to the resolution being used by DirectX.)

Different types of games are suited for different input devices. (That was so profound I think I'll save it in my list of "famous quotations.") *Real-time strategy (RTS)* games are not well suited for joysticks because such games involve detailed control (often called *micromanagement*) over the game that is only really possible with the mouse.

The keyboard and mouse combination is the preferred choice for *first-person shooter (FPS)* games such as *Doom 3* and *Half-Life 2,* in case you haven't already noticed. As I'm sure most gamers have learned, any other form of input just does not work well enough in an FPS game. Sure, you can use an advanced joystick in an FPS game, but you aren't likely to score anywhere near the level of a player who is adept with a keyboard and mouse. The reason? A joystick is a single (albeit powerful) device. Even with multiple triggers and grips, a joystick does not have the precision of a mouse on the screen for targeting. The ability to quickly run, jump, and crouch by pressing closely coupled keys along with aiming and firing with a mouse simply cannot be beat.

But how does that relate to an RPG such as Celtic Crusader? I'm a big fan of console games, such as *Fire Emblem* for the Game Boy Advance. Games like this work really well with just a simple directional pad (D-pad) and a couple of buttons. You should keep this in mind when you are designing a PC game: Simpler is almost always better. I'm not suggesting using a joystick for a computer RPG, because most players won't go to the trouble of installing a gamepad or other type of joystick just for your game, when the de facto standard is keyboard and mouse. Although many gamers have a joystick, you can't rely on it exclusively. To do so will alienate some players and cause them to dislike your game. (You can almost guarantee they will not go buy a joystick just for your game.) On the PC platform, keyboard and mouse are the ruling family and should be respected.

It is important that you consider the best type of user input for the games you develop and then optimize each game for that type of input. Of course, you must also provide an alternate means of input for those players who are not adept with your own favorite devices (and don't fault someone for not knowing any better). No matter the argument, you should provide at least the two primary forms of input. A keyboard can be used just like the joystick for player movement, while the mouse might be used in various parts of the game to select inventory and so on. Figure 5.1 shows you how the input devices communicate with the system.

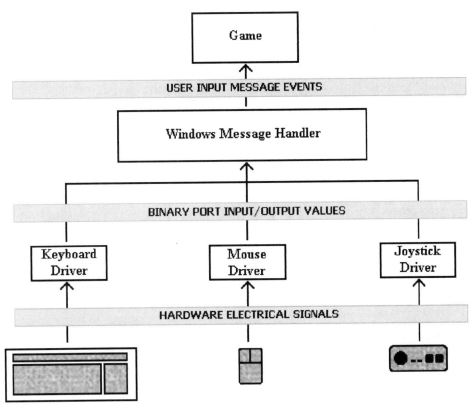

Figure 5.1
Input devices use device drivers to communicate with Windows and DirectX.

Keyboard Input

Keyboard devices have been around since the 1950s, at the dawn of the computer age. Supporting one might seem like a given until you actually start to consider how the keyboard should be utilized in a game. The trusty keyboard is always available, while other devices like joysticks are not always available. Therefore, regardless of your input device of choice, you *must* support a keyboard in every game, at least minimally. Don't be lame.

Most games provide a means to quickly end the game by pressing a simple key combination. This has been somewhat lacking in games of late, but it is a feature I highly recommend. Back in the MS-DOS days, it was common for games to use Alt+X, Alt+Q, Ctrl+X, or Ctrl+Q to end the game (which might result in a pop-up message asking for verification).

No matter how awesome you think your game is, and no matter whether you believe users will just leave your game running 24/7, you must realize that some players try out the game and then uninstall it five minutes later with utmost urgency. This might be the case with *World of Warcraft*. If you think your game is on par with it, you need to chill out because you're cracking up. The tastes of players vary widely. There are some players who think *Doom 3* is the worst game ever, while at the same time believing that *Pac-Man* is the best game ever. Don't fault them for being lame, just expect it. I am one of these types of users. If I can't quickly and easily exit out of a game, it will irritate me and I will very likely stop playing and uninstall it. I realize it's a trivial reason to abandon a game that otherwise might be extremely fun, but that is the situation.

DirectX usually runs in full-screen mode, so you should provide a quick method for ending the game in a hurry, and be sure to use a common key combination to at least bring up a menu. (I wholeheartedly recommend the Escape key.) In the old MS-DOS days, programmers could lock up a PC once a game started up. (No Task Manager back in those days!) But today, it's easy to kill a process, so you can't mess with users anymore.

Mouse Input

The mouse is another user input device that has been around for decades and must be considered required hardware—something you can count on being present in a computer system. Building a game entirely around the mouse is acceptable, as long as basic keyboard functionality is provided as a supplement for power users (gamers who are experts with a game and prefer to use quick keyboard shortcut keys)—which is a polite way of saying they complain an awful lot, and you don't want them on your discussion forum.

It is often tedious to use a mouse for absolutely everything in a game when shortcut keys may also be used. Power users demand it, so it is a good idea to provide at least minimal keyboard support, even if you plan to target the mouse as the primary means of input for your game. If you so choose, you may exclude mouse input entirely, but most users expect *some* use for the mouse. I don't know anyone who uses a joystick to play *Command & Conquer: Generals* (in fact, I'm pretty sure the game does not support one).

Show Me the Devices

DirectInput provides a common interface for many different input devices that might be installed on a system. In the past, a game programmer would have needed to write a custom interface for each device separately. Most books and tutorials on DirectX (including the documentation that comes with DirectX) are very hard to read, but if you can wade through them, you might find out how to enumerate the devices on a system before using them. The reasoning behind this is that DirectInput detects the installed devices on a system, and it is then up to you to determine which device to use. Who cares? I don't. In every case I have seen, the default device is the correct one. Is there really a need to enumerate the devices? I mean, if a keyboard isn't installed on a PC, how do you think the user was able to log in in the first place? (Case in point: Microsoft's latest game development tool, XNA Game Studio, has built-in support for a keyboard, mouse, and Xbox 360 controller.)

Programming the Keyboard

DirectInput is the DirectX component responsible for providing a common interface for user input devices, allowing you to write the same code for many different types of devices (present or future). (Another great quote! I should start sending these gems to Wikipedia.) Like the other components of DirectX (such as Direct3D), DirectInput is included when you install the DirectX runtime library. DirectInput is versatile. You can even plug in an Xbox 360 controller into your PC and use it as an alternate joystick with DirectInput. Although we are not covering joystick input code in this chapter, the process of acquiring a joystick and using it is a similar process to that of the mouse and keyboard.

The keyboard is the easiest device to program with DirectInput, because it really just provides a status value for all of the keys, allowing your program to detect key presses. Multiple, simultaneous key presses are supported, allowing you to move a character (or spaceship, for example) while shooting. Most arcade games do not work well with a mouse. There is a natural tendency to use two hands in an arcade game (which is most likely engendered through arcade or console experience).

The arrow keys and spacebar have been used in countless games as the primary means of user input. In a typical example like *Asteroids,* the left and right arrow keys would be used to rotate the ship. The up arrow key applies thrust to move the ship. The spacebar is a good candidate for firing a weapon. One important concept I want you to understand is that *all* of the keys are treated as equal by DirectInput, including Ctrl, Alt, Shift, Space, Enter, the Function keys, even NumLock. You can use any of these keys you wish in your game, because no one key is more important than any other—it's all just an array of numbers to DirectInput. (If you don't remember what an array is, I refer you back to Chapter 2.)

Initializing the Keyboard Device

Programming the keyboard with DirectInput is very straightforward. I go over the most difficult part of setting up DirectInput and creating the keyboard interface here, so you understand how DirectInput works. There are two objects you'll need to create in order to use a keyboard. First, you need to create a DirectInput.Device object and tell DirectInput to acquire it. Then, you will create a DirectInput.KeyboardState object to detect key presses.

```
Private keyboard As DirectInput.Device
Private keystate As DirectInput.KeyboardState
```

You create the keyboard device when you create the object with the *new* operator and the device's constructor, passing a SystemGuid.Keyboard value as the sole parameter. Note that this same class (DirectInput.Device) will also be used for the mouse.

```
keyboard = New DirectInput.Device(DirectInput.SystemGuid.Keyboard)
```

But before you can use the keyboard, it must be initialized. So far, we've just created the keyboard device, but it is not yet being used to detect keyboard input.

The first step is to create a `CooperativeLevelFlags` variable to tell DirectInput how to acquire the keyboard:

```
Dim cooplevel As CooperativeLevelFlags
CooperativeLevelFlags = CooperativeLevelFlags.Background Or _
    CooperativeLevelFlags.NonExclusive
```

These cooperative flags tell DirectInput to capture the keyboard device in a passive manner, without preventing other applications from using it. If you run your game in full-screen mode, then you will want to use CooperativeLevel-Flags.Exclusive and CooperativeLevelFlags.Foreground. But since we're using a window, the setting is Background and NonExclusive. The "Or" is a binary operation. It doesn't mean that these two are optional; it means they are both used to determine the cooperative level.

Once the cooperative level is stored in a variable, we can set the cooperative level and then acquire the keyboard device:

```
keyboard.SetCooperativeLevel(Me, cooplevel)
keyboard.Acquire()
```

At this point, the keyboard should be acquired and available for use. Yay.

Detecting Key Presses

Key presses are detected using a `DirectInput.KeyboardState` variable:

```
Private keystate As DirectInput.KeyboardState
```

But now we have a bit of a problem. Up to this point in our example programs, we've just sort of thrown something up in a window and then waited for the user to close the window, without any interaction or even a game loop. But now we have to poll the keyboard regularly to update the `KeyboardState` variable with all of the key-press information, and this requires an active loop of some sort running.

The best way to do this is within a `while` type loop somewhere, possibly when the form first loads. That is something to think about for the near future, when we begin drawing graphics onto the screen in real time, but right now let's keep it simple: We'll use a Timer control!

You may add a Timer control to the form via the Toolbox if you are an apps programmer, or you can just add the following code to add a Timer to the program:

```
Private WithEvents clock As Timer
```

Once added, we can write a function that will receive Timer events automatically (because the variable was declared using WithEvents). The routine will be called clock_Tick and will be responsible for polling the keyboard. Rather than just report key presses right here in the Tick event, we'll go one step further: A for loop will examine all of the keys in the KeyboardState variable and fire off a call to a custom Key_Press function whenever one of the keys is being pressed. This will be our own little key-press event.

```
Private Sub clock_Tick(ByVal sender As Object, ByVal e As System.EventArgs) _
Handles clock.Tick
    'poll keyboard for keypresses
    keystate = keyboard.GetCurrentKeyboardState()

    Dim n As Integer
    For n = 1 To 255
        If keystate(n) Then
            Key_Press(n)
        End If
    Next
End Sub
```

This parsing through the KeyboardState array is not absolutely necessary. If you want to just add code to your game that checks an individual key state, that will run faster (for instance, keystate(Key.A) will work). I find that calling a helper routine such as Key_Press helps to abstract keyboard input code a bit, so that I can focus on responding to all of the current key presses without having to use a separate if statement for every single key. By doing it in this manner, a more efficient Select Case statement can be used. But at this point, we'll just print out any keys being pressed (using a TextBox control that has been added to the form).

```
Public Sub Key_Press(ByVal key As DirectInput.Key)
    TextBox1.Text += key.ToString + " "
End Sub
```

Testing Keyboard Input

I want to give you a simple example now so you'll be able to easily adapt this code to your own games. We'll create a sample program called KeyboardTest. This program checks for key presses and then prints out the name of the key using a TextBox on the form. The program is shown in Figure 5.2.

```
Imports Microsoft.DirectX
Imports Microsoft.DirectX.DirectInput

Public Class Form1

    Private keyboard As DirectInput.Device
    Private keystate As DirectInput.KeyboardState

    Private WithEvents clock As Timer
```

Figure 5.2
The KeyboardTest program demonstrates how to use a keyboard with DirectInput.

```vb
Public Function Init_Keyboard() As Boolean
    Try
        'create new keyboard device
        keyboard = New DirectInput.Device(DirectInput.SystemGuid.Keyboard)

        'set cooperative level for keyboard
        Dim cooplevel As CooperativeLevelFlags = _
            CooperativeLevelFlags.Background Or _
            CooperativeLevelFlags.NonExclusive
        keyboard.SetCooperativeLevel(Me, cooplevel)

        'try to acquire the keyboard
        keyboard.Acquire()

        Return True
    Catch ex As Exception
        Return False
    End Try
End Function

Public Sub Key_Press(ByVal key As DirectInput.Key)
    TextBox1.Text += key.ToString + " "
End Sub

Private Sub Form1_Load(ByVal sender As System.Object, _
ByVal e As System.EventArgs) Handles MyBase.Load

    'create the timer
    clock = New Timer()
    clock.Interval = 100

    If Not Init_Keyboard() Then
        TextBox1.Text += "Error acquiring keyboard device." + ControlChars.CrLf
    Else
        TextBox1.Text += "Keyboard device acquired." + ControlChars.CrLf
        clock.Start()
    End If
End Sub

Private Sub Form1_FormClosing(ByVal sender As Object, _
ByVal e As System.Windows.Forms.FormClosingEventArgs) Handles Me.FormClosing

    keyboard.Unacquire()
```

```
        keyboard.Dispose()
        keyboard = Nothing

    End Sub

    Private Sub clock_Tick(ByVal sender As Object, ByVal e As System.EventArgs)_
Handles clock.Tick

        'poll keyboard for keypresses
        keystate = keyboard.GetCurrentKeyboardState()

        Dim n As Integer
        For n = 1 To 255
            If keystate(n) Then
                Key_Press(n)
            End If
        Next
    End Sub

End Class
```

That's the end of the KeyboardTest program. Run the program. If all goes well, when you press and hold multiple keys, the program prints out those keys in the TextBox.

Keyboard Class

To help with future projects that will need to use the keyboard (including Celtic Crusader), I have created a reusable class called CKeyboard that you will want to add to your projects. The CKeyboard.vb class file is located on the CD-ROM under the folder for this chapter.

```
Imports Microsoft.DirectX
Imports Microsoft.DirectX.DirectInput

Public Class CKeyboard
    Private ref_form As Windows.Forms.Form
    Private p_keyboard As DirectInput.Device
    Private p_keystate As DirectInput.KeyboardState

    Public Sub New(ByRef frm As Windows.Forms.Form)
        ref_form = frm
    End Sub
```

```vb
Public Function Init() As Boolean
    Try
            'create new keyboard device
            p_keyboard = New DirectInput.Device( _
                DirectInput.SystemGuid.Keyboard)

            'set cooperative level for keyboard
            Dim cooplevel As CooperativeLevelFlags = _
                CooperativeLevelFlags.Background Or _
                CooperativeLevelFlags.NonExclusive

            p_keyboard.SetCooperativeLevel(ref_form, cooplevel)

            'try to acquire the keyboard
            p_keyboard.Acquire()

            'initialize key state
            Poll()

            Return True

    Catch ex As Exception
            Return False
    End Try
End Function

Public Sub Poll()
    p_keystate = p_keyboard.GetCurrentKeyboardState()
End Sub

Public Function KeyState(ByVal key As Microsoft.DirectX.DirectInput.Key) _
As Boolean
    Return p_keystate(key)
End Function

Protected Overrides Sub Finalize()
    MyBase.Finalize()
    p_keyboard.Unacquire()
    p_keyboard.Dispose()
    p_keyboard = Nothing
End Sub
End Class
```

Programming the Mouse

Programming a mouse interface with DirectInput is similar to handling the key presses, but the mouse has to provide movement and scroll wheel information as well, so a structure is used rather than just a simple array. If you don't remember what a structure is, please refer back to Chapter 2 for an explanation.

DirectInput abstracts mouse events specifically for game programming, providing relative motion values for the mouse rather than absolute values. For instance, when tracking the mouse with DirectInput, if you move it slowly to the right, the X position is a small number (usually less than 5), but that number does not increase! When you stop moving the mouse, the X motion returns to 0. This movement is called *mickeys*. I've never understood the joke: mouse, mickeys... whatever.

Likewise, moving to the left generates a negative X motion, which returns to 0 when you stop moving the mouse. The process works in the same manner for vertical Y motion. The fascinating aspect of the DirectInput mouse handler is that the faster you move it, the higher the X and Y motion values.

Note

When you stop moving the mouse, DirectInput reports the motion values to be 0 for both the X and Y axes.

Suppose you are writing a *Breakout*-style game in which the player controls a paddle at the bottom of the screen. By looking at the mouse's motion values, you can move the paddle left or right using the motion values *directly*—that is, without having to massage the numbers first! If you use VB events like Form_MouseMove, you have to convert the absolute position of the mouse into a relative motion value. DirectInput handles that automatically. For this reason, it's preferable to use DirectInput. But if you do need to just track the mouse's movement on your game's form, it is very easy to use Form_MouseMove (which is used in Celtic Crusader when choosing a character when the game starts up).

This brings up a question: How do you figure out where the mouse is located on the screen without absolute values? The answer is that you must track the pointer just like you would move a sprite on the screen. You have to make sure the pointer doesn't go off the edge of the screen, and you update the pointer position based on the mouse's motion. The hardware mouse's cursor is not visible in full-screen mode, but it is in windowed mode. It is up to you to create and display a cursor using a simple sprite (and in a game, you would want to do this anyway). You also have to keep track of the absolute position of the cursor (which is why a sprite is a good solution).

Tip

One thing to keep in mind is that you should draw the cursor after you have finished drawing all the other objects in the game. That way, the mouse cursor always appears on top of the other objects.

Mouse Buttons and Movement

DirectInput provides mouse information through a state object called Direct-Input.MouseState (which is comparable to MouseInput.KeyboardState). Once defined, you can poll the mouse's current state with:

```
mousestate = mouse.CurrentMouseState
```

The MouseState object contains an X, Y, and Z value, for the mouse's position and wheel state, as well as an array of button status values. First, define a byte array variable, like so:

```
Dim b() As Byte
```

Then, use this variable to retrieve the button information via:

```
b = mousestate.GetMouseButtons()
```

To test for button 1, check array element zero:

```
If (b(0) > 0) Then 'button 1
If (b(1) > 0) Then 'button 2
If (b(2) > 0) Then 'button 3
```

Detecting movement is a little easier because we can just look at the X, Y, and Z values directly:

```
mousex = mousestate.X
mousey = mousestate.Y
mousewheel = mousestate.Z
```

Testing Mouse Input

Now let's put all of this fragmented knowledge into a cohesive program. The MouseTest program is shown in Figure 5.3.

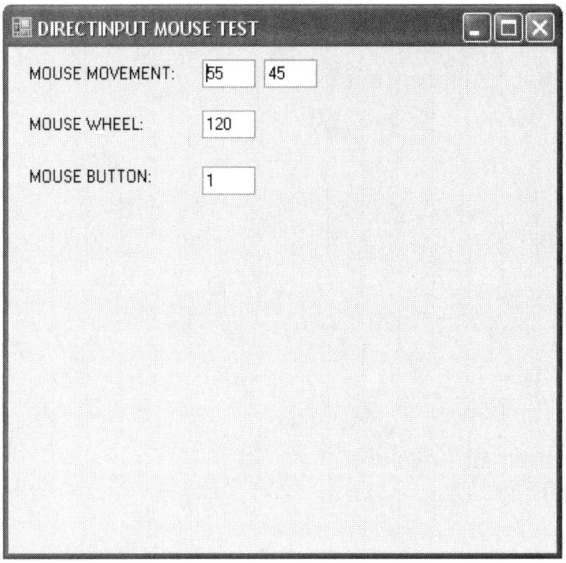

Figure 5.3
The MouseTest program demonstrates the mouse support in DirectInput.

The MouseTest program is a Windows Application project with a reference to Microsoft.DirectX and Microsoft.DirectX.DirectInput. There are several helper subroutines provided in this program listing that you will want to use in future projects whenever you need to use the mouse.

```
Imports Microsoft.DirectX
Imports Microsoft.DirectX.DirectInput

Public Class Form1

    Private mouse As DirectInput.Device
    Private mousestate As DirectInput.MouseState

    Private WithEvents clock As Timer

    Public Function Init_Mouse() As Boolean
        Try
            'create new mouse device
            mouse = New DirectInput.Device(SystemGuid.Mouse)

            'set cooperative level for mouse
            Dim cooplevel As CooperativeLevelFlags = _
                CooperativeLevelFlags.Background Or _
```

```
                    CooperativeLevelFlags.NonExclusive
            mouse.SetCooperativeLevel(Me, cooplevel)

            'try to acquire the mouse
            mouse.Acquire()

            Return True
        Catch ex As Exception
            Return False
        End Try
    End Function

    Public Sub Mouse_Click(ByVal button As Integer)
        TextBox4.Text = button.ToString
    End Sub

    Public Sub Mouse_Move(ByVal X As Integer, ByVal Y As Integer)
        TextBox1.Text = X.ToString
        TextBox2.Text = Y.ToString
    End Sub

    Public Sub Mouse_Wheel(ByVal Z As Integer)
        TextBox3.Text = Z.ToString
    End Sub

    Private Sub Form1_Load(ByVal sender As System.Object, _
ByVal e As System.EventArgs) Handles MyBase.Load

        If Not Init_Mouse() Then
            MessageBox.Show("Error acquiring mouse device.")
            Me.Close()
        End If

        'create the timer
        clock = New Timer()
        clock.Interval = 100
        clock.Start()

    End Sub

    Private Sub Form1_FormClosing(ByVal sender As Object, _
ByVal e As System.Windows.Forms.FormClosingEventArgs) Handles Me.FormClosing
```

```
            mouse.Unacquire()
            mouse.Dispose()
            mouse = Nothing
    End Sub

    Private Sub clock_Tick(ByVal sender As Object, ByVal e As System.EventArgs) _
Handles clock.Tick

            'poll mouse for movement and button presses
            mousestate = mouse.CurrentMouseState
            Dim b() As Byte = mousestate.GetMouseButtons()
            If (b(0) > 0) Then Mouse_Click(1)
            If (b(1) > 0) Then Mouse_Click(2)
            If (b(2) > 0) Then Mouse_Click(3)

            If mousestate.X <> 0 Or mousestate.Y <> 0 Then
                Mouse_Move(mousestate.X, mousestate.Y)
            End If
            If mousestate.Z <> 0 Then
                Mouse_Wheel(mousestate.Z)
            End If

    End Sub
End Class
```

Mouse Class

To help make the mouse input code more reusable from one project to the next, and to cut down on the amount of code in future projects, I have created a class called CMouse that is located on the CD-ROM in the folder for this chapter in a file called CMouse.vb.

```
Imports Microsoft.DirectX
Imports Microsoft.DirectX.DirectInput

Public Class CMouse
    Private p_mouse As DirectInput.Device
    Private p_mousestate As DirectInput.MouseState
    Private buttons() As Byte

    Public Sub New(ByRef frm As Windows.Forms.Form)
        Try
```

```
                    'create new mouse device
                    p_mouse = New DirectInput.Device(SystemGuid.Mouse)

                    'set cooperative level for mouse
                    Dim cooplevel As CooperativeLevelFlags = _
                        CooperativeLevelFlags.Background Or _
                        CooperativeLevelFlags.NonExclusive
                    p_mouse.SetCooperativeLevel(frm, cooplevel)

                    'try to acquire the mouse
                    p_mouse.Acquire()

                Catch ex As Exception
                    MessageBox.Show("Error initializing mouse", _
                        "DirectInput Error")
                End Try

            End Sub

            Public Sub Poll()
                p_mousestate = p_mouse.CurrentMouseState
                buttons = p_mousestate.GetMouseButtons()
            End Sub

            Public Function Button() As Integer
                If (buttons(0) > 0) Then
                    Return 1
                ElseIf (buttons(1) > 0) Then
                    Return 2
                ElseIf (buttons(2) > 0) Then
                    Return 3
                Else
                    Return 0
                End If
            End Function

            Public Function X() As Integer
                Return p_mousestate.X()
            End Function

            Public Function Y() As Integer
                Return p_mousestate.Y()
            End Function
```

```
Public Function Wheel() As Integer
     Return p_mousestate.Z
End Function

Public Sub Dispose()
     p_mouse.Unacquire()
     p_mouse.Dispose()
End Sub
End Class
```

Printing Text

Why do we need a section just about printing text? Although it might seem logical to provide a simple and fast text output function in DirectX, there really isn't one! Microsoft has provided a C++ class that can print out a TrueType font, but it is not available under Managed DirectX. In any event, the issue is moot because we would create our own font printing code even if DirectX did provide one, because we want a distinctive look to our text. Remember, we'll soon be working on an RPG, and we want our text to look really bright, large, and easy to read (because there's usually a lot of dialogue in an RPG).

Tip

We're going to use a helpful utility program to assist with the creation of bitmapped fonts. This tool, which is called Bitmap Font Builder, was written by Thom Wetzel, Jr., and is available from his website at www.lmnopc.com.

The bitmapped font that we'll use is shown in Figure 5.4. The characters in this bitmap file are 16×16 pixels per character, with 16 columns across in each row. The real trick to printing out text is no trick at all; we'll just be treating the font as an animated sprite and the bitmap image as a sprite sheet, where each character of text is one frame of the sprite's animation sequence.

You can create any type of bitmapped font that you want by drawing each character yourself, and it is usable in your games as long as each character has the same size. You may want a larger font with better details, so you might opt for a character size of 32×32 or so. Keep in mind that the characters are treated as a texture in memory, meaning that you can scale your font at runtime to produce a variety of sizes. *At the same time,* as a texture, your font image must follow the same rule that sprites must obey. Texture resolutions must be one of the following: 128×128, 256×256, 512×512, or 1024×1024. But I find it much

Figure 5.4
The bitmapped font includes only the most commonly needed text characters.

easier to use a tool like Bitmap Font Builder than to edit fonts manually (see Figure 5.5).

One important aspect of font rendering that requires explanation is the issue of transparency. Bitmap Font Builder does not output the bitmap files we need *directly*. It does a good job of creating the fonts and positioning each character evenly inside the tiles of the sprite sheet. But these images do not have an alpha channel for transparency. As I mentioned in the previous chapter, we're abandoning all use of color-keyed transparency (where a certain pixel color is used for background transparency), focusing our attention instead on professional transparency support through the alpha channel. The Windows BMP format does not support an alpha channel, so we use either Targa or PNG files. After Bitmap Font Builder outputs an image, I load it up into the GIMP and use the Magic Wand tool to highlight all of the empty spaces in the image, in between and inside every character in the font, and then generate a mask layer or an alpha layer directly.

Printing the Bitmapped Font

I have written two subroutines that work together to print out a text message on the screen. There are a lot of parameters in these two subroutines because I want

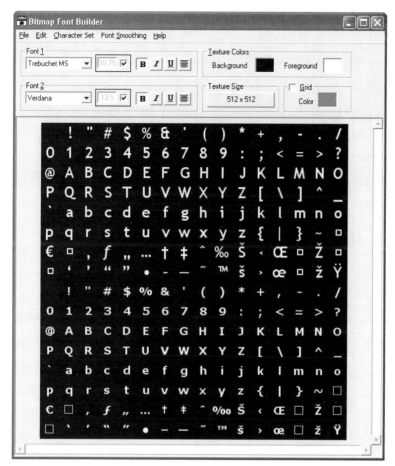

Figure 5.5
Bitmap Font Builder is a utility that generates bitmapped fonts stored in a bitmap file.

them to be completely reusable and capable of supporting multiple fonts (which you can load, each from a different bitmap file). Therefore, they will be most effective inside a class, because then we'll be able to eliminate a lot of the parameters that these routines would otherwise require. Since this code is all based on the sprite code you have seen in previous chapters, I don't think it's necessary to explain what each line of code does here. This new class is called CBitmapFont.vb.

```
Imports Microsoft.DirectX
Imports Microsoft.DirectX.Direct3D

Public Class CBitmapFont
    Private m_font As CSprite
```

```
Private m_d3d As CDirect3D
Private rendercolor As Color

Public X As Integer
Public Y As Integer
Public SpacingModifier As Integer

Public Sub New(ByRef d3d As CDirect3D)
    m_d3d = d3d
    m_font = New CSprite(m_d3d)
    SetLetterSize(16, 16)
    SetStartFrame(0)
    rendercolor = Color.White
    SpacingModifier = 0
End Sub

Public Sub Load(ByVal filename As String)
    m_font.Load(filename)
End Sub

Public Function GetImage() As Direct3D.Texture
    Return m_font.GetImage()
End Function

Public Sub SetImage(ByRef image As Direct3D.Texture)
    m_font.SetImage(image)
End Sub

Public Sub SetColumns(ByVal columns As Integer)
    m_font.Columns = columns
End Sub

Public Sub SetLetterSize(ByVal width As Integer, ByVal height As Integer)
    m_font.FrameWidth = width
    m_font.FrameHeight = height
End Sub

Public Sub SetStartFrame(ByVal frame As Integer)
    m_font.StartFrame = frame
End Sub

'Overloaded version of Print with X, Y, and color
Public Sub Print(ByVal X As Integer, ByVal Y As Integer, _
```

```
ByVal rendercolor As Color, ByVal text As String)
        Me.X = X
        Me.Y = Y
        m_font.RenderColor = rendercolor
        Print(text)
    End Sub

    'Overloaded version of Print with X and Y
    Public Sub Print(ByVal X As Integer, ByVal Y As Integer, _
    ByVal text As String)            Me.X = X
        Me.Y = Y
        Print(text)
    End Sub

    'Normal version of Print
    Public Sub Print(ByVal text As String)
        Dim n As Integer
        Dim x1 As Integer
        Dim ch As Byte

        For n = 1 To Len(text)
            x1 = X + (n - 1) * (m_font.FrameWidth - SpacingModifier)
            ch = m_font.StartFrame + Asc(Mid$(text, n, 1))
            PrintChar(x1, Y, ch)
        Next n
    End Sub

    Private Sub PrintChar(ByVal X As Integer, ByVal Y As Integer, _
    ByVal c As Byte)
        m_font.SetPosition(X, Y)
        m_font.CurrentFrame = c - 32
        m_font.DrawFrame()
    End Sub

End Class
```

Basically, the Print subroutine looks at each character in the passed string and passes it as a single byte to the helper routine, PrintChar, which does the real work of drawing each character to the screen (via the code in CSprite). The CBitmapFont class is totally self-contained as long as you have the CDirect3D and CSprite classes also available (in other words, the texture and other objects needed to render the font are internal to the font class).

The FontTest Program

The FontTest program demonstrates how to use the CBitmapFont class. Figure 5.6 shows the program running. Note the variety of sizes and colors. By simply adjusting the rendering color of the sprite, the font is drawn in a different color. Therefore, you need not create a custom font for each color that you want to use.

This program is a Windows Application project with a reference to the following libraries:

- Microsoft.DirectX

- Microsoft.DirectX.Direct3D

- Microsoft.DirectX.Direct3DX

- Microsoft.DirectX.DirectInput

The project also depends upon the following additional modules to run: CDirect3D.vb and CSprite.vb.

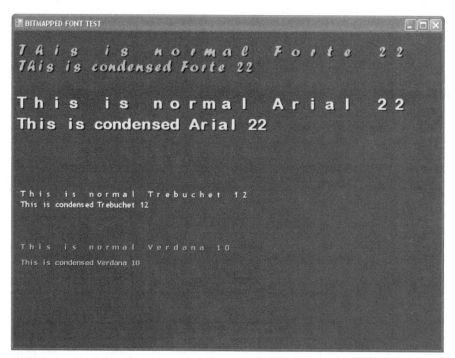

Figure 5.6
The FontTest program demonstrates how to print text with a bitmap font.

```
Imports Microsoft.DirectX
Imports Microsoft.DirectX.Direct3D

Public Class Form1
    Const SCREENW As Integer = 800
    Const SCREENH As Integer = 600

    Private WithEvents clock As New Timer()
    Private d3d As CDirect3D
    Private forte22 As CBitmapFont
    Private arial22 As CBitmapFont
    Private trebuchet12 As CBitmapFont
    Private verdana10 As CBitmapFont

    Private Sub Form1_Load(ByVal sender As System.Object, _
ByVal e As System.EventArgs) Handles MyBase.Load

        Me.Size = New Size(SCREENW, SCREENH)
        Me.Text = "BITMAPPED FONT TEST"

        d3d = New CDirect3D(Me)
        d3d.Init(SCREENW, SCREENH, True)

        forte22 = New CBitmapFont(d3d)
        forte22.Load("font.png")
        forte22.SetColumns(16)
        forte22.SetLetterSize(32, 32)

        arial22 = New CBitmapFont(d3d)
        arial22.SetImage(forte22.GetImage())
        arial22.SetColumns(16)
        arial22.SetStartFrame(128)
        arial22.SetLetterSize(32, 32)

        trebuchet12 = New CBitmapFont(d3d)
        trebuchet12.Load("trebuchet_verdana_10.png")
        trebuchet12.SetColumns(16)
        trebuchet12.SetLetterSize(16, 16)

        verdana10 = New CBitmapFont(d3d)
        verdana10.SetImage(trebuchet12.GetImage())
        verdana10.SetColumns(16)
        verdana10.SetStartFrame(128)
        verdana10.SetLetterSize(16, 16)
```

```
        clock.Interval = 50
        clock.Start()
    End Sub

    Private Sub clock_Tick(ByVal sender As Object, _
ByVal e As System.EventArgs) Handles clock.Tick

        d3d.StartRendering(Color.DarkBlue)
        d3d.StartSprites()

        forte22.SpacingModifier = 0
        forte22.Print(2, 22, Color.Black, "This is normal Forte 22")
        forte22.Print(0, 20, Color.Orange, "This is normal Forte 22")

        forte22.SpacingModifier = 15
        forte22.Print(2, 52, Color.Black, "This is condensed Forte 22")
        forte22.Print(0, 50, Color.Orange, "This is condensed Forte 22")

        arial22.SpacingModifier = 0
        arial22.Print(2, 122, Color.Black, "This is normal Arial 22")
        arial22.Print(0, 120, Color.Yellow, "This is normal Arial 22")

        arial22.SpacingModifier = 14
        arial22.Print(2, 162, Color.Black, "This is condensed Arial 22")
        arial22.Print(0, 160, Color.Yellow, "This is condensed Arial 22")

        trebuchet12.SpacingModifier = 0
        trebuchet12.Print(11, 301, Color.Black, "This is normal Trebuchet 12")
        trebuchet12.Print(10, 300, Color.White, "This is normal Trebuchet 12")

        trebuchet12.SpacingModifier = 8
        trebuchet12.Print(11, 321, Color.Black, "This is condensed Trebuchet 12")
        trebuchet12.Print(10, 320, Color.White, "This is condensed Trebuchet 12")

        verdana10.SpacingModifier = 0
        verdana10.Print(11, 401, Color.Black, "This is normal Verdana 10")
        verdana10.Print(10, 400, Color.LightGreen, "This is normal Verdana 10")

        verdana10.SpacingModifier = 8
        verdana10.Print(11, 431, Color.Black, "This is condensed Verdana 10")
```

```
        verdana10.Print(10, 430, Color.LightGreen,
        "This is condensed Verdana 10")

        d3d.StopSprites()
        d3d.StopRendering()
    End Sub
End Class
```

Level Up

This chapter explained how to use DirectInput to handle keyboard and mouse input. While Visual Basic has rudimentary user input events that are available with a form, these events are too slow to handle a real-time, fast-paced game like Celtic Crusader, so we need to use DirectInput for high-speed input. User input is such a critical part of a game that it deserves adequate attention during design. It is important that you consider what the game's optimum input device is and then optimize the game for that particular device. In addition to tackling the subject of input, we also covered *output* in the form of a bitmapped font renderer that has been encapsulated into a class called CBitmapFont. You will be able to use this font class in all future projects, and we'll use it extensively in the Celtic Crusader game to display dialogue between game characters.

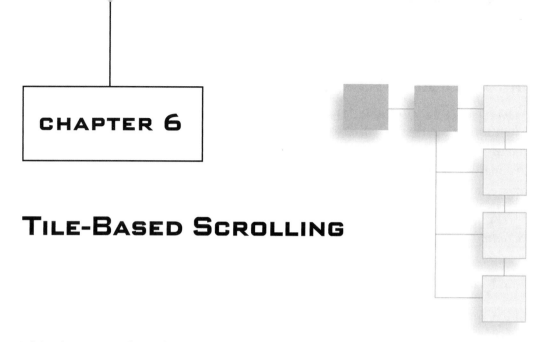

CHAPTER 6

TILE-BASED SCROLLING

This chapter explains how to create a tile-based scrolling engine using 2D tiles rendered with Direct3D. You will learn some of the basic techniques used in tile-based scrolling, and you will gain an understanding of how a scrolling display is created, from simple concepts to complete "partial-tile" triple-buffered scrolling. We'll be using a map editing program called Mappy to create tile-based maps and the associated tile bitmaps used to construct the game world. Then, you'll learn the next step in the theory of scrolling—how to generate the game-world image at runtime using the source tiles and the map data exported by Mappy. By using a small surface about the same size as the screen, the tiles are drawn at the current scroll position using a third screen buffer (in other words, triple buffering) to produce a scrolling game world. The resulting tile scrolling engine is the foundation for Celtic Crusader. Here are the key topics we have to cover:

- Introduction to scrolling

- The scroller engine

- Direct partial-tile scrolling

- The ScrollWorld program

- The CTileScroller class

Introduction to Scrolling

What is scrolling? In today's gaming world, where 3D is the focus of everyone's attention, it's not surprising to find gamers and programmers who have never heard of scrolling. What a shame! The heritage of modern games is a long and fascinating one that is still relevant today, even if it is not understood or appreciated. The console industry puts great effort and value into scrolling, particularly on handheld systems, such as the Nintendo DS.

Scrolling is the process of displaying a small window of a larger virtual game world. There are three basic ways to scroll the display:

- Load a large bitmap image

- Create a large bitmap out of tiles at runtime

- Draw tiles directly on the screen (the most advanced method)

Figure 6.1 illustrates the concept of scrolling, which, in essence, involves the use of a large game world of which only a small portion is visible through the screen at a time.

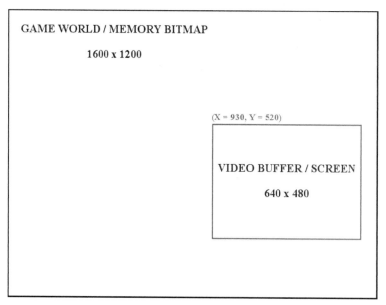

Figure 6.1
The scroll window shows a small part of a larger game world.

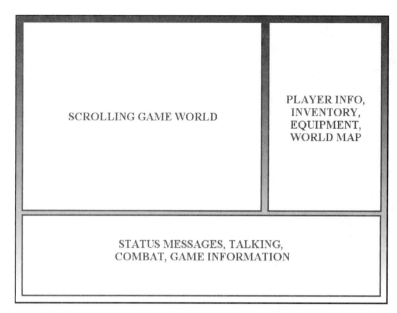

Figure 6.2
Some games use a smaller portion of the game screen for a scrolling window.

The key to scrolling is having something in the virtual game world to display in the scroll window (or the screen). Also, I should point out that the entire screen need not be used as the scroll window. It is common to use the entire screen in scrolling-shooter games, but role-playing games (RPGs) often use a smaller window on the screen for scrolling, using the rest of the screen for game-play (combat, inventory, and so on) and player/party information, as shown in Figure 6.2.

You could display one huge bitmap image in the virtual game world representing the current level of the game (or the *map*), and then copy a portion of that virtual world onto the screen. This is the simplest form of scrolling. Another method uses tiles to create the game world at runtime. Suppose we had a large bitmap file containing a pre-rendered image of the game world. You would then load up that large bitmap and copy a portion of it to the screen, and that portion would represent the current scroll position.

For instance, I took a map from Mappy and used the Export menu to save a giant bitmap image of the whole tile map, which works great for this example program. Figure 6.3 shows the Export dialog box in Mappy, where you can choose the

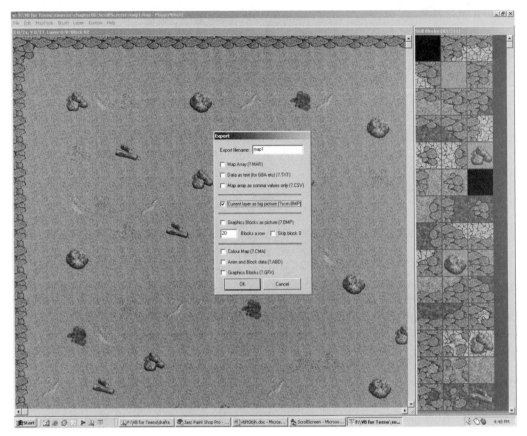

Figure 6.3
Exporting a Mappy map as one large bitmap image.

Current Layer as Big Picture (?scrn.BMP) option to save the entire tile map as one large bitmap file.

When you use Mappy to generate a single large bitmap image of a map, it saves the map exactly as it appears inside the Mappy tile editor window, as you can see in Figure 6.4.

Tip

Mappy is a map editing program that has been used by professional game developers for years to create retail 2D games. The trial edition of Mappy, included on the CD-ROM, is fully functional, but the professional version includes more advanced features. You may visit Mappy's home page at www.tilemap.co.uk.

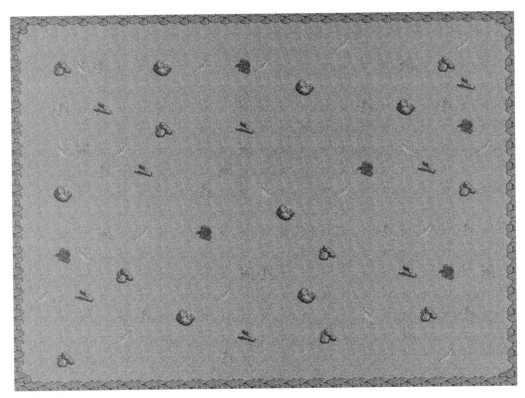

Figure 6.4
The Mappy-generated tile map has been saved as a single large bitmap image.

Constructing the Tiled Image

This theory of using a single large bitmap seems reasonable at first glance, but that method of scrolling has a very serious limitation. When you create a game world, the whole point is to interact with that game world. A single, large bitmap used to render the game world prevents you from actually tracking where the player is located on the map, as well as what other objects are on the map. In a tile-based game world, each tile is represented by a number, and that number has *meaning.* A tile containing a tree is *impassable,* while a tile of grass can be walked on. Of course, you could create a new array or some other method to keep track of the player, various enemies, and objects in the game world, but that requires a lot of extra work. There's a better way to do it.

A high-speed scrolling arcade game automatically scrolls horizontally or vertically, displaying ground-, air-, or space-based terrain below the player (usually represented by an airplane or spaceship). The point of such games is to keep the action moving so fast that the player doesn't have a chance to rest from one wave of enemies to the next. There are ways to optimize a tile scroller for these types of games, but for an RPG that can scroll in any direction, we need our tile scroller to be more robust and versatile.

Tiling is a process in which there really is no background, just an array of small images that make up the background as it is displayed. In other words, it is a virtual background and takes up very little memory compared to a full bit-mapped background. You are probably wondering: How can I load tiles and make a scrolling game world out of a Mappy level?

Now, you could just go into Mappy and save another large bitmap file every time you need to make a change to your game world, but that is not the best way to do it. The best way is to save the tiles to a separate bitmap image and save the map data to a data file using those parts to re-create the game world as you designed it in Mappy, sort of like a blueprint. We want to be able to scroll a *very large* game world without any memory limitations.

Most levels in a scrolling arcade game are quite large, comprised of thousands of tiles in one orientation or the other (usually just scrolling up and down—vertically—or left to right—horizontally). These types of games are called *shooters* for the most part, although the horizontally scrolling games are usually *platformers* (such as the original Mario games). Not only does your average Mario game have large scrolling levels, but those levels have parallax layers that make the background in the distance scroll by more slowly than the layer on which the player's character is walking.

When working on a new game, I find it helpful to start storing my tiles in a new image one by one as I need them, so that I can construct a new set of tiles for the game while I'm working on it. This also helps to keep the number of tiles down. If you have a huge tile map with hundreds of tiles in it, and you only need a few of them (at least during the early stages of a game's development), then you have to figure out which numbers those tiles are referred to, and you have to deal with a large texture in memory. Figure 6.5 shows an example of a "work in progress"

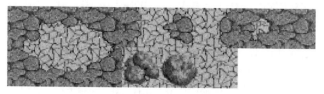

Figure 6.5
This example 256 × 256 texture has tiles being added one at a time as they are needed.

image containing just a handful of tiles that are used in the examples that we'll soon examine. There is some empty space in the image, but that's because more tiles will be added to it.

Exporting Tiles

A single large bitmap is just not used; it's what you might call amateur work. Another possibility is that you could continue to use a single large bitmap, but *create* that bitmap at runtime and fill it with tiles according to the map file and tile images. Although this solution would generate the game world on the fly, a large bitmap image representing the game world is still required in memory, which is not quite the ideal solution. Shortly, you will learn how to draw tiles directly without using a large representation in memory.

Let's take a look at Mappy again to see some ways to get tile data into a file so that we can use it. We're still somewhat in theory mode here, but I have an idea and I want to put it to the test. To do that, we need tile data. Mappy's export features are versatile. When you have the map just the way you want it, you can bring up the Export dialog box from the File menu, as shown in Figure 6.6.

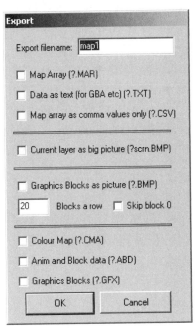

Figure 6.6
Mappy's Export dialog box has a lot of useful options.

The options you are interested in are the following:

- Map Array as Comma Values Only (?.CSV)

- Current Layer as Big Picture (?scrn.BMP)

- Graphics Blocks as Picture (?.BMP)

You may ignore the rest of the options, as they are not needed just yet. An interesting item of note here is the first option, Map Array (?.MAR). This will be of interest soon—it's an option that exports the map tile data into a binary file that looks like an array of integers (each comprised of two bytes). These binary files are very small, with just two bytes per tile, about a thousand times smaller than a text file filled with comma-delimited numbers.

You can use the second option, Current Layer as Big Picture, to generate one large bitmap image of the entire map. The other two options are for saving the tile images into a new bitmap file, as well as for saving the map data into a text file. You can choose all three options if you want, and Mappy obliges by creating all three files for you.

Using the Tile Data

Mappy exported a file called map1.CSV with the tile data inside. I would like you to first rename this file to map1.txt so it is easy to open with a simple text editor such as Notepad. When you open the file, you see something like the image in Figure 6.7.

Do you recall what settings you used to create this map file in Mappy? The dimensions are important because you must know how many tiles are in the data file. You can specify the number of columns and rows when you create a new map in Mappy, or you can view the properties of the current map in Mappy by using the MapTools menu and selecting Map Properties. You should see the dialog box shown in Figure 6.8.

This dialog box shows you a lot of information, but the parts I want you to focus on are the Map Array values shown. Here, you can see that this map has a width of 25 and a height of 18. Therefore, you want to use those values in your program when you're ready to draw the tiles.

Formatting the Map Data

Now let's talk about actually getting the tile data into your program. You already know how to load a bitmap file, so reading the tile images is not a problem. The

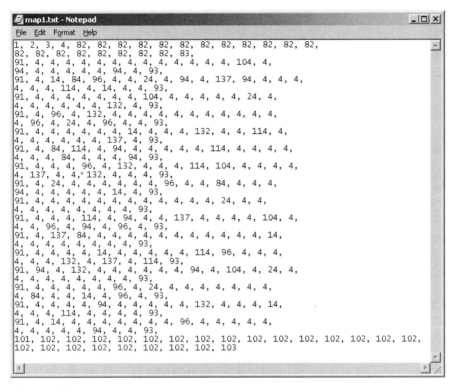

Figure 6.7
The tile data saved as comma-delimited values in a text file.

tile data stored in that text file, however, is a bit of a problem. You have two choices here:

- Read the data directly out of the file.

- Store the data into your program as a constant array.

You can copy the map data out of that map1.txt file (which you renamed from map1.CSV) right into your source code file and then convert it to a *constant array,* as shown in Figure 6.9. Does that sound strange? Well, I'll admit that is rather odd. This is just one possible way to get map data into your program. For small game levels or maps, this may be a good solution to the problem. You would just locate tile numbers inside the array using an index number. Now, why in the world would you want to do it this way, with all that manual editing? The idea is to be able to edit the tile data *directly* after the initial tile map has been created. If you want to make small changes here and there in the map, you can just edit the numbers; there's no need to open it up in Mappy ever again. But

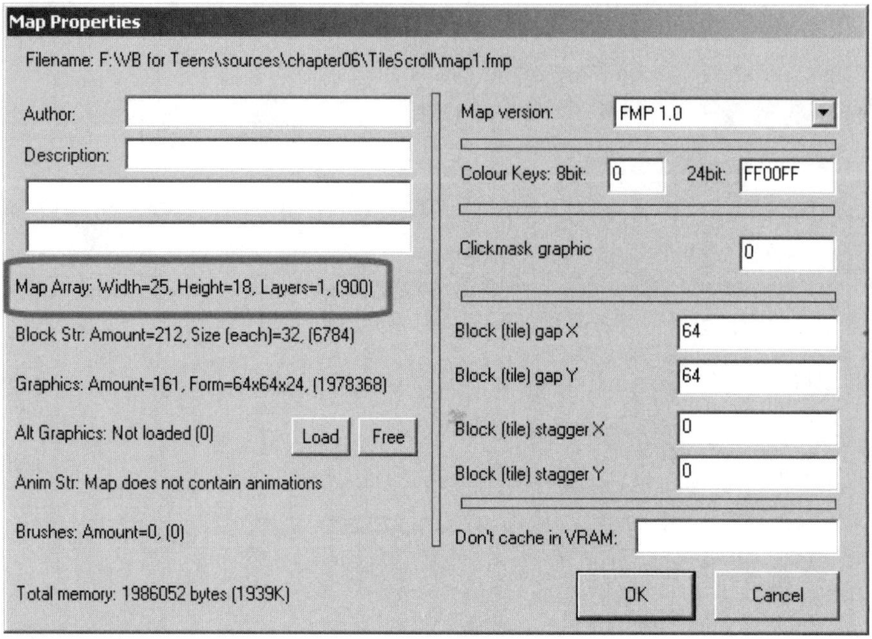

Figure 6.8
The Map Properties dialog box in Mappy.

the obvious drawback is that this doesn't work very well for large maps. Even the 30 × 30 tilemap shown here doesn't quite fit in the text editor.

A Comment about Map Size

That might look like a lot of numbers, but it really is tiny compared to most game levels! If you can see this on a single screen or single page, that's a good sign that it's tiny by most standards. However, it works well for the purpose of teaching the subject of scrolling.

As you can see, I have declared two constants, MAPW and MAPH, that define the size of this tilemap. After that, I declared mapdata as the name of the array, followed by 900 numbers representing the values in the 30 × 30 map. (I have used a *continuation* character at the end of every line—the underscore character allows you to continue a statement onto the next line in VB.NET.)

This is *almost* good enough to use in a game, and it is certainly nice to have the map data right here, where it is compiled into the EXE file. That is the best way to keep someone from tampering with your game levels! Another way is to export

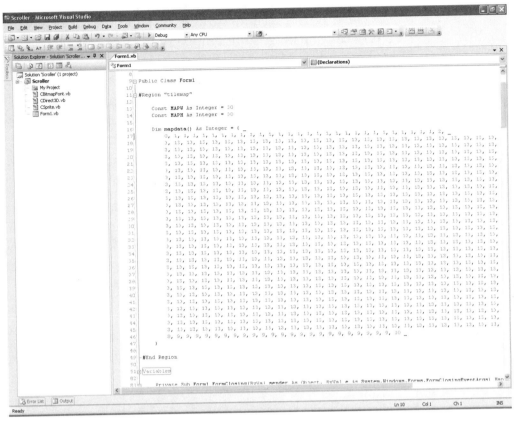

Figure 6.9
The tile map data embedded in a VB project.

the data to a binary file and load it into your game; this is the method we'll use with Celtic Crusader.

Stepping Stones of the World

The process of drawing tiles to fill the game world reminds me of laying down stepping stones, although tiling is admittedly a perfect analogy for what happens. Basically, tiles of a larger pattern are laid down from left to right, top to bottom, in that order. The first row is added, one tile at a time, all the way across, then the next row down is filled in from left to right, and so on until the entire map is filled.

The Scroller Engine

Now that you have a good understanding of what scrolling is and how we can edit tile maps and export them, let's take a look at the basic theory and code to actually draw a scrolling tile map on the screen.

The problem with scrolling a large game world is that too much memory is required to create a surface in memory sufficient to hold a large enough map for the game (even if you break the map into sections). You cannot create a single surface to hold the entire game world because most levels are far too large! The tile map for the Celtic Crusader game, for example, is more than 60,000 pixels across! That would consume so much memory that the program would not even run, and even if it did, that would be a *horrible* way to write a game. We're talking about old-school scrolling here, after all, so it should not need much memory!

Let's examine a method of tile rendering that supports giant maps using very little memory. All the memory required for the tile-based scroller developed here is a bitmap for the tiles and an array with all of the tile values. A map comprised of several million tiles can be rendered by this tile engine and will require only a small memory footprint.

Dynamic Partial-Tile Scrolling

The key to implementing a dynamic partial-tile scrolling engine is the use of a scroll buffer (or perhaps it could be called a *triple buffer system* because the frame buffer and back buffer represent the first two), upon which the tiles are drawn at the current scroll position.

The word *dynamic* here refers to the way the tile engine draws what is needed at that particular point in the game world, while *partial-tile* refers to the way it draws full tiles and partial tiles to fill the borders around the current scroll position. If you think about it, each individual tile is 32 × 32 pixels in size (at least, in my examples they are; you may use any tile size you wish), so without the partial-tile capability, drawing tiles directly to the screen one portion at a time results in very jumpy scrolling, where the screen is only updated whenever complete tiles can be drawn. This might work for a turn-based game such as *Civilization III* or *Panzer General* (both classic 2D games), but it is not suitable for a scrolling RPG game world.

To make this technique work, we start with two variables used to keep track of the scroll position: ScrollX and ScrollY. When drawing tiles directly, these variables give a precise position at which the tiles should start drawing in a left-to-right, top-to-bottom orientation. If the scroll position is at (500,500), what does this mean, exactly? It means that the tiles specified in the map should be drawn at the upper-left corner of the screen, *from* the position of the 500 × 500 point in the game world. Try to keep this concept in mind when you are working on scrolling, because the screen position is always the same—the scolling view is rendered onto the screen at the upper left, 0×0. Although the scroll position changes all the time, the destination location on the screen never changes. We're drawing one screen worth of the game world at a time, from any location in that game world. At the same time, we want to render the tiles that make up that portion of the game world *dynamically*, in order to keep the scroll engine efficient.

Testing the Dynamic Tile Renderer Theory

Figure 6.10 shows a small game world, one of several we could use as an example. Do you see the rock border around the map? The border is helpful when you are developing a new tile scroller because it shows the boundaries, allowing you to determine whether the scrolling view is being displayed at the correct location based on the scroll position. (In other words, it should stop scrolling when it reaches the edge of the "world," but it should not skip any tiles.)

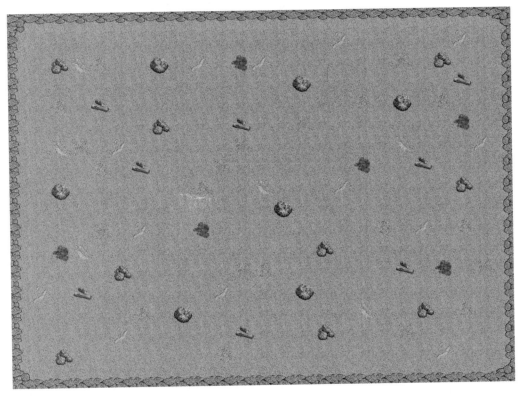

Figure 6.10
The small game world used as an example map file.

Now let's assume that you're using a screen resolution of 800 × 600, because this is a good resolution to use; it's relatively small so the screen updates quickly, but it is large enough to display a lot of details on the screen without crowding. There is a simple calculation that gives you the tile number as well as the partial tile values relatively easily. Are you familiar with *modulus*? This is a mathematical operation that produces the *remainder* of a division operation. Let me give you a simple example:

$$10 / 5 = 2$$

This is simple enough to understand, right? What happens when you are using numbers that are not evenly divisible?

$$10 / 3 = 3.33333333...$$

This is a problem, because the remainder is not an even number, and we're talking about pixels here. You can't deal with fractions of a pixel! However, you can work with fractions of a tile because tiles are made up of many pixels. Thinking in terms of complete tiles here, let's take a look at that division again:

$$10 / 3 = 3, \text{ with a remainder of } 0.33333333...$$

Let me now use numbers more relevant to the problem at hand. Let's assume we're creating a scroller using tiles that are each 64 × 64 pixels in size. Celtic Crusader uses 32 × 32 pixel tiles, but for the sake of argument, let's give this a try:

$$800 / 64 = 12.5$$

This represents a calculation that returns the number of tiles that fit across the screen with a width of 800 pixels (assuming the tiles are 64 pixels wide). What does 12.5 tiles mean when you are writing a scroller? The .5 represents a *part* of a tile that must be drawn; hence, I call it *partial-tile scrolling*. Switching to 32 × 32 pixel tiles results in an evenly divisible screen, at least horizontally (32 × 32 results in 25 tiles across, 18.75 tiles down).

Here is where it gets really interesting—at least, I think so! After you have drawn your tiles across the screen, and you want to fill in the remaining 0.5 of a tile, you can calculate the size of the tile like so:

$$\text{remainder} = 0.5$$

$$64 \times \text{remainder} = 32$$

That is, half of the partial tile must be drawn to handle the scrolling edge that was not lined up with a tile edge on the map. Rather than keeping track of the remainder at all, there is a simpler way to calculate the portion of the tile that must be drawn, in the measurement of pixels:

Screen Width *Modulus* Tile Width = Partial Tile Size

Here is a real example using the numbers we've been discussing:

800 Mod 64 = 32

N o t e

The *modulus* operator (Mod in VB) is similar to operators such as multiply, divide, add, and subtract, but it simply returns the *remainder* of a division calculation, which works great for our purposes here.

Try not to think of scrolling in screen terms, because the whole discussion revolves around the tile map in memory (the tile data itself). The tile data is expanded to full tiles when drawn to the screen, but until that happens, these tiles might be thought of as a huge virtual game world from which the scrolling window is drawn. Figure 6.11 shows the game world with the scroll window superimposed, so you can see how the screen represents a portion of the game world. While viewing this figure, imagine there is no image containing this game world map, just a virtual array of tile numbers. Those tiles are drawn *just* to the screen, based on what is visible in the darkened part of the figure.

Let's try another problem so you get the hang of calculating partial tiles before we get into the source code for this chapter. Suppose the scroll position is at (700,0) on the map, and our tiles are 64 × 64 pixels each. Which would be the starting tile, and what is the value of the partial tile (in pixels)? To calculate first the tile position in the map data array, just drop the decimal part, which represents the remainder:

700 / 64 = 10.9375 = 10 *tiles*

Next, you *do* want to keep the remainder, and actually drop the tile position because now you're interested in pixels.

700 / 64 = 10.9375

64 × 0.9375 = 60

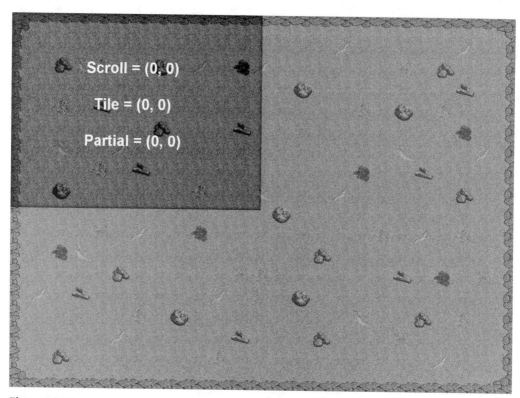

Figure 6.11
Dynamic scrolling generates the tiled scroll buffer on the fly using map data.

Therefore:

700 Mod 64 = 60

The modulus operator greatly helps with this calculation by skipping that middle step. It simply provides the remainder value directly, giving the exact number of pixels that must be drawn from the partial tile to fill in the top and left edges of the screen. The calculation is illustrated in Figure 6.12.

Ready for another try at it? It's very important that you understand how partial-tile scrolling works before moving on, so study this code carefully. This time, calculate the tile numbers and partial-tile values for both the X and Y position of the scroll window at (372,489). Figure 6.13 shows the answer graphically.

First the X value:

372 / 64 = 5.8125 (tile X = 5)

64 × 0.8125 = 52 (pixels)

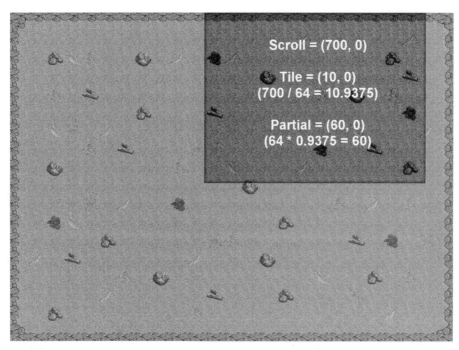

Figure 6.12
An example of how the partial tile calculation is performed at position (700,0).

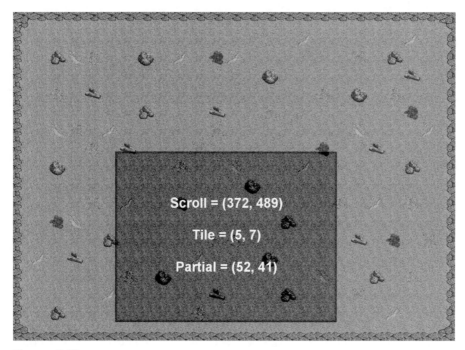

Figure 6.13
The partial tile calculation makes it possible to perform true tile-based scrolling.

Now for the Y value:

489 / 64 = 7.640625 (tile Y = 7)

64 × 0.640625 = 41 (pixels)

Coding the Partial-Tile Scrolling Subroutine

Are you ready to put this algorithm into code and see how it works? The first sub-routine in this brave new world is called to update the scroll position due to user input. Don't worry about missing dependencies at this point; we'll fill in the global variables you see here when we complete the first Scroller Test program in a bit.

```
Public Sub UpdateScrollPosition()
    Dim GameWorldW As Long = MAPW * TILEW
    Dim GameWorldH As Long = MAPH * TILEH

    'update horizontal scrolling position and speed
    ScrollX = ScrollX + SpeedX
    If (ScrollX < 0) Then
        ScrollX = 0
        SpeedX = 0
    ElseIf ScrollX > GameWorldW - WINDOWWIDTH Then
        ScrollX = GameWorldH - WINDOWWIDTH
        SpeedX = 0
    End If

    'update vertical scrolling position and speed
    ScrollY = ScrollY + SpeedY
    If ScrollY < 0 Then
        ScrollY = 0
        SpeedY = 0
    ElseIf ScrollY > GameWorldW - WINDOWHEIGHT Then
        ScrollY = GameWorldH - WINDOWHEIGHT
        SpeedY = 0
    End If
End Sub
```

Filling the Screen with Tiles

The UpdateScrollBuffer subroutine copies tiles from the source tile image onto the scroll buffer, a surface image that is just slightly larger than the screen resolution. It does this to take into account the tile overlap that may occur at some resolutions. This routine is responsible for filling in the scroll buffer. It does this by using two For loops, and inside the second loop it draws row after row of tiles, one at a time, from the source tile image to the destination scroll buffer image. This is all necessary before we even see the game world appear on the screen—that's another step entirely!

```
Public Sub UpdateScrollBuffer()
    Dim indexX As Integer
    Dim indexY As Integer
    Dim tilesAcross As Integer
    Dim tilesDown As Integer
    Dim X As Integer
    Dim Y As Integer
    Dim tilenum As Integer

    'calculate the number of columns and rows
    'integer division drops the remainder
    tilesAcross = WINDOWWIDTH \ TILEW
    tilesDown = WINDOWHEIGHT \ TILEH

    'draw tiles onto the scroll buffer surface
    For Y = 0 To tilesDown
        For X = 0 To tilesAcross

            indexX = ScrollX \ TILEW + X
            indexY = ScrollY \ TILEH + Y

            '*** This condition shouldn't be necessary.
            'If indexY >= MAPH Then indexY = maph-1

            tilenum = mapdata(indexY * MAPW + indexX)
            DrawTile(tilenum, TILEW, TILEH, TILECOLUMNS, X * TILEW, Y * TILEH)

        Next X
    Next Y
End Sub
```

For the sake of consistency, let me show you the DrawTile subroutine here because it is called by the preceding subroutine to draw each tile. Do you see some familiar code in this function? You should! It's the same sort of code we wrote to draw an animated sprite frame on the screen. We are using the same technique to draw tiles, only now we're drawing them from a Surface rather than from a Texture, which is more suitable for a sprite. For one thing, we don't need to draw tiles transparently. There are six parameters for the DrawTile routine: the tile number, the tile width and height, the number of columns in the source image, and the destination x and y positions. You could actually call DrawTile to draw any single tile anywhere on the screen without using the scroll buffer because it's versatile (due to the parameter list).

```
Public Sub DrawTile( _
    ByVal tilenum As Long, _
    ByVal tilew As Long, _
    ByVal tileh As Long, _
    ByVal columns As Long, _
    ByVal destx As Long, _
    ByVal desty As Long)

    'create a rectangle to the source
    Dim srcRect As New Rectangle
    srcRect.X = (tilenum Mod columns) * tilew
    srcRect.Y = (tilenum \ columns) * tileh
    srcRect.Width = tilew
    srcRect.Height = tileh

    'create a rectangle to the destination
    Dim dstRect As New Rectangle(destx, desty, tilew, tileh)

    'draw the tile
    d3d.Device().StretchRectangle(tiles, srcRect, scrollbuffer, _
        dstRect, TextureFilter.None)
End Sub
```

Drawing the Scroll Buffer

After you have filled the scroll buffer with tiles for the current scroll position within the game world, the next thing you must do is actually draw the scroll buffer to the screen. This is where things get a little interesting. The scroll buffer is filled only with complete tiles, but it is from here that the partial tiles are taken into account. This is interesting because the whole tiles were drawn onto the scroll buffer, but the partial tiles are handled when drawing the scroll buffer to the screen. The partialx and partialy variables are given the result of the modulus calculation, and these values are then used as the upper-left corner of the scroll buffer that is copied to the screen.

I don't usually like to use global variables in a subroutine, because good coding practice produces subroutines that are independent and reusable from one project to the next. The `DrawTile` subroutine is much more independent than `DrawScrollWindow`, but it also uses the global `mapdata` array. In the final analysis, some of this can't be helped if you want the game to run at a fast frame rate, because passing variables to subroutines is a very time-consuming process, and you want the game to run as fast as possible. We'll put all of this code into a class so the global constants and variables will not be visible to the main program.

Remember, the scrolling window is just the beginning. The rest of the game still has to be developed, and that includes a lot of animated sprites for the player's character, non-player characters (NPCs), plus buildings, animals, and any other objects that appear in the game. The bottom line is that the scroller needs to be as efficient as possible. (Yes, even with today's fast PCs, the scroller needs to be fast—never use the argument that PCs are fast to excuse poorly written code!)

Therefore, the `DrawScrollBuffer` subroutine uses the global variables for the map data, tile source bitmap, scroll buffer, and back buffer. To pass these values to the subroutine every time consumes too many processor cycles, slowing down the game. This is the last step in the partial-tile scroller rendering system.

```
Public Sub DrawScrollBuffer()
    Dim partialx As Integer
    Dim partialy As Integer

    'calculate the partial sub-tile lines to draw
    partialx = ScrollX Mod TILEW
    partialy = ScrollY Mod TILEH

    'set dimensions of the source image
    Dim srcRect As New Rectangle(partialx, partialy, WINDOWWIDTH, WINDOWHEIGHT)

    'set the destination rect
    Dim dstRect As New Rectangle(0, 0, SCREENW, SCREENH)

    'draw the scroll window
    d3d.Device().StretchRectangle(scrollbuffer, srcRect, backbuffer, _
        dstRect, TextureFilter.None)
End Sub
```

The ScrollWorld Program

Let's put these subroutines into a complete program to see how this scrolling technique works in the real world. Create a new project called Scroller Test and add the usual DirectX, Direct3D, and other library references to the project. Then type in the subroutines we just went over into the program:

- UpdateScrollPosition

- UpdateScrollBuffer

- DrawTile

- DrawScrollBuffer

Aligning Tiles to the Scroll Buffer

There is one factor that you must take into consideration while designing the screen layout of your game with a scrolling window. The size of the scrolling window must be evenly divisible by the size of the tiles, or you end up with a *floating overlap* at the uneven edge. This is an issue that I considered solving in the scrolling code itself. But it turns out that this is unnecessary because you can just change the destination rectangle when drawing the scroll buffer to the screen (something we'll explore later in this chapter with the Scrolling Viewport program).

From now on, we'll focus on tiles that are each 32×32 pixels in size because that is the tile size used in Celtic Crusader. If you're using a screen resolution of 800×600 with 32×32 tiles, your width is fine, but height is a problem. Cut off the bottom of the scroll window at 576 (which is 18 tiles high), leaving the remaining 24 pixels unused at the bottom. This shouldn't be a problem because you can use that screen real estate for things like an in-game menu system, player status information, or perhaps in-game dialogue. (Don't confuse this with the discussion earlier about partial tiles, because the partial-tile drawing is different than the overall alignment of tiles on the scroll buffer surface.)

Figure 6.14 illustrates how you could position the scroll window, leaving a small portion at the bottom of the screen, which might be used for other things. In Celtic Crusader, we draw a border around the screen that covers up the empty space at the bottom.

I recommend limiting the scrolling window to a portion of the screen anyway, as it makes more sense than displaying game information over the top of the

Figure 6.14
The scrolling window should be evenly divisible by the tile size.

scrolling window. This holds true unless you are doing something cool, like drawing transparent windows over the top of the background.

Tip

Since most scrolling games will render the scroll buffer into a window that is smaller than the actual screen, we'll just need to explore this feature next and not worry about it right now.

Figure 6.15 shows the Scroller Test program running at 800×600, with some blank space showing at the right and bottom edges of the scroll window. This is intentional, keeping the scroller code as efficient as possible (without too many conditions placed upon it). By simply making the scroll window evenly divisible by the tiles, there is no special-case code required to keep the scrolling tiles in view beyond the scroll window.

The next screenshot of Scroller Test, in Figure 6.16, shows the program running at a resolution of 640×480. As you can see, the screen was evenly divisible with the 64×64 tiles, so the right edge is flush with the screen, while the bottom edge (in which 480 is not evenly divisible by 64) leaves a portion of the screen unused. There is another solution to some of these resolution problems, aside from drawing the scroll buffer into a window—you could also use smaller tiles. In fact, in most of the examples (and in the Celtic Crusader game to come) I use 32×32 tiles because they're easier to use and they consume less memory.

Finally, Figure 6.17 shows the program running at 1024×768, with an even distribution of tiles from left to right and top to bottom, completely filling in the screen. Although this particular resolution does work well with this tile size, that shouldn't be your goal with a scrolling game; a portion of the screen is used for

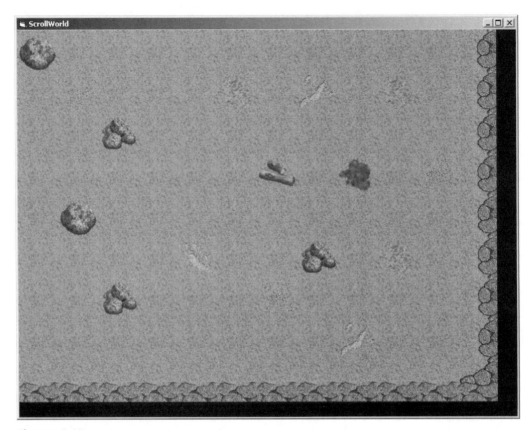

Figure 6.15
The Scroller Test program cannot uniformly fill the 800 × 600 screen.

other aspects of the game anyway (such as status information or the score). Once you have the main screen designed for your game, you have a better idea about how large of a scroll window you need.

The Scroller Test Source Code

The Scroller Test program is almost already written with the four subroutines we examined earlier. These will need to be added to the Scroller Test program (inside the Form code file) in addition to the following code. Here we have some global constants and variables, the Form1_Load event, a timer that simulates a game loop, and the MouseMove event.

In addition to these core routines, you will need the CDirect3D class developed previously, because this file has all of the core Direct3D code (namely, the device object) needed by the tile renderer.

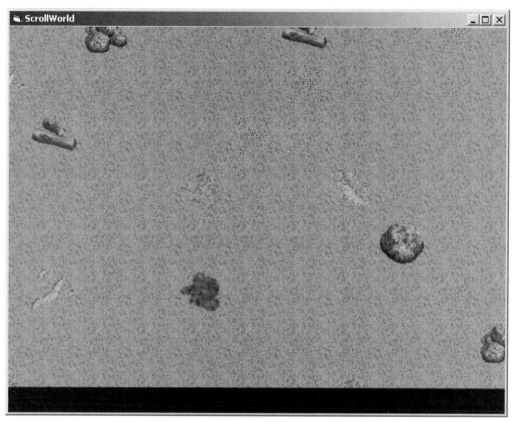

Figure 6.16
The Scroller Test program fills most of the screen at 640 × 480.

You may refer to the project on the CD-ROM for the complete tile map and a few of the support routines not provided here. In most of the examples from this point forward, I won't be providing complete code listings; I'll just go over the key portions of code and recommend you open the projects from the CD-ROM to see all of the remaining (and relatively unimportant) details.

```
'screen size
Const SCREENW As Integer = 800
Const SCREENH As Integer = 600

'tile size
Const TILEW As Integer = 32
Const TILEH As Integer = 32
Const TILECOLUMNS As Integer = 8
```

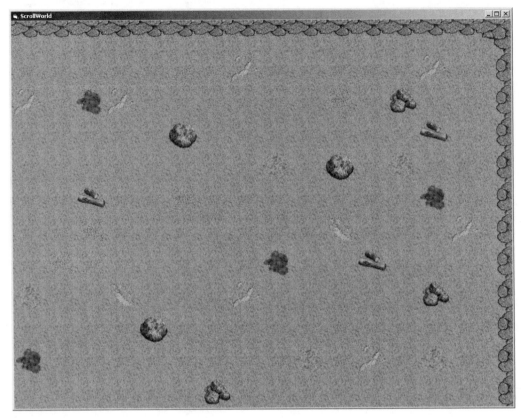

Figure 6.17
At 1024 × 768, the scroller fills the entire screen evenly.

```
'scrolling window size divided into whole tiles
Const WINDOWWIDTH As Integer = (SCREENW \ TILEW) * TILEW
Const WINDOWHEIGHT As Integer = (SCREENH \ TILEH) * TILEH

'tile scroller surfaces
Public scrollbuffer As Direct3D.Surface
Public tiles As Direct3D.Surface

'scrolling values
Public ScrollX As Long
Public ScrollY As Long
Public SpeedX As Integer
Public SpeedY As Integer

Private d3d As CDirect3D
Dim backbuffer As Direct3D.Surface

Private WithEvents clock As Timer
```

Next we have the Form1_Load event, the clock_Tick event, and the MouseMove event.

```
Private Sub Form1_Load(ByVal sender As System.Object, ByVal e As System.
EventArgs) _
    Handles MyBase.Load
        Dim time As Integer
        Dim start As Integer = time = System.DateTime.Now.Millisecond()
        Dim mode As DisplayMode = Manager.Adapters.Default.CurrentDisplayMode
        Dim rect As Rectangle

        Me.Size = New Size(SCREENW, SCREENH)
        Me.Text = "SCROLL TEST"

        d3d = New CDirect3D(Me)
        d3d.Init(SCREENW, SCREENH, True)
        backbuffer = d3d.Device.GetBackBuffer(0, 0, BackBufferType.Mono)

        'load the tiles
        tiles = d3d.Device().CreateOffscreenPlainSurface( _
            512, 512, mode.Format, Pool.Default)

        SurfaceLoader.FromFile(tiles, "maptiles256.bmp", Filter.None,
        RGB(0, 0, 0))

        'scroll buffer size is slightly larger than screen
        Dim ScrollBufferW As Integer = SCREENW + TILEW
        Dim ScrollBufferH As Integer = SCREENH + TILEH

        'create the scroll buffer
        scrollbuffer = d3d.Device().CreateOffscreenPlainSurface( _
            ScrollBufferW, ScrollBufferH, mode.Format, Pool.Default)
        rect = New Rectangle(0, 0, scrollbuffer.Description.Width, _
            scrollbuffer.Description.Height)
        d3d.Device().ColorFill(scrollbuffer, rect, Color.Blue)

        'initialize timer
        clock = New Timer()
        clock.Interval = 30
        clock.Start()
    End Sub
```

```
    Private Sub clock_Tick(ByVal sender As Object, ByVal e As System.EventArgs) _
        Handles clock.Tick

        UpdateScrollPosition()
        d3d.StartRendering(Color.Black)

        UpdateScrollBuffer()
        DrawScrollBuffer()

        d3d.StopRendering()
    End Sub

    Private Sub Form1_MouseMove(ByVal sender As Object, _
        ByVal e As System.Windows.Forms.MouseEventArgs) Handles Me.MouseMove

        Const STEPPING As Integer = 8

        'move mouse on left side to scroll left
        If e.X < SCREENW / 2 Then SpeedX = -STEPPING

        'move mouse on right side to scroll right
        If e.X > SCREENW / 2 Then SpeedX = STEPPING

        'move mouse on top half to scroll up
        If e.Y < SCREENH / 2 Then SpeedY = -STEPPING

        'move mouse on bottom half to scroll down
        If e.Y > SCREENH / 2 Then SpeedY = STEPPING
    End Sub
```

The Scrolling Viewport Program

Using the entire screen for the tile scroller might be a goal for the game, part of its design, if the screen resolution divides evenly by the tile size (such as 1024 × 768, as we examined earlier). But most games don't fill the entire screen with tiles. It's far more common to scroll the game world in a viewport or window on the screen. This is especially true of RPGs.

I've provided an example program on the CD-ROM called Scrolling Viewport that demonstrates exactly what the name implies. You can see the program running in Figure 6.18. The key difference between this program and the

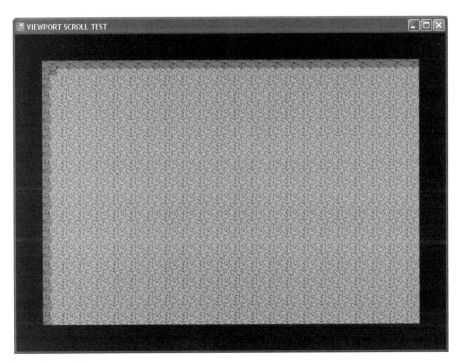

Figure 6.18
The Viewport Scroll Test program.

previous one is the code that actually draws the scroll buffer to the screen—all of the rest of the code is unchanged. Here is the DrawScrollBuffer routine again, now with a new parameter—a Rectangle that specifies the output viewport for the scroller. Notice that I've commented out the previous code so you can see the change in effect.

```
Public Sub DrawScrollBuffer(ByVal rect As Rectangle)
    Dim partialx As Integer
    Dim partialy As Integer

    'calculate the partial sub-tile lines to draw
    partialx = ScrollX Mod TILEW
    partialy = ScrollY Mod TILEH

    'set dimensions of the source image
    'Dim srcRect As New Rectangle(partialx, partialy,
    WINDOWWIDTH, WINDOWHEIGHT)
    Dim srcRect As New Rectangle(partialx, partialy, rect.Width, rect.Height)
```

```
'set the destination rect

'Dim dstRect As New Rectangle(0, 0, SCREENW, SCREENH)

'draw the scroll window
d3d.Device().StretchRectangle(scrollbuffer, srcRect, backbuffer, _
    rect, TextureFilter.None)
```

End Sub

The CTileScroller Class

To wrap up this subject, I've created a class that wraps up all of the routines and global variables and other aspects of tile-based scrolling. This reusable class is called TileScroller and will be used extensively throughout the rest of the book while we build the Celtic Crusader game. Once you've added the TileScroller class to your project, you can use it very easily using code such as this:

```
Private scroller As TileScroller

'create the tile scroller
scroller = New TileScroller(d3d, SCREENW, SCREENH, TILEW, TILEH, COLUMNS)
scroller.MapWidthInTiles = MAPW
scroller.MapHeightInTiles = MAPH

'load the tiles
scroller.LoadTiles("maptiles256.bmp", 256, 256)
```

Then, when you want to update the scroll buffer and render the scrolling viewport to the screen, there are just two methods in the class that you need to call. Note that now I'm passing the mapdata array to the Update routine (which is now called UpdateTilemap). The Draw method was adapted from Draw-ScrollBuffer previously, with a simple name change. Of course, all of these routines now use properties (in other words, class variables) internally, so there are not as many parameters required as there were in the Scroller Test program earlier.

```
scroller.UpdateTilemap(mapdata)
scroller.Draw(New Rectangle(50, 50, 700, 500))
```

Here is the code for the entire TileScroller class. You can open the TileScroller Class example program from the CD-ROM if you wish.

```vb
Imports Microsoft.DirectX
Imports Microsoft.DirectX.Direct3D

Public Class TileScroller
    Private ref_d3d As CDirect3D

    'scroll buffer image
    Private p_scrollbuffer As Direct3D.Surface

    'source tile artwork image
    Private p_tiles As Direct3D.Surface

    'map size is measured in tiles, not pixels
    Private p_maptilesw As Integer
    Private p_maptilesh As Integer

    'tile size
    Private p_tilew As Integer
    Private p_tileh As Integer

    'number of columns in source image
    Private p_tilecolumns As Integer
    Private p_scrollx As Integer
    Private p_scrolly As Integer

    Private p_ScrollBufferW As Integer
    Private p_ScrollBufferH As Integer
    Private p_windoww As Integer
    Private p_windowh As Integer

    Public Sub New(ByRef d3d As CDirect3D, ByVal windoww As Integer, _
        ByVal windowh As Integer, ByVal tilew As Integer, ByVal tileh As Integer, _
        ByVal tilecolumns As Integer)

        Dim mode As DisplayMode = Manager.Adapters.Default.CurrentDisplayMode

        'create local reference to Direct3D object
        ref_d3d = d3d

        'save tile details
        p_tilew = tilew
        p_tileh = tileh
        p_tilecolumns = tilecolumns
```

```vb
        'scroll buffer size is slightly larger than screen
        p_ScrollBufferW = windoww + p_tilew
        p_ScrollBufferH = windowh + p_tileh

        'create the scroll buffer
        p_scrollbuffer = d3d.Device().CreateOffscreenPlainSurface( _
            p_ScrollBufferW, p_ScrollBufferH, mode.Format, Pool.Default)

        Dim rect As New Rectangle(0, 0, p_scrollbuffer.Description.Width, _
            p_scrollbuffer.Description.Height)

        d3d.Device().ColorFill(p_scrollbuffer, rect, Color.Blue)

        'scrolling window size is divided into whole tiles
        p_windoww = (windoww \ p_tilew) * p_tilew
        p_windowh = (windowh \ p_tileh) * p_tileh
    End Sub


    Public Property MapWidthInTiles() As Integer
        Get
            Return p_maptilesw
        End Get
        Set(ByVal value As Integer)
            p_maptilesw = value
        End Set
    End Property

    Public Property MapHeightInTiles() As Integer
        Get
            Return p_maptilesh
        End Get
        Set(ByVal value As Integer)
            p_maptilesh = value
        End Set
    End Property

    Public Property TileWidth() As Integer
        Get
            Return p_tilew
        End Get
        Set(ByVal value As Integer)
```

```vb
            p_tilew = value
        End Set
End Property

Public Property TileHeight() As Integer
    Get
            Return p_tileh
    End Get
    Set(ByVal value As Integer)
            p_tileh = value
    End Set
End Property

Public Property TileColumns() As Integer
    Get
            Return p_tilecolumns
    End Get
    Set(ByVal value As Integer)
            p_tilecolumns = value
    End Set
End Property

Public Property ScrollX() As Integer
    Get
            Return p_scrollx
    End Get
    Set(ByVal value As Integer)
            p_scrollx = value
    End Set
End Property

Public Property ScrollY() As Integer
    Get
            Return p_scrolly
    End Get
    Set(ByVal value As Integer)
            p_scrolly = value
    End Set
End Property

Public Sub LoadTiles(ByVal filename As String, ByVal tilew As Integer, _
    ByVal tileh As Integer)
```

```vb
        Dim mode As DisplayMode = Manager.Adapters.Default.CurrentDisplayMode

        p_tiles = ref_d3d.Device().CreateOffscreenPlainSurface( _
            tilew, tileh, mode.Format, Pool.Default)

        SurfaceLoader.FromFile(p_tiles, filename, Filter.None, RGB(0, 0, 0))
    End Sub

    Public Sub UpdateTilemap(ByRef mapdata() As Byte)
        Dim indexX As Integer
        Dim indexY As Integer
        Dim tilesAcross As Integer
        Dim tilesDown As Integer
        Dim X As Integer
        Dim Y As Integer
        Dim tilenum As Integer

        'calculate the number of columns and rows
        'integer division drops the remainder
        tilesAcross = p_windoww \ p_tilew
        tilesDown = p_windowh \ p_tileh

        'draw tiles onto the scroll buffer surface
        For Y = 0 To tilesDown
            For X = 0 To tilesAcross

                indexX = p_scrollx \ p_tilew + X
                indexY = p_scrolly \ p_tileh + Y

                If indexY >= p_maptilesh Then indexY = p_maptilesh - 1

                Try
                    tilenum = mapdata(indexY * p_maptilesw + indexX)
                    DrawTile(tilenum, X * p_tilew, Y * p_tileh)
                Catch ex As Exception
                End Try
            Next X
        Next Y
    End Sub

    Private Sub DrawTile( _
        ByVal tilenum As Long, _
        ByVal destx As Long, _
        ByVal desty As Long)
```

```
            'create a rectangle to the source
            Dim srcRect As New Rectangle
            srcRect.X = (tilenum Mod p_tilecolumns) * p_tilew
            srcRect.Y = (tilenum \ p_tilecolumns) * p_tileh
            srcRect.Width = p_tilew
            srcRect.Height = p_tileh

            'create a rectangle to the destination
            Dim dstRect As New Rectangle(destx, desty, p_tilew, p_tileh)

            'draw the tile
            ref_d3d.Device().StretchRectangle(p_tiles, srcRect, p_scrollbuffer, _
                dstRect, TextureFilter.None)
        End Sub

        Public Sub Draw(ByVal destRect As Rectangle)
            Dim partialx As Integer
            Dim partialy As Integer

            'calculate the partial sub-tile lines to draw
            partialx = p_scrollx Mod p_tilew
            partialy = p_scrolly Mod p_tileh

            'set dimensions of the source image
            Dim srcRect As New Rectangle(partialx, partialy, destRect.Width, _
                destRect.Height)

            'draw the scroll window
            ref_d3d.Device().StretchRectangle(p_scrollbuffer, srcRect, _
                ref_d3d.BackBuffer, destRect, TextureFilter.None)
        End Sub

        Protected Overrides Sub Finalize()
            MyBase.Finalize()
            p_scrollbuffer.Dispose()
            p_scrollbuffer = Nothing
            p_tiles.Dispose()
            p_tiles = Nothing
        End Sub

End Class
```

Level Up

This chapter has really knocked out the subject of tile-based scrolling by pro-viding the code you need to present the game world to the player in the upcoming Celtic Crusader game. You continue to learn the things needed to get this game functional in the chapters to come, but you have learned the most important techniques needed to make the game a reality. The ability to scroll a game world of any size was the primary goal of the book thus far, because Celtic Crusader has a very large game world. This chapter has fulfilled that requirement.

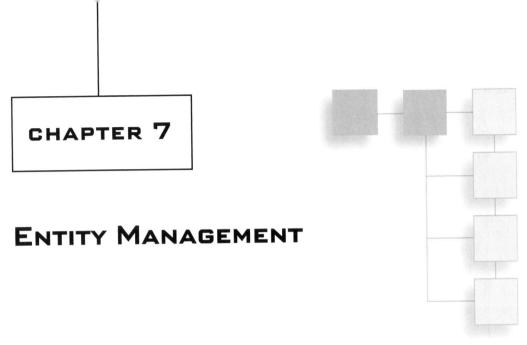

CHAPTER 7

ENTITY MANAGEMENT

Entity management is a core technique of every game of sufficient complexity, in which simpler methods (such as an array of sprites) will not suffice. You can imagine creating a *Breakout*-style game using an array for the blocks (and I'll demonstrate such an example in this chapter). But when you have hundreds or thousands of "entities" (which usually take the form of sprites in 2D games), an array is just not practical. How do you handle bullets in a fast-paced arcade game if your main array is used for alien ships? Create another array for bullets? Instead, we'll look at a technique in this chapter that lets you add all of your sprites into a *managed list,* with far more capabilities than a simple array.

This chapter also explains the core technique of detecting collisions between two sprites. This is a higher-level technique than previous topics you have learned so far, which have focused more on just getting something up on the screen. In addition to testing for sprite-to-sprite collisions, this chapter also shows you how to identify when the player has hit a tile that is impassable (such as an ocean square), which will be a vital feature of the Celtic Crusader engine. Here is a breakdown of the major topics in this chapter:

- Reacting to solid objects

- Rectangle intersection

- Entity management

Reacting to Solid Objects

Let's begin our discussion with collision detection first, then we'll study the subject of entity management. After creating the example game in this chapter, you'll see why I've reserved that subject until after we've studied collisions. Collision detection is an important technique that you should learn. It is a requirement for every game ever made. I can't think of any game that does not need collision detection, because it is such an essential aspect of gameplay. Without collisions, there is no action, goal, or purpose in a game. There is no way to interact with the game without collisions taking place. In other words, collision detection makes the sprites in a game come to life and makes the game believable. Not every situation in which collision detection occurs necessarily means that something is hit or destroyed. We can also use collision testing to prevent the player from going into certain areas (such as a lake or mountain area that is impassible).

Rectangle Intersection

Collision detection or testing is done using the Rectangle class. First, you will create a rectangle based on the position and size of one object, such as a sprite. Then you will need to create a similar rectangle for a second object. Once you have two rectangles, which represent the position and size of two objects, then you can test to see whether the rectangles are intersecting. You can do this with a method built into the Rectangle class—it's called IntersectsWith. Since we already have a sprite class called CSprite available, let's use it to create a function called CollidedWith that performs this testing and returns true or false:

```
Public Function CollidedWith(ByRef sprite1 As CSprite, ByRef sprite2 As CSprite)
As Boolean
    'set up the first rectangle
    Dim rect1 As New Rectangle( _
    sprite1.GetPosition.X, sprite1.GetPosition.Y, _
    sprite1.FrameWidth, sprite1.FrameHeight)

    'set up the second rectangle
    Dim rect2 As New Rectangle( _
    sprite2.GetPosition.X, sprite2.GetPosition.Y, _
    sprite2.FrameWidth, sprite2.FrameHeight)

    'check for collision
    Return rect1.IntersectsWith(rect2)
End Function
```

Let's dissect this function to determine what it does. First, notice that CollidedWith returns a Boolean value (true or false). Notice also that two sprites are passed as parameters ByRef, which means *by reference.* Thus, the entire sprite class is not passed to the function, only a reference to the sprite's location in memory. Two rectangles are created based on the position and size of each sprite, and then the first rectangle is used to call the IntersectsWith function, to which is passed the second rectangle, and a true or false result is returned.

Modifying the Sprite Class

Instead of reusing this CollidedWith function in our source code in each new project, it is easier and more logical to add it to the CSprite class. To do that we'll need to modify it a bit, so that the function uses the sprite's internal properties, thus eliminating one of the parameters passed to the function. Open up the CSprite.vb file and add the following new function:

```
Public Function CollidedWith(ByRef other As CSprite) As Boolean
    'create the first rectangle
    Dim rect1 As New Rectangle(Me.GetPosition.X, Me.GetPosition.Y, _
    Me.FrameWidth, Me.FrameHeight)

    'create the second rectangle
    Dim rect2 As New Rectangle(other.GetPosition.X, other.GetPosition.Y, _
    other.FrameWidth, other.FrameHeight)

    'check for collision
    Return rect1.IntersectsWith(rect2)
End Function
```

Sprite Collision Test Program

To demonstrate sprite collision testing with our new function, I've put together a quick demo based on the old game of *Breakout,* and it's shown in Figure 7.1. Let me show you how to create this project. We'll reuse classes written previously to simplify the game and cut down on the amount of code that would otherwise be required.

First, create a new project in VB.NET and add these DirectX library references:

- Microsoft.DirectX

- Microsoft.DirectX.Direct3D

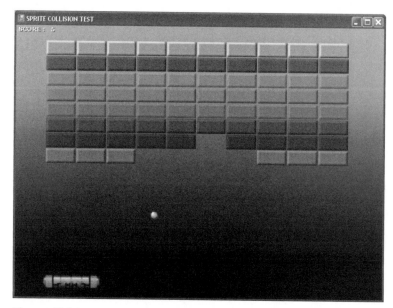

Figure 7.1
The Sprite Collision Test program demonstrates bounding rectangle collision testing.

- Microsoft.DirectX.Direct3DX

- Microsoft.DirectX.DirectInput

Next, gather the class files from previous chapters and add them to your project:

- CDirect3D

- CSprite

- CKeyboard

- CMouse

- CBitmapFont

Let's start with the library import statements, class definition, and global variables:

```
Imports Microsoft.DirectX
Imports Microsoft.DirectX.Direct3D
Imports Microsoft.DirectX.DirectInput

Public Class Form1
    Const TITLE As String = "SPRITE COLLISION TEST"
    Const SCREENW As Integer = 800
```

```
    Const SCREENH As Integer = 600

    Private WithEvents clock As Timer

    Private d3d As CDirect3D
    Private keyboard As CKeyboard
    Private mouse As CMouse

    Private background As CSprite
    Private ball As CSprite
    Private paddle As CSprite
    Private font1 As CBitmapFont
    Private block_image As CSprite
    Private blocks(10, 8) As CSprite
    Private score As Integer = 0
```

Next up is the Form1_Load subroutine, which is the first thing that runs, so this is where we initialize DirectX, load up all of the game's resources, and set the starting values for variables.

```
Private Sub Form1_Load(ByVal sender As System.Object, _
ByVal e As System.EventArgs) Handles MyBase.Load
    Dim x As Integer
    Dim y As Integer

    'initialize form
    Me.Size = New Size(SCREENW, SCREENH)
    Me.Text = TITLE
    Me.SetStyle(ControlStyles.AllPaintingInWmPaint Or _
        ControlStyles.Opaque, True)

    'initialize Direct3D
    d3d = New CDirect3D(Me)
    d3d.Init(SCREENW, SCREENH, True)

    'initialize input devices
    keyboard = New CKeyboard(Me)
    mouse = New CMouse(Me)

    'load fonts
    font1 = New CBitmapFont(d3d)
    font1.Load("trebuchet_verdana_10.png")
    font1.SetColumns(16)
```

```
        font1.SetLetterSize(16, 16)
        font1.SpacingModifier = 6
        font1.SetStartFrame(128)

        'load background
        background = New CSprite(d3d)
        background.Load("background.bmp")

        'load ball sprite
        ball = New CSprite(d3d)
        ball.Load("ball.png")
        ball.SetPosition(400, 300)
        ball.SetVelocity(4.0, 2.5)

        'load paddle sprites
        paddle = New CSprite(d3d)
        paddle.Load("paddle.png")
        paddle.SetPosition(350, SCREENH - 50)

        'load blocks with shared texture
        block_image = New CSprite(d3d)
        block_image.Load("blocks.bmp")

        ' Create the block sprites
        For y = 1 To 8
            For x = 1 To 10
                blocks(x, y) = New CSprite(d3d)
                blocks(x, y).Alive = True
                blocks(x, y).SetImage(block_image.GetImage())
                blocks(x, y).Columns = 4
                blocks(x, y).FrameWidth = 64
                blocks(x, y).FrameHeight = 32
                blocks(x, y).CurrentFrame = y - 1
                blocks(x, y).SetPosition(x * (64 + 2), y * (32 + 2))
            Next
        Next

        'create timer
        clock = New Timer()
        clock.Interval = 10
        clock.Start()
    End Sub
```

Next up is the clock_Tick event, which is our current form of game loop. We'll just use a simple timer to refresh the screen in this example. In fact, you could get away with using a timer for an entire game. It really does a fine job and provides a very fast loop if you specify a short interval (such as 10 milliseconds).

```
Private Sub clock_Tick(ByVal sender As Object, ByVal e As System.EventArgs) _
    Handles clock.Tick

    CheckInput()

    'move the ball
    ball.Move()
    ball.KeepInBounds(New Rectangle(0, 0, SCREENW, SCREENH))

    CheckCollisions()

    'begin rendering
    d3d.StartRendering(Color.Black)
    d3d.StartSprites()

    background.Draw()
    ball.Draw()
    paddle.Draw()
    DrawBlocks()
    PrintScore()

    'done rendering
    d3d.StopSprites()
    d3d.StopRendering()

    If keyboard.KeyState(Key.Escape) Then
    clock.Stop()
    Me.Close()
    End If
End Sub
```

Now let's add some helper routines. CheckInput checks the keyboard and mouse devices and moves the paddle based on the left or right arrow keys or mouse movement. Then we have the MovePaddle routine, which moves the paddle left or right and keeps it within the screen boundary. DrawBlocks iterates through all 80 blocks and draws each one (if it's still alive). PrintScore does just what its name implies, while Form1_FormClosed is the shutdown event where we release objects from memory.

```
Private Sub CheckInput()
    'update keyboard
    keyboard.Poll()

    If keyboard.KeyState(Key.Left) Then MovePaddle(-6)
    If keyboard.KeyState(Key.Right) Then MovePaddle(6)

    'update mouse
    mouse.Poll()
    If mouse.X <> 0 Then MovePaddle(mouse.X)

    'move paddle
    paddle.KeepInBounds(New Rectangle(0, 0, SCREENW - paddle.GetWidth(),
SCREENH))
End Sub

Private Sub MovePaddle(ByVal x As Integer)
    Dim pos As PointF = paddle.GetPosition
    pos.X += x
    paddle.SetPosition(pos)
End Sub

Private Sub DrawBlocks()
    Dim x As Integer
    Dim y As Integer

    For y = 1 To 8
        For x = 1 To 10
            If blocks(x, y).Alive Then
                blocks(x, y).DrawFrame()
            End If
        Next
    Next
End Sub

Private Sub PrintScore()
    font1.Print(2, 2, Color.Black, "SCORE: " + score.ToString())
    font1.Print(1, 1, Color.White, "SCORE: " + score.ToString())
End Sub

Private Sub Form1_FormClosed(ByVal sender As Object, _
    ByVal e As System.Windows.Forms.FormClosedEventArgs) Handles Me.FormClosed
```

```
    keyboard.Dispose()
    keyboard = Nothing
    background = Nothing
    ball = Nothing
    paddle = Nothing
    d3d = Nothing
End Sub
```

Finally, we have the CheckCollisions routine, which is called from the clock_Tick event. This routine looks at all of the blocks, and for each block that has not been knocked out already, a collision test is performed to see whether the ball is intersecting the block. If so, then the block is destroyed and the ball bounces away.

```
Private Sub CheckCollisions()
Dim x As Integer
Dim y As Integer

'test for collision with paddle
If paddle.CollidedWith(ball) Then
    ball.SetVelocity(ball.GetVelocity.X, ball.GetVelocity.Y * -1)
End If

'test for collision with blocks
For y = 1 To 8
    For x = 1 To 10
        If blocks(x, y).Alive Then
            If ball.CollidedWith(blocks(x, y)) Then
            score += 1
            blocks(x, y).Alive = False
            ball.SetVelocity(ball.GetVelocity.X, ball.GetVelocity.Y * -1)
            End If
        End If
    Next
Next
End Sub
```

Entity Management

There are so many limitations in the code for that sprite collision example game that I had a hard time writing it as-is without groaning. It is a perfectly valid way to write a game, but after you see the power and convenience of using an entity management system, you'll never want to use an array again! So you suffered through numerous pages of collision detection code and discussion in order to prove a point. I hope it was well taken! Would you have appreciated what I'm about to show you otherwise?

Entity management refers to the management of game objects, which usually take the form of a 2D sprite or a 3D mesh or model. Entities should be thought of as independent actors in the scene of the game. Because of this, entity management is a limited version (like a little brother) of the larger subject of *scene management*. A 3D scene manager is a *major* part of a 3D engine, which has to iterate through all of the mesh objects, each of which contains many polygons (also called *faces*). A 3D entity might be an animated skeleton warrior attacking your hero character. The management of the skeleton "entity" should be built into the game engine so the programmer (who is either the engine developer or someone who is using an engine to build a game) doesn't have to deal with things like iterating through all the faces in the skeleton mesh and rendering each one. Instead, a scene manager will provide a mesh class of some sort with a simple render or draw function.

Benefits of Entity Management

For our purposes here, we are only concerned with 2D graphics with the goal of building our Celtic Crusader RPG. So what we need is a 2D entity manager—in other words, a *sprite manager*. I've mentioned that phrase before, but now it takes on a whole new meaning because management of the sprites will be automated. We'll go over a single-type entity manager in this chapter. As we get deeper into the Celtic Crusader engine, we'll add more sprite types to the entity manager. What I'm saying here is that our first entity manager will only tackle one type of sprite, such as the blocks in the example game. A future version of the entity manager will handle *all* of the sprites in the game and will process them differently based on their purpose or type using new properties that we'll add to the sprite class.

For instance, the ball in this *Breakout*-style game needs to move around, but the blocks don't move at all. So, the entity manager will need to know this simple fact. One easy way to tell it is to set the velocity for the blocks to zero so even though the blocks are "moved," they don't go anywhere with zero velocity. This actually works, but it would be helpful to have a "movable" property that the entity manager will examine prior to moving them. Likewise, we might have an "animating" property that causes the sprite to be drawn using either Draw() or DrawFrame(), depending on this property. In the end, what you want is an automated game engine that does the heavy lifting for you, freeing up your "front end" game code from these menial tasks—such as updating animation frames, moving, checking bounds, checking collisions, and so on.

Creating a Linked List

You can create a simple entity manager using the List class. VB.NET supports many kinds of container classes, from the generic Collection, to a Dictionary, to a Stack, and all are useful for solving various programming challenges. For instance, a stack or queue container is often used to create a packet buffer in a networked game. For our purposes here, we're going to use a simple List class, which is fully defined as System.Collections.Generic.List.

This list is similar to the std::vector class in the C++ standard template library (STL), which makes it easier to port code from VB to C++, and vice versa. (Yes, it is indeed possible, despite the vast differences in these languages!) I originally developed the tile scroller featured in the previous chapter in VB, and then ported it to C++, oddly enough.

When you define a list object, you must tell it what types of objects it will contain. Although you could define a list to handle generic objects, it is very helpful to tell it exactly what you intend to store in the list. In the definition below, I've created a list called entityList that will contain CSprite objects.

```
Private entityList As System.Collections.Generic.List(Of CSprite)
```

When you are initializing your game in Form1_Load, you'll want to create your game sprites in the usual manner. But the great thing about a list is that you no longer need to use global variables for your sprites. Instead, you can reuse a single sprite object for all of your game's sprites, and simply add them to the list, one at a time, using the same variable. For instance:

```
Dim sprite As CSprite
sprite = new CSprite(d3d)
sprite.Load("fighter1.png")
entityList.Add(sprite)
sprite = new CSprite(d3d)
sprite.Load("fighter2.png")
entityList.Add(sprite)
sprite = nothing
```

The great thing about this code is that it only requires a temporary sprite variable in order to create the sprite and add it to the list. You might be wondering how this is possible because I've destroyed the sprite in the last line. It is possible because we're creating memory for each sprite using the `new` operator. When you "new" an object, Visual Basic allocates memory for it from the main system memory (sometimes called *heap*). The sprite variable is, actually, just a reference to the object in memory. (Recall our basic programming lessons back in Chapter 2?) The sprite doesn't exist in our `Form1_Load` routine; it exists in the broader system memory store. So, when we add the sprite to our linked list, it is really the *reference* to the sprite object in memory that is being stored in the list, not all of the data for the image itself (including the texture). The texture itself is stored separately from the sprite in system memory because we create a new Texture object for it. The CSprite class doesn't "own" its image, it just happens to be the only thing that knows where the image lives. Without the sprite, the image's *address* is lost in memory. As a result, when we add a sprite to the list, then the list can refer to the sprite in memory and we no longer need the separate variable.

There are many more methods besides `Add()` that are available in the List class. Although you can remove an object from the list at any time using `Remove()`, this could cause problems if you're going through the list in a `For` loop. If you suddenly remove an object from the list inside a `For` loop, then the counter will be invalid (because you've just reduced the list count by one), and as a result, when the loop reaches the last object, it will no longer exist and a runtime error will occur. You can get around this problem by exiting out of the loop after removing an object from the list. This circumstance happens most often when you are doing collision detection.

We'll spend quite a bit more time with entity management in future chapters, so that introduction and overview will suffice for now. Let's put it to use in a real example so you can see entity management in action.

Creating an Entity Manager

The Entity Test program uses a single list called `entityList` and adds 1,000 sprites to it. Each sprite is represented as a marble image, and they are all moved and drawn on the screen over a fiery background image. (It doesn't make much sense, but I thought it looked cool.) Figure 7.2 shows what the demo looks like. This is running on a lowly 2.0 GHz Pentium M with a GeForce 6400 256 MB video card, so I'm sure you will get better results on just about any other system.

Figure 7.2
The marbles in this demo are stored in a linked list, handled by an entity manager.

Note

I've included a modified version of the Sprite Collision Test program on the CD-ROM that uses an entity manager to handle all of the blocks in the game. The demo is located in a folder called Entity-Based Collision Test. I decided to use the bouncing ball demo here instead because it was a simpler example of entity management and also to provide a little variety.

Here's the source code for the program. It's short enough that I think you can make your way through the code without an explanation of every subroutine. I'll highlight all of the entity management code for reference.

```
Imports Microsoft.DirectX
Imports Microsoft.DirectX.Direct3D
Imports Microsoft.DirectX.DirectInput

Public Class Form1
    Const TITLE As String = "ENTITY MANAGEMENT TEST"
    Const SCREENW As Integer = 800
    Const SCREENH As Integer = 600
    Const MARBLES As Integer = 1000

    Private WithEvents clock As Timer
    Private WithEvents frameclock As Timer
```

```vb
Private d3d As CDirect3D
Private keyboard As CKeyboard
Private background As CSprite
Private frameCount As Integer
Private frameRate As Integer
Private entityList As System.Collections.Generic.List(Of CSprite)

Private Sub Form1_Load(ByVal sender As System.Object, _
    ByVal e As System.EventArgs) Handles MyBase.Load

    Dim n As Integer
    Dim s As CSprite
    Dim rand As New Random()

    'initialize form
    Me.Size = New Size(SCREENW, SCREENH)
    Me.Text = TITLE
    Me.SetStyle(ControlStyles.AllPaintingInWmPaint Or _
        ControlStyles.Opaque, True)

    'initialize DirectX
    d3d = New CDirect3D(Me)
    d3d.Init(SCREENW, SCREENH, True)
    keyboard = New CKeyboard(Me)

    'load background
    background = New CSprite(d3d)
    background.Load("background.bmp")

    'create the entity list
    entityList = New List(Of CSprite)

    'load ball sprite
    Dim marble_image As CSprite
    marble_image = New CSprite(d3d)
    marble_image.Load("marbles.png")

    'add blocks to the entity list
    For n = 1 To MARBLES
        s = New CSprite(d3d)
        s.Alive = True
        s.SetImage(marble_image.GetImage())
        s.Columns = 8
```

```
                s.FrameWidth = 64
                s.FrameHeight = 64
                s.CurrentFrame = rand.Next(16)
                s.SetPosition(rand.Next(SCREENW - 64), rand.Next(SCREENH - 64))
                s.SetVelocity(rand.NextDouble(), rand.NextDouble())
                entityList.Add(s)
        Next

        'now we're done with the marble texture, go ahead and destroy it
        marble_image = Nothing

        'start the timers
        clock = New Timer()
        clock.Interval = 5
        clock.Start()
        frameclock = New Timer
        frameclock.Interval = 999
        frameclock.Start()
End Sub

Private Sub clock_Tick(ByVal sender As Object, ByVal e As System.EventArgs) _
Handles clock.Tick

        Static screenBoundary As New Rectangle(0, 0, SCREENW - 64, SCREENH - 64)
        Dim s As CSprite

        'move the sprite entities
        For Each s In entityList
            If s.Alive Then
                s.Move()
                s.KeepInBounds(screenBoundary)
            End If
        Next

        'begin rendering
        d3d.StartRendering(Color.Black)
        d3d.StartSprites()

        'draw the background image
        background.Draw()

        'draw the sprite entities
```

```
        For Each s In entityList
            If s.Alive Then
                s.DrawFrame()
            End If
        Next

        'done rendering
        d3d.StopSprites()
        d3d.StopRendering()

        keyboard.Poll()
        If keyboard.KeyState(Key.Escape) Then
            clock.Stop()
            Me.Close()
        End If

        'increment framerate counter
        frameCount += 1
    End Sub

    Private Sub frameclock_Tick(ByVal sender As Object, _
    ByVal e As System.EventArgs) Handles frameclock.Tick
        frameRate = frameCount
        frameCount = 0
        Me.Text = TITLE + " (" + frameRate.ToString() + " FPS)"
    End Sub

    Private Sub Form1_FormClosed(ByVal sender As Object, _
    ByVal e As System.Windows.Forms.FormClosedEventArgs) Handles
Me.FormClosed
        keyboard = Nothing
        d3d = Nothing
        background = Nothing
        entityList.RemoveRange(0, entityList.Count)
        entityList = Nothing
    End Sub
End Class
```

Debug versus Release

While we're looking at the results of this demo, I'd like to bring up a very important subject—the Visual Basic debugger. Did you know that whenever you

Figure 7.3
The entity test program running in debug mode is much slower.

press F5 to run a program, it only runs about one third as fast as it would otherwise run without the debugger? F5 is the default way to run code in VB.NET, but this type of run is hobbled by the debugger. If you want to see how fast your program will really run, then press Ctrl+F5 to run it rather than F5, since Ctrl+F5 starts the program without debugging. The previous figure was run without debugging. Now take a look at the same code running with debugging (F5) in Figure 7.3. What a huge drop in performance, only a third what it was before!

The moral of the story is this: Always run your code without debugging with Ctrl+F5, unless you specifically want to use breakpoints or run your program with line-by-line debugging to track down a bug. Furthermore, when your game is finished and you're ready to share it with your friends, be sure to change the configuration from Debug to Release and then rebuild it. There's a huge difference!

If you perform a Release build of your game and then get errors, it is likely due to missing media files. I've been storing artwork and sound files in bin\debug by default, but when you rebuild a game for Release, you'll need to also copy your resource files into bin\release. Or, you could just copy the .exe file out of either Debug or Release into a folder with your resources and just run it from there. But that is not very convenient while you're in the middle of writing your code and performing test runs over and over again.

Also, if you store all of your resources in one of these folders, *never* use the Clean Solution option in the Build menu, because it wipes clean the entire Debug or Release folder, including all of your bitmap and sound files! It's best to keep a copy of all your resources in the main folder of a project, and then copy them to Debug or Release as needed.

Level Up

This chapter provided an introduction to entity management and collision detection. You learned about the basic collision between two sprites—or more accurately, between two rectangles—using the `Rectangle.IntersectsWith` method, which simplifies the collision code that you would otherwise have to write yourself. Next, we learned about entity management using linked lists, and I'm sure you were as amazed as I was the first time I saw the improvements that a linked list make toward cleaning up and shortening the length of the code.

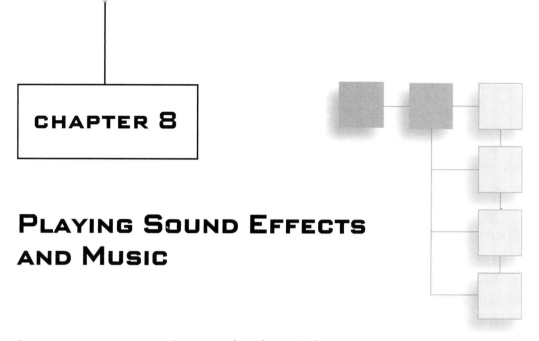

CHAPTER 8

PLAYING SOUND EFFECTS AND MUSIC

In years past, programming sound and music for games was an enormous task. Custom sound code was usually too difficult to write due to the conflicting standards among the various sound cards in the industry. Today, that is no longer a problem. Now a single, dominant hardware maker sets the PC audio standard and a single, dominant sound library sets the software standard. While some may argue the point, I believe that Creative Labs has the sound card market wrapped up with the Sound Blaster products. At the same time, the complicated audio driver industry has been eclipsed by the incredibly versatile and powerful DirectX Audio library. This chapter is a quick jaunt through the DirectSound part of DirectX, with a small program to demonstrate how to use DirectSound to play .WAV files in Visual Basic. We'll also take a look at a trick way to play background music with MP3 files. Here are the major topics in this chapter:

- Introduction to DirectSound

- Programming DirectSound

- Playing waves

- DirectSound helper classes

- Additional audio file options

Introduction to DirectSound

Audio is always a fun subject to explore because sound effects and music have such an impact on impression and influence our opinions of games so strongly. What is a game without sound? It is nothing more than a technology demo. Sound is absolutely essential for the success of any game, no matter how large or small.

Sound Effects

DirectX Audio is made up of the DirectSound and DirectMusic components. To gain access to DirectSound, you will need to add a reference to `Microsoft.-DirectX` and `Microsoft.DirectSound` in the Project References. DirectSound is a library for playing and manipulating sound and music files, from simple mono .WAV files, to multisample audio segments, to MIDI files. DirectSound can be used for more than just games—this library is capable of handling just about any audio programming need. But it is just a library for Windows file formats, without any support for files like .MP3 or .OGG, which are both very popular with game developers. My preferred format is Ogg Vorbis, which is a high-compression, high-quality format, and I use the FMOD sound engine to load and play .OGG files in C++ projects. Although a VB.NET library may be available for .OGG files, I am not aware of one, so we'll just stick with .WAV files.

DirectSound is the main component of DirectX Audio and the one used most often in games. This component is capable of mixing .WAV sound buffers in real time. DirectSound3D is a support component that works with DirectSound to provide real-time 3D positional audio processing. DirectSound supports accelerated sound hardware, and DirectSound3D is the component that takes advantage of that.

Background Music

Even the simplest game needs some form of background music, or it is difficult for the player to remain interested. Remember this important rule of gaming: Any game without sound and music is just a technology demo. It is absolutely essential that you spend some of your development time on a game working on the music and sound effects. In fact, it is probably a good idea to do so during development. As the game takes shape, so should the sounds and music. Background music should reflect what is going on in the game and can even be used to invoke the emotions of the player. Consider a scene in which a beloved game character dies. Upbeat music would spoil the mood, while dark and menacing background music would engender feelings of remorse and sorrow (and perhaps even anger).

Keep this in mind when working on sections of a game and try to have a different background sequence for different circumstances. Victory should be rewarded with upbeat music, while menacing or dangerous situations should be accompanied by low-beat, low-tempo songs that reinforce the natural emotions that arise in such a circumstance. Later in this chapter, in the "Additional Audio File Options" section, I'll show you how to use Windows Media Player to play an MP3 file in your game projects.

Programming DirectSound

Now, if you are going into this chapter with a desire to grab some code and use it in the Celtic Crusader game right away, you may be pleased with the sample program in this chapter. Rather than theorize about sound hardware and .WAV forms, how about if I just jump right in and show you how to play some cool sounds to spruce up the game? That's exactly what I show you in this section— how to get started programming DirectSound right away.

Ambient sound is a term that I borrowed from *ambient light,* which you might already understand. Just look at a light bulb in a light fixture on the ceiling. The light emitted by the bulb pretty much fills the room (unless you are in a very large, poorly lit room). When light permeates a room, it is said to be *ambient;* that is, the light does not seem to have a source.

Contrast this idea with directional light and you get the idea behind ambient sound. *Ambient sound* refers to sound that appears to have no direction or source. Ambient sound is emitted by speakers uniformly, without any positional effects. This is the most common type of sound generated by most games (at least most older games—the tendency with modern games is to use positional sound).

The DirectX component that handles ambient sound is called DirectSound. DirectSound is the primary sound mixer for DirectX. While this component is technically called DirectX Audio, it really boils down to using the individual components. DirectSound is one such component, capable of mixing and playing multichannel .WAV sound buffers (a portion of memory set aside to contain the binary sound data).

Creating the DirectSound Object

To use DirectSound, you must first add the references to `Microsoft.DirectX` and `Microsoft.DirectSound` to your project. Once the libraries are available, then you can add `Imports` statements to the top of the program so these libraries will be readily available.

```
Imports Microsoft.DirectX
Imports Microsoft.DirectX.DirectSound
```

To create a link to the DirectSound library, you must add a `DirectSound.Device` object variable to your program like this:

```
Private dsound As DirectSound.Device
```

Once the main DirectSound device is available, then you can initialize it like this:

```
dsound = New DirectSound.Device()
dsound.SetCooperativeLevel(Me, CooperativeLevel.Priority)
```

The Cooperative level tells DirectSound how to initialize the sound device, and the Priority setting tells it to use the best hardware audio features of your sound card.

Loading a Wave File

The next step to playing sound with DirectSound involves creating a buffer to hold a sound loaded from a .WAV file. The object that holds the wave is called a `SecondaryBuffer`. To create a `SecondaryBuffer` object, you must declare it in the variable declarations section of the program:

```
Private sound1 As SecondaryBuffer
```

The .WAV file is loaded into this `SecondaryBuffer` object by the constructor. To load the file, pass the filename to the constructor. However, before you can do that, there are two more parameters that the constructor expects, so let's go over them now.

The second parameter expected by the `SecondaryBuffer` constructor is a `BufferDescription` object. This object tells the loader how to configure the sound buffer after it is loaded into memory, giving you (the programmer) some capabilities, such as the ability to adjust the volume, pan, and frequency of the sound. Here is how you configure the `BufferDescription` object for one-time use:

```
Dim desc As New BufferDescription
desc.ControlPan = True
```

```
desc.ControlVolume = True
desc.ControlFrequency = True
desc.ControlEffects = True
```

The third parameter is your `DirectSound.Device` object, which we called `dsound`. So, now that you know how to get prepared for loading the sound, it can be loaded with a call to the constructor:

```
sound1 = New SecondaryBuffer(filename, desc, dsound)
```

Playing the Sound

To play a sound buffer, you use the `Play` procedure available in each `SecondaryBuffer` object (which is the sound itself, as you'll recall). There are two parameters to `Play`. First is the priority setting of the sound, which is used when there are a lot of sounds being played at the same time and the sound mixer might need to give higher priority to some sounds over others. You can just set this to 0 because we don't care about priorities here. The second parameter is a playback flag that, among other things, lets you play a sound normally (`BufferPlayFlags.Default`) or with looping (`BufferPlayFlags.Looping`).

```
sound.Play(0, BufferPlayFlags.Default)
```

The PlayWave Program

The PlayWave program demonstrates how to create and initialize the `DirectSound` device, load a .WAV file into memory, and then play the wave. To demonstrate how sounds are automatically mixed, the program actually loads up another sound file as well. There are two buttons on the form; each plays one of the sound buffers. Because there is not much to this program other than the simple form, I haven't bothered with a figure. You will need to add two buttons to the form, simply called Button1 and Button2, as shown in Figure 8.1.

```
Imports Microsoft.DirectX
Imports Microsoft.DirectX.DirectSound

Public Class Form1
    Private dsound As DirectSound.Device
    Private sound1 As SecondaryBuffer
    Private sound2 As SecondaryBuffer
```

Figure 8.1
The PlayWave program demonstrates how to use DirectSound.

```
Public Sub Init_DirectSound()
    dsound = New DirectSound.Device()
    dsound.SetCooperativeLevel(Me, CooperativeLevel.Priority)
End Sub

Public Function LoadWave(ByVal filename As String) As SecondaryBuffer
    Dim desc As New BufferDescription
    desc.ControlPan = True
    desc.ControlVolume = True
    desc.ControlFrequency = True
    desc.ControlEffects = True

    Dim sound As SecondaryBuffer
    sound = New SecondaryBuffer(filename, desc, dsound)

    Return sound
End Function

Public Sub PlayWave(ByRef sound As SecondaryBuffer, _
Optional ByVal looping As Boolean = False)
    If looping Then
        sound.Play(0, BufferPlayFlags.Looping)
    Else
        sound.Play(0, BufferPlayFlags.Default)
    End If
End Sub
```

```
    Private Sub Form1_Load(ByVal sender As System.Object, _
ByVal e As System.EventArgs) Handles MyBase.Load
        Me.Text = "DIRECTSOUND TEST PROGRAM"

        Init_DirectSound()

        sound1 = LoadWave("halleluia.wav")
        sound2 = LoadWave("energy.wav")
    End Sub

    Private Sub Button1_Click(ByVal sender As System.Object, _
ByVal e As System.EventArgs) Handles Button1.Click
        PlayWave(sound1)
    End Sub

    Private Sub Button2_Click(ByVal sender As System.Object, _
ByVal e As System.EventArgs) Handles Button2.Click
        PlayWave(sound2)
    End Sub
End Class
```

Since this program already included helper functions and subroutines for using sound files, we don't need to go over them here. Just use `Initialize_DirectSound`, `LoadWave`, and `PlayWave` whenever you need to support sound in one of your games.

DirectSound Helper Classes

Let's wrap up this code into a pair of classes that will make DirectSound programming much easier in VB.NET. First is the CDirectSound class, which wraps up the initialization of DirectSound and provides a device for use with sound playback. The class is quite small because DirectSound handles all of the hard work for us.

CDirectSound

We'll use CDirectSound to load individual sound buffers from .WAV files into memory, and play them as well, while the CSound class will simply hold the sound buffer itself without providing much functionality.

```
Imports Microsoft.DirectX
Imports Microsoft.DirectX.DirectSound
```

```
Public Class CSoundDevice
    Private dsound As DirectSound.Device

    Public Sub New(ByRef frm As Windows.Forms.Form)
        dsound = New DirectSound.Device()
        dsound.SetCooperativeLevel(frm, CooperativeLevel.Priority)
    End Sub

    Public Function Load(ByVal filename As String) As CSound
        Dim sound As New CSound
        sound.SoundBuffer = New SecondaryBuffer(filename, sound.p_desc, Me.
        dsound)
        Return sound
    End Function

    Public Sub Play(ByRef sound As CSound, Optional ByVal looping As Boolean =
    False)
        If looping Then
            sound.SoundBuffer.Play(0, BufferPlayFlags.Looping)
        Else
            sound.SoundBuffer.Play(0, BufferPlayFlags.Default)
        End If
    End Sub

End Class
```

CSound

Next we have the CSound class, which handles loading and playback of a single sound file.

```
Imports Microsoft.DirectX
Imports Microsoft.DirectX.DirectSound

Public Class CSound
    Private p_sound As SecondaryBuffer
    Friend p_desc As BufferDescription

    Public Property SoundBuffer() As SecondaryBuffer
        Get
            Return p_sound
        End Get
```

```
                Set(ByVal value As SecondaryBuffer)
                    p_sound = value
                End Set
            End Property

            Public Sub New()
                p_desc = New BufferDescription()
                p_desc.ControlPan = True
                p_desc.ControlVolume = True
                p_desc.ControlFrequency = True
                p_desc.ControlEffects = True
            End Sub
        End Class
```

Testing the Sound Classes

The Wave Class Test program is a modified version of the PlayWave program, which we examined earlier in this chapter. However, in this version of the program, with the use of the CDirectSound and CSound classes, the code is only a few lines long! This demonstrates how to create the CDirectSound object and initialize it, and how to create CSound objects and load .WAV files and play them.

```
Imports Microsoft.DirectX
Imports Microsoft.DirectX.DirectSound

Public Class Form1
    Private dsound As CSoundDevice
    Private sound1 As CSound
    Private sound2 As CSound

    Private Sub Form1_Load(ByVal sender As System.Object, _
    ByVal e As System.EventArgs) Handles MyBase.Load
        Me.Text = "DIRECTSOUND CLASS TEST"

        'create the CSoundDevice object
        dsound = New CSoundDevice(Me)

        'load some wave files
        sound1 = dsound.Load("halleluia.wav")
        sound2 = dsound.Load("energy.wav")
    End Sub
```

```
    Private Sub Button1_Click(ByVal sender As System.Object, _
    ByVal e As System.EventArgs) Handles Button1.Click
        dsound.Play(sound1)
    End Sub

    Private Sub Button2_Click(ByVal sender As System.Object, _
    ByVal e As System.EventArgs) Handles Button2.Click
        dsound.Play(sound2)
    End Sub
End Class
```

Additional Audio File Options

DirectSound has its uses for sound effects and looping music tracks, but what if you want to use a more advanced audio file, such as an MP3, for your game's music? Although we don't have a library available for this, there is an alternative that works quite well that I'll introduce to you. Actually, there are two alternatives!

The DirectX.AudioVideoPlayback Library

Although Microsoft ditched DirectMusic when Managed DirectX was made available to C# and VB programs, they did provide a good alternative in the DirectX.AudioVideoPlayback library. By adding this library to your project, you can easily create an Audio object and use it to play MIDI or MP3 music files! Here is a simple example program called PlayMusic, and it is located on the CD-ROM under the folder for this chapter.

Although I've referenced a MIDI file in this program, you can replace the MIDI with any of your own favorite MP3 files. Just keep in mind that you cannot distribute unlicensed music with any games you create, no matter how cool the game is with the music! If you want to commission a custom soundtrack for your game project, there are composers available who will do that kind of work for a fee. One such composer is Chris Hurn, who has created the soundtrack for *Starflight: The Lost Colony* (www.starflightgame.com). You may find Chris Hurn's website at www.chrishurn.com.

```
Imports Microsoft.DirectX
Imports Microsoft.DirectX.AudioVideoPlayback

Public Class Form1
    Private music As Audio
    Private filename = Application.StartupPath & "\song.mid"
```

```
Private Sub Form1_Load(ByVal sender As System.Object, _
ByVal e As System.EventArgs) Handles MyBase.Load

    'load the music file
    music = New Audio(filename)

    'play the music
    music.Play()
End Sub


Private Sub Form1_FormClosing(ByVal sender As Object, _
ByVal e As System.Windows.Forms.FormClosingEventArgs) _
Handles Me.FormClosing

    music.Stop()
End Sub


End Class
```

The Windows Media Player Control

The other way to handle professional music files in your game project is by using the Windows Media Player control. You may be wondering, "Why would I want to use a Media Player control when DirectX.AudioVideoPlayback is available? For simple music playback, that library is preferred. But there is a drawback—it doesn't have very many options. Sure, you can play back an audio file, but you can only really determine whether an Audio track is playing or stopped. Beyond that, it's pretty slim. The Media Player control, on the other hand, is chock full of features, as the Jukebox program demonstrates.

So how does this work? VB.NET has the ability to embed an object on a form, and this capability is called OLE (*Object Linking and Embedding*). You can, for instance, embed an Excel spreadsheet on a VB form, and it will be fully functional! There are some obvious licensing issues when you embed a whole application onto a form, and usually applications that do this sort of thing just assume that the software (such as Excel) has already been preinstalled on the end user's PC. But there are some Windows applications that are so common that we can pretty much count on them being available. One example is Windows Media Player, which is automatically installed on Windows XP and Vista. And if anyone is still using an older version of Windows, odds are they have Windows Media Player installed because it is free.

I've included a project with this chapter called The Jukebox, which demonstrates how to use am embedded Media Player object. The Media Player is not available as a .NET Component, so you'll have to add it from the list of COM or ActiveX components (see the COM tab in the Add Reference dialog box). See Figure 8.2. You want to add the ActiveX control called Windows Media Player to your project.

When the WMP control is available to the project, you can drag it from the Toolbox to the form. The complete design of the form in The Jukebox is shown in Figure 8.3. Note that the WMP control is on the bottom of the form, and in the Properties window on the right, its Visible property has been set to false. This will allow us to use the WMP control in the program without it being visible, so our program will look as if it's a real media player, while in fact it is just using the features built into the control (namely, the ability to load and play any type of media file).

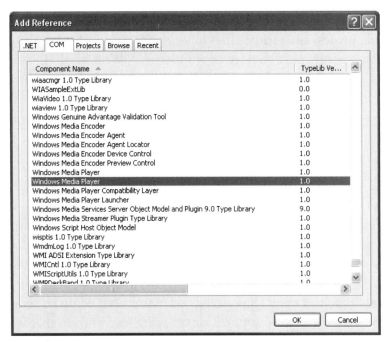

Figure 8.2
Adding a reference to the Windows Media Player ActiveX control.

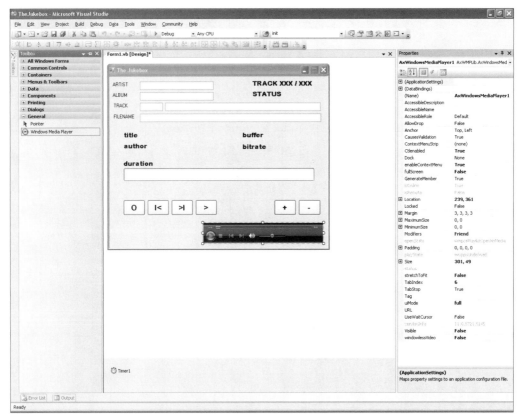

Figure 8.3
Adding the Windows Media Player control to the form.

The My Jukebox program lets you type in details for each media file, including a filename (which can be a local or remote media file streamed over the Internet, as shown in Figure 8.4).

Playing Media Files

You can play any media file with the WMP control by setting its URL property equal to a filename (or a URL to a file on a website, for instance). This is deceptively simple, because there is really no "play" function at all. Once you set the URL property to a filename, playback will automatically start. Likewise, if you want to stop playback, set URL to an empty string (" ").

```
AxWindowsMediaPlayer1.URL = "symphony.rmi"
```

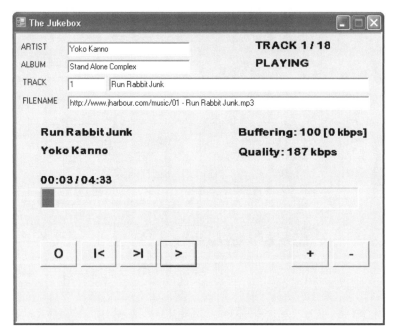

Figure 8.4
Media files can be played locally or streamed over the Internet.

Level Up

This chapter was a quick overview of DirectSound, giving you just enough information to add sound effects to your own games. By loading multiple sound files into memory and playing them at certain points in your game, you greatly enhance the game-play experience. DirectSound handles all of the details for you, including loading the .WAV file and playing it through the sound system. All you have to do is instruct it what to do. In that sense, you are the conductor of this orchestra. In this chapter, you learned how to tap into the AudioVideoPlayback library to play music files, and you also learned how to use the Windows Media Player ActiveX control for advanced audio file support (including streaming music files off the Web). Just keep in mind that you cannot distribute copyrighted music.

PART II

THE GAME WORLD

The second part of the book focuses on the design of Celtic Crusader and the construction of the game world, with an emphasis on recreating Ireland as it might have looked about a thousand years ago.

- Chapter 9: Designing the Celtic Crusader Game

- Chapter 10: Creating the Game World

- Chapter 11: Exploring the Game World

- Chapter 12: Adding Scenery and Objects

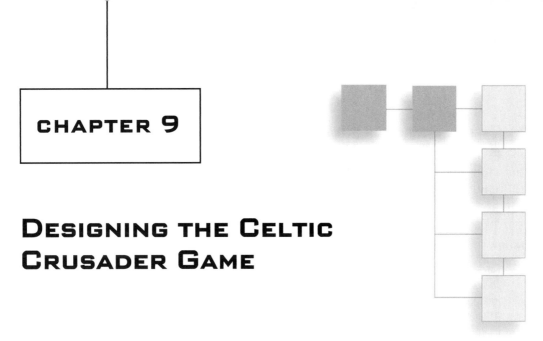

CHAPTER 9

DESIGNING THE CELTIC CRUSADER GAME

In this chapter we will design the game world featured in Celtic Crusader. Designing a game is no simple task, and it should not be thrown together after the source code has been nearly completed. The design should direct what code gets written and what the game world looks like. I have written several successful game design documents, and they are very valuable to the development team on a game project. In this chapter we will merely design the game world and describe how the game will be played, rather than creating an entire design doc. Here are the important topics:

- The quest-based storyline

- Designing the RPG world

- The player's character (PC)

- The non-player characters (NPCs)

- Inventory and gold

- Weapons and armor

- Magic

- Communication

- Combat

The Quest-Based Storyline

You can learn a lot about your subconscious motivations and creative impulses by designing a game with pencil and paper. I get so much enjoyment out of the design process that my enthusiasm gets the best of me and I want to jump into the code and start writing the game! At the same time, I enjoy drawing even though I'm not a very good artist. (I can't draw people or living creatures at all, so I don't even try.)

Note

For a complete discussion of how to design a role-playing game, see *Swords & Circuitry: A Designer's Guide to Computer Role-Playing Games* (Thomson Course PTR, 2002) by Neal and Jana Hallford. I also recommend *Character Development and Storytelling for Games* (Thomson Course PTR, 2004) by Lee Sheldon if you are interested in learning how to create realistic storylines and characters for your games.

It's important to put as much on paper as possible before you start writing source code. It is good to get started on the artwork for a game while doing the design, because that helps you realize what is possible and somewhat helps with the creative process. If you start working on a game without any design at all, at worst it ends up being left unfinished, at best is a clinical game (meaning it is functional but lacks substance).

Celtic Crusader is based in ninth-century Ireland, a country occupied by Norwegian Vikings, who ruled the seas at the time. The Vikings were not just barbarous raiders, although this game's story is about Viking occupation in Ireland and generally depicts Vikings as the bad guys. The Viking civilization was spread across a much wider area than even the Roman Empire, although it was not as strong and it was not based entirely on military conquest. The Vikings were explorers and traders who settled lands, such as Iceland and Greenland, that had never before been visited by humans. Although humans had migrated to North and South America at around this time, the Vikings are also credited as being the first Europeans to discover and settle North America. (Actually, the Viking settlers in Greenland were the first Canadians.)

The storyline is usually not as important as the quests, which are what drives the story forward. Your character does not have a specific goal, because nothing in life is that clearly defined. Instead, the game develops while your character develops, mainly by fighting animals and fantasy creatures, as well as the occasional Viking raiding party. Your character's attributes determine how good he is in combat. (See "The Player's Character (PC)" section later in this chapter.) In Celtic Crusader, we're building more of a "hack-and-slash" game, which may be compared to games such as *Diablo* and *Baldur's Gate*. There are more complex adventure-based RPGs as well (such as *The Elder Scrolls* and the *Might & Magic* series), and they tend to take a very long time to finish.

Designing the RPG World

The game world in Celtic Crusader is based on the island country of Ireland. I chose this land because it has a rich mythology going back more than 2,000 years, providing a huge pool of possible plot elements for the storyline and subquests in a game. I thought of basing the game on ancient America, designing a game around the Mayan or Incan civilizations, but decided to go with Ireland because it is easier to design a smallish game story around an island. That also makes it possible to set boundaries on the game map limiting the player's movement (as opposed to putting mountains or some sort of no-man's land at the boundary of a land-locked game world).

There is a lot to be said for a randomly generated world or a world based on a completely fictional land with no historical basis. It allows you (the game's designer) to let loose with your imagination to create a world that does not influence, nor is affected by, the "real world." Generating a random world is definitely possible, but I don't like the random factor because it prevents me from designing the game around real locations in the world. Celtic Crusader has characters that are from specific towns based on character class, and I want those towns to be real places on the map, not just generated locations in a random world. The goal is to build a game that has a lot of replay value by offering strong character development rather than anonymous random combat. The fact of the matter is, most people love a good story. Giving your game a good story with believable characters makes it far more fun to play than a randomly generated world, even if the same characters appear in that fictional world.

Map of the World

Figure 9.1 shows the map of the world in Celtic Crusader as a traditional hand-drawn illustration. This rough sketch represents Ireland in the ninth century, when the Vikings invaded England and Ireland from their empire in Norway, Denmark, and Sweden.

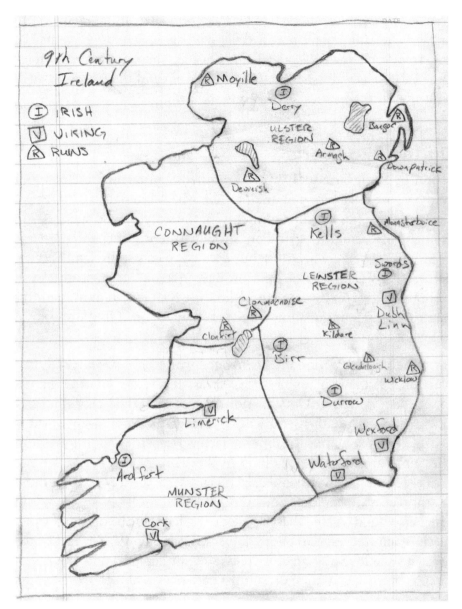

Figure 9.1
Hand-drawn illustration of the world in Celtic Crusader, based in Ireland.

This map shows Viking towns (a V inside a square), Irish towns (an I inside a circle), and ruins (an R inside a triangle), to give you an idea about how quests are based on the game world itself rather than by some random quest-generation system. In reality, I have taken some creative liberties with the true historical significance of the towns shown in this map. The Irish "towns" were, in reality, monasteries that the Vikings either did not discover or did not plunder for one reason or another. The ruins shown on the map are, in fact, monasteries that the Vikings had plundered (by stealing all gold, silver, and valuables they could find). I thought the idea of a plundered monastery lent itself well to a ruin (filled with evil creatures). The ruins in Celtic Crusader are based somewhat on historical fact (which I believe really helps with the story), with the idea being that the plundered monasteries, by becoming ruins, have been invaded by vile monsters that are not generally found elsewhere in the game.

The ruins are basically a training ground where the player's character gains experience, goes up in levels, and acquires gold to buy better equipment in the towns. The goal with this game engine is to have certain parts of the map cause a new map to load, with the player inserted into a certain part of the new map. However, I have found that this is a very difficult thing to do without causing the source code to grow in complexity (and I want to keep this game on the simple side). Therefore, the towns in the game world are represented on the map itself rather than as a *warp* type of system that enters and exits the towns. I really like this idea better because it keeps the suspension of disbelief going.

Note

> *Suspension of disbelief* is a term that describes one's immersion in a fictional setting. You may have experienced this while reading a good book or playing a good game: You lose track of the real world around you and become totally immersed in the fiction. This is a *very good thing* to strive for in your game designs, and you should strive to achieve it with every game. Anything that takes away the player's suspension of disbelief should be removed from the game. A clunky user interface, a difficult combat system, an overload of information on the screen—these all lead to ruining the player's feeling of total immersion.

By taking the hand-drawn map and scanning it into the computer, I have been able to clean it up and turn it into a digital version of this game's world. That world is shown in Figure 9.2.

My goal is to teach you how to create an RPG as well as an RPG game engine that you can customize for your own vision and imagination for a game. I want to give you just enough to get the job done, while avoiding doing everything for you, so you are motivated to improve the game.

While you're working on a game like this, always consider ways to make whatever you're working on reusable. If you are constructing a player creation screen, think of ways to make the screen dynamic and flexible, without hard-coding anything specific. It is a good idea to keep things concrete and solidly built in the

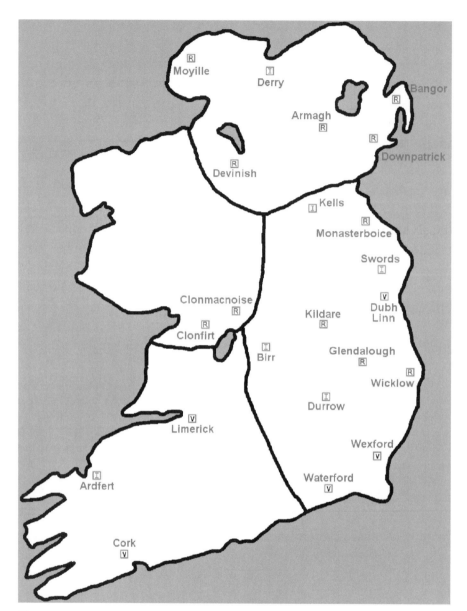

Figure 9.2
The hand-drawn map has been scanned and converted to a digital map.

game, but not to the point where it's impossible to modify later. If you have buttons on the screen that the player needs to click with the mouse, make those buttons easy to move around—use constants at the top of the source code for that particular screen. Another option is to make everything in your game *skinnable*. You know, skins are all the rage in user interfaces today, and most music players for your PC support skinning. This is a process where the program controls can be repositioned and the images used to represent those controls can be modified—with some fantastic results. Why not take that excellent design methodology with you in the design of a game and make it totally customizable by storing skins and settings in files outside of the source code for the game? This excellent concept may be beyond the scope of this short book, but I want you to keep it in mind while you are working.

Figure 9.3 shows my design for the scrolling game world. The player's sprite remains in the center of the screen at all times, with the world scrolling underfoot. With this design in mind, the map has to be laid out so there is room around the borders for the player to reach the edge of the map. In other words, when the player reaches the ocean, the map needs to have ocean squares going out a little so the player can walk right up to the seashore. The eight-way scrolling of the map is perfect for the sprites in this game, which have been rendered with animation in eight directions.

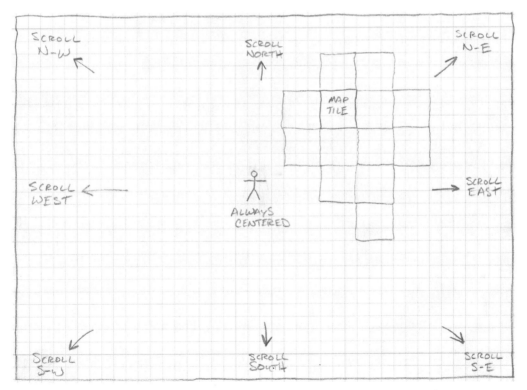

Figure 9.3
The player is centered on the screen within the scrolling game world.

Regions

There are four provinces, or regions, in the version of Ireland represented in this game: Leinster, Munster, Ulster, and Connaught. It is not crucial, but I have always found that a background story and historical depth make a game far more compelling for the player, greatly improving the sense of immersion in the game world. A game is not just backgrounds, sprites, and collision detection, and players expect much more depth to an RPG than they expect from an arcade game. One aspect of the *Ultima* series that made it so popular is the wealth of historical information provided to the player within the game (usually through dialog with NPCs). You want to create the illusion that the player is just one person in a huge, populated world that goes on with or without him.

Leinster Region

Leinster region, located on the east side of Ireland, is where most of the fighting takes place between the native Irish people (who are, admittedly, descended from Anglo-Saxons in the first place, never mind that the Celts are long gone . . .) and the Viking invaders who created three settlements: Dubh Linn, Wexford, and Waterford. Leinster, shown in Figure 9.4, borders all three of the other regions.

The Irish monastery towns include Kells, Swords, Birr, and Durrow. There are also some ruins (pillaged monasteries) in this region: Monasterboice, Kildare, Glendalough, and Wicklow. This region produces the most axe-bearing warriors and sword-wielding paladins in the world.

Munster Region

The Munster region of Ireland, located in the southwest, is adjacent to Leinster and Connaught. See Figure 9.5.

Munster is the second strongest region of Viking occupation on Ireland with the two Viking settlements of Limerick and Cork. Although there are no ruins in this region at all, there is one Irish monastery town called Ardfert, which is famous for producing skilled archers (known by the character class scout), the likes of which fought against the Vikings during their initial invasion and occupation. The Vikings have never learned about the secret bow craft of Ardfert, so many patriotic archers are still trained there.

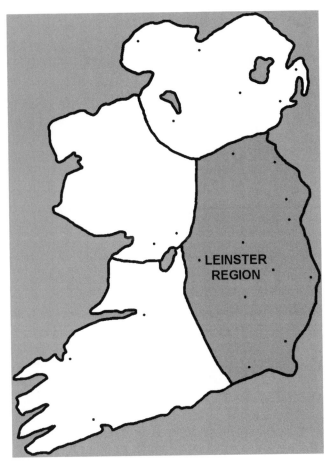

Figure 9.4
The Leinster region of the map.

Ulster Region

Ulster region, located on the north side of Ireland, is the location for most of island's religious artifacts; its inhabitants practice the ancient art of mastering the natural world. Ulster, shown in Figure 9.6, was devastated by the Vikings during their initial invasion, with many mages killed while trying to protect their monasteries. There were vast arrays of gold and silver artifacts given to the mages of Ulster as offerings throughout the generations. Despite mastery of the natural world, Ulster mages were peaceful in nature and abhorred violence of any kind, even in one's defense. As a result, the mages of Ulster were defenseless against an unknown enemy that brought brutality to the region, plundering the monasteries of Moyille, Devenish, Armagh, Downpatrick, and Bangor, leaving them in ruins. Only Derry remained unscathed by the plundering.

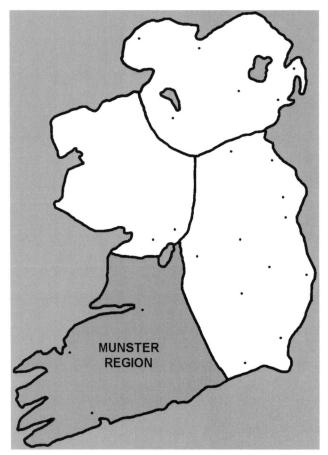

Figure 9.5
The Munster region of the map.

The tenants of Derry, the last vestige of Celtic mages left alive, have been forced to abandon their prior unity with the natural world and focus their attention on combat in order to drive out the Viking invaders. Mages of Derry are masters of the staff in hand-to-hand combat and are able to wield some of the unseen forces of the world to aid them in battle.

Connaught Region

The Connaught region, shown in Figure 9.7, is located on the western side of Ireland. Connaught was once a vast grazing land for cows, sheep, and goats, with its wide-open plains and plentiful feeding ranges. Connaught is not a widely settled region, though, and the Viking invasion rallied those few living in

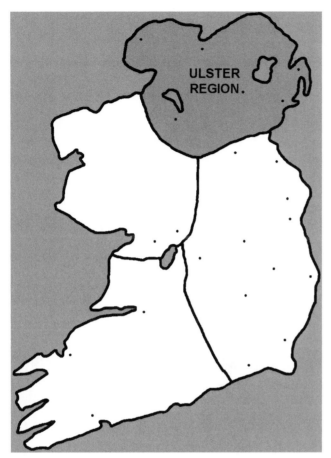

Figure 9.6
The Ulster region of the map.

Connaught to the battle in defense of the land. The result is that forests have grown into Connaught from the south, and it is mainly a breeding ground for evil creatures and a hiding place for criminals.

Two monasteries in southern Connaught—Clonmacnoise and Clonfert—were pillaged by the Vikings, who left them in ruins. The inhabitants of these two ruins are a constant nuisance to the hardworking citizens of Birr, located nearby in Leinster region.

At the start of the game, the player will begin in a town within one of these four regions depending on the character class chosen, and the history of the region will be reflected in the people that the player will encounter early in the game.

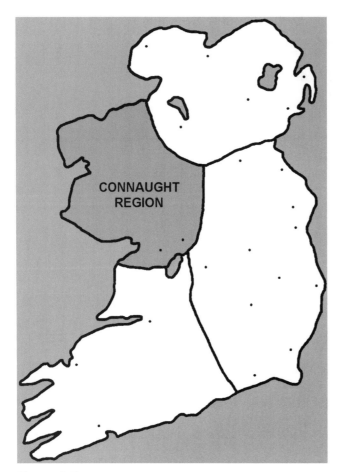

Figure 9.7
The Connaught region of the map.

The Player's Character (PC)

One of the most enjoyable aspects of playing an RPG is creating your very own custom character to use in the game. This is why true RPGs have more depth and more replay value than games featuring a specific set of characters (as in the *Zelda* series). Because player character creation is so much a part of the experience, it's important to design the character creation screen with as much versatility as possible so the player can create his or her own persona for the game.

Celtic Crusader is taking shape as an old-school RPG, and will eventually allow you to design your own character from scratch. The game should allow your character to interact within the confines of the main storyline of the game (as well as within the subquests). Figure 9.8 shows one possible design for a character creation screen.

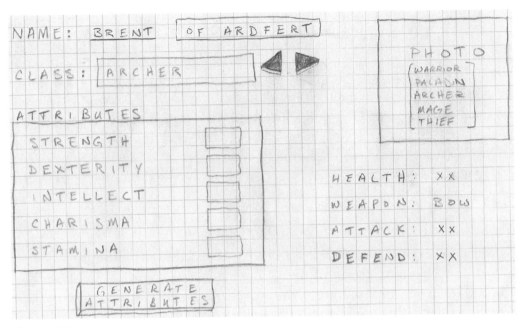

Figure 9.8
A rough-draft design for a possible character creation screen.

Character Attributes

All characters (including non-player characters and monsters) in the game have the same set of attributes in order to make combat possible: strength, dexterity, stamina, intellect, and charisma.

Strength

Strength represents the character's ability to carry a weight and swing a weapon, and is generally good for the warrior and knight classes, which carry hand-to-hand combat weapons, such as axes and swords. The strength attribute is used to calculate the attack value for the character (meaning, the amount of damage the player inflicts on enemies with each swing of a weapon). Each time the character attacks, a dice roll (which is a random number in code) against the attack value determines whether the attack succeeds. If the attack is a hit, then the weapon's damage value is used to inflict damage against the opponent.

Suppose your character has an attack value of 12, which is calculated using the character's strength (mainly, although you may include dexterity in a custom calculation to make the game more interesting). Typical "attack rolls" are done with a 20-sided die. In a Visual Basic program, you can simulate the roll of dice using the Random class.

Dexterity

Dexterity represents the agility of the character, the ability to manipulate objects (such as a weapon), and the skill with which the player uses his or her hands in general. A very low dexterity means the character is clumsy, while a very high dexterity means the character can manipulate complicated devices and perform fast, complex actions. Use of any weapon (such as a sword, a mace, or even a bow) is improved with a high dexterity.

Stamina

Stamina represents a character's endurance, or the ability to continue performing an activity for a long period of time. Stamina is also known as *constitution* in some RPGs. A very high stamina provides a character with the ability to engage in lengthy battles without rest, while a character with low stamina tires quickly (and likely falls in battle).

Intellect

Intellect represents the character's ability to learn, remember things, and solve problems. The mage class requires a very high intellect, while relatively low intellect is common in fighter classes, in which brute force is more important than mental faculties.

Charisma

Charisma represents the character's attractiveness and appearance, and generally affects how others respond to the character. A character with very high charisma attracts others, while one with very low charisma shuns others. Knights usually have very high charisma, reflecting their heroic stature.

Character Status

When the character is actually in the game, you want the player to be able to view the information about his or her character by bringing up some sort of status screen, as is the norm with most RPGs. Figure 9.9 shows an example screen that I designed to show the player's stats in a sort of pop-up window over the game screen. The window shows information about the player in the game, such as attributes, equipment, health, gold, and so on.

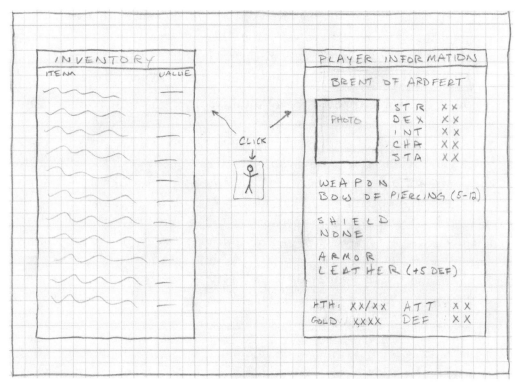

Figure 9.9
The design for the in-game player information screen.

This screen design also has one possible way of handling inventory management in the game. Since inventory is such a huge and complex issue, I've had to scrap the idea at this point and make the game simpler—or else it would never have made it into this book! Instead of a complex inventory system in the game, the player just picks up gold and uses it to upgrade weapons and armor in the towns. I'm a little disappointed at this, but inventory is unbelievably difficult to deal with in an RPG. Although it is essential for some game designs, I've scaled down my aspirations for Celtic Crusader in the interest of getting the game done. In reality, my experience has shown that this is a justified decision because most inventory management is used just to sell weapons and items found in the world, with the sole purpose of equipping the character with better gear. This shortened method skips the steps required to pick up and sell items.

There is yet a third reason for skipping this part of the game: It's just not realistic. I've played games where inventory was so time consuming and required so much micromanagement that it absolutely ruined my suspension of disbelief while playing the game. Realistically, if you are a soldier of one class or another, do you have the strength to carry 100 swords, shields, and suits of armor while also carrying 1,000 arrows and 250 rings? Some RPGs *are* that ridiculous. A limited form of inventory management is definitely needed, though, so I suggest making that a serious first upgrade to the game if you want to make it better.

I like how Peter Molyneux designed an intuitive inventory system for the game *Fable*. In *Fable,* your character can carry quite a lot of stuff, because there is a fascinating aspect of this game that allows you to become a trader, making money by buying and selling goods. But with respect to combat gear, the game automatically recognizes "suits" of related armor items so you can auto-equip all related items of armor at once. I could literally go on for pages describing this amazing game. One thing that caused me to fall off my seat with laughter was what happened to my character when I equipped him with a very heavy hammer weapon. The game accurately modeled the character *dragging* the hammer behind him, and he was barely able to swing it!

Character Classes

Each character class comes from a certain part of the world, where it is assumed that the raw materials and skills are available for that class. For instance, sword-wielding paladins come from the Irish towns within the region of Leinster. There is no real reason for this historically, but I just like the idea of certain character classes coming from different parts of the world.

Table 9.1 shows the character classes and their home regions. The two fighter classes—warrior and paladin—both originate in Leinster. In reality, a character might be born anywhere, but is located in one of the towns in a certain region when the character is created. In the context of the game, creating a character means simply that you, as the player, are finding and assuming the identity of someone in the fictional world (or rather, someone of whom you are taking control).

Table 9.1 Character Classes and Their Home Regions

Character Class	Region
Warrior	Leinster
Knight	Leinster
Thief	Connaught
Scout	Munster
Mage	Ulster

Note that there are no Irish towns in the region of Connaught (only two ruins), so no characters can originate from this region. This is generally going to be a chaotic region ruled by anarchy, populated with thieves, cutthroats, and evil creatures aplenty.

The character attribute modifiers for each class are based on a fixed set of 15 points distributed among the attributes to reflect that class' strong and weak characteristics. If you add the modifiers together, they equal 15, no matter the class, so there is no numerical advantage of one class over another. These base attributes are essential to defining each class. You should feel free to change this numerical basis for your own vision for this game. Just be sure to start off the base character classes with low "stats"—you don't want the player to become too strong early in the game.

Warrior Class

Warriors originate in the Leinster region due to the ongoing conflict with the Vikings, which have the strongest presence here of all Ireland. (There are three Viking settlements: Dubh Linn, Wexford, and Waterford.) It does make sense, if you think about it, because where there is the greatest conflict there is likely to be the most surplus of weapons available. A character in this region should be able to find a weapon and begin training—and there is the added possibility that a character was formerly an Irish patriot in a defeated and disbanded army. Figure 9.10 shows an example of a concept drawing of a Viking warrior.

Warriors can wield any type of heavy weapon but are basically limited by the available artwork, meaning that the warrior in this game carries an axe. Warriors have the attribute modifiers detailed in Table 9.2.

Knight/Paladin Class

Knights (frequently called *paladins* in RPGs) are holy warriors who pledge their loyalty to God and country, so to speak, although this has been fantasized in literature and fantasy gaming to mean that knights have certain magical capabilities (notably the ability to heal others). It is generally accepted that a knight in an RPG should always defend good and fight against evil. You should never have an evil knight (otherwise, you should just create a character from another class), although it might be possible to have a "dark knight" who has become corrupted, which is an interesting story element.

Figure 9.10
An artistic concept drawing of a Viking warrior (courtesy of Eden Celeste).

Table 9.2 Warriors' Attribute Modifiers

Attribute	Modifier
Strength	+8
Dexterity	+4
Intellect	−3
Charisma	0
Stamina	+6

Figure 9.11 shows an example of a concept drawing of a dark knight. You can see from this single drawing that concept artwork is extremely valuable, as it helps to fully realize the potential of the game and gives the sprite artist an example of what the sprite should look like. When you have 100+ frames of animation for a

Figure 9.11
An artistic concept drawing of a dark knight (courtesy of Eden Celeste).

Table 9.3 Knights' Attribute Modifiers

Attribute	Modifier
Strength	+6
Dexterity	+4
Intellect	−3
Charisma	+5
Stamina	+3

sprite, you want to be sure that it is correct on the first frame because animation is very difficult to modify after the artist has completed the work.

In this game, I loosely define a knight as a sword-wielding character, or swordsman for short. Knights are well-rounded characters, with the character attribute modifiers in Table 9.3.

Thief/Rogue Class

The thief is a classic character class in RPGs because this type of character sort of fills in the gap between the very powerful warrior/knight classes and the scout

Table 9.4 Thieves' Attribute Modifiers

Attribute	Modifier
Strength	−1
Dexterity	+7
Intellect	+3
Charisma	+1
Stamina	+5

(archer). A thief typically carries a small dagger or a club and is skilled at opening locks (such as locked doors and treasure chests). A thief is not strong enough to be a powerful warrior or knight, nor is a thief skilled with a bow or trained in the art of magic; a thief is sort of an odd character that has a different set of skills based on stealth.

Thieves generally come from Connaught and are found lurking in the corners and alleys of Birr and Limerick, though they tend to travel quite often, following merchant caravans from one region to another. As a result, a thief character may be from any Irish or Viking town. Table 9.4 shows the attribute modifiers for the thief class.

Scout/Archer Class

Scouts are common in the land of Ireland since the bow is the most common hunting weapon throughout the world. However, the military-caliber archer is only found in one place: the forest-encroached Irish town of Ardfert, the only unscathed Irish settlement in the region of Munster. The craft of building bows and carving straight arrows may be found throughout the land, but the craft of building armor-piercing knight arrows and multi-string compound bows is now limited exclusively to Ardfert.

The skilled archers of Ardfert are themselves as skilled in bowcraft as they are in warcraft, often recruited by Irish militia at the outlying towns and by rebel factions still fighting against the Vikings. The attribute modifiers for the scout class are given in Table 9.5.

Mage/Wizard Class

The mages of Ulster region were once peaceful caretakers of Ireland's monasteries, turning their attention to a mastery of the natural world, including the use of healing herbs and cultivating gardens. The invasion of the Vikings and subsequent pillaging of monasteries left many of the mages slaughtered, and those remaining fled to the few monasteries that were not discovered by the Vikings. Those who were left refocused their attention on combat techniques they observed in the natural world—that, along with their mastery of unseen forces, makes the mages of Ulster skilled in hand-to-hand combat as well as in using magic. In addition, mages still know the art of healing.

Figure 9.12 shows an artist's concept drawing of a female mage character. What is the most significant thing that you notice about the concept drawings? They are hand-drawn, often in pencil, and scanned, rather than edited in a graphic editor

Table 9.5 Scouts' Attribute Modifiers

Attribute	Modifier
Strength	+3
Dexterity	+8
Intellect	−2
Charisma	+1
Stamina	+5

Figure 9.12
An artistic concept drawing of a female mage (courtesy of Eden Celeste).

Table 9.6 Mages' Attribute Modifiers

Attribute	Modifier
Strength	−6
Dexterity	+3
Intellect	+9
Charisma	+4
Stamina	+5

program. Even if you have some fantastic character models already available for your game (that you plan to render into animated sprites), your game will still benefit greatly from hand-drawn concept renditions of each character. Table 9.6 reveals the attribute modifiers for the mage class.

Note

A good baseline for character attributes is 10, from which the final character attribute numbers are calculated. So if you create a wizard based on the Mage class, which has an Intellect modifier of +9, then your new wizard will have a total intellect value of 19.

The Non-Player Characters (NPCs)

Non-player characters (NPCs) represent everyone in the world other than the player's character (and the party in a game with more than one person playing, as in multiplayer games). NPCs are usually controlled by the game itself using a scripted or behavioral subroutine. The NPCs might be common townsfolk walking around the towns, doing their work and conducting business. NPCs might also be enemies, opposed to the player's character, who attack the PC on sight. Most of the time, fantasy creatures and monsters are not called NPCs because they are just obstacles that the player must overcome to complete a quest, and they generally help build up the PC's experience to level and increase his skills.

The NPCs in Celtic Crusader should follow a simple predefined path in the towns and do not venture outside the towns in which they are placed. This is accomplished by having them move around only within a limited range from their starting points. So, if the town of Durrow is located at a certain x, y position on the map, then the game generates a certain number of NPCs and places them at the same location identified as that town (along with a small random value, so they aren't all bunched up). The NPCs then move about in random directions and distances within a close proximity to their original starting points. In many cases, NPCs walk back and forth between two points on the map.

This rather simplistic behavior produces a surprisingly realistic town, and you can always insert some NPCs with more advanced behavior necessary to complete a certain quest. But most of the NPCs simply move around in this simple manner and make themselves available to the PC for dialogue. Each NPC is provided with a simple set of responses to dialogue that the player can choose to engage in (by walking up to an NPC and hitting a button).

The player is unable to attack non-combat NPCs because the game simply does not have the capability at this point to cause the townsfolk to react to attack, but this is a good idea for a future upgrade to the game. As you will see in the second half of this book, there are a lot of concepts that must be covered in a short time and in a limited amount of space, so I cannot fully develop the idea of populating the towns and furthering the storyline. However, you will learn enough from the continual upgrades to the Celtic Crusader game project in each chapter to fully develop an interactive game world.

Weapons and Armor

The standard weapons are very weak in combat while the player is just getting started in the first few levels. This is balanced by the levels of creatures and enemy NPCs that the player encounters in the early stages. As the player increases in experience and goes up in levels, the foes are equally challenging to keep the player on edge all the time and to keep the good players from finishing the game too quickly.

The player should be able to equip a standard weapon, shield, and armor and automatically swap gear when better items are found (which is not a significant part of the game, so it is not strongly emphasized). Table 9.7 shows the standard weapons that may be used by each character class.

Table 9.7 Standard Weapons by Class

Character Class	Standard Weapon
Warrior	Axe
Knight	Sword
Rogue	Club
Scout	Bow
Mage	Staff

Magic

Magic is a huge part of most RPGs and adds a lot to the character development aspects of a game. However, I have played many games that emphasize way too much magic, to the point of almost abandoning traditional weapons for offense and defense. In my opinion, magic should be downplayed as much as possible because it ruins the story. When there are hundreds of available magic spells that a character can learn, it tends to become the whole focus of the gameplay, and that's a shame! The game shouldn't be totally about character development and becoming the most powerful wizard in the world, although that is exactly what happens with some games.

One way to handle magic is by treating spells as animated projectile sprites with embedded damage modifiers that cause things to happen to the target. For instance, arrows fired by the scout do damage based on the scout's character attack value, which is affected by the quality of the character's bow and skill. Several factors determine the possible amount of damage that an arrow can inflict on an opponent, if the opponent doesn't block the attack. (A strong defense value causes the arrow to miss entirely in some attacks.)

The amount of magic that can be used in an RPG is greatly dependent upon the available artwork to render magic spells used as weapons (such as a fireball). It is better to start off with a limited magic system that allows the mage classes (which you might subclass into cleric, wizard, and so on) to heal themselves and others, as well as to enchant weapons. It is very common for magic in an RPG to grow in usage and depth as the game develops from one sequel to the next. Don't assume that you absolutely must get every single idea into the game on your first attempt. It's fun to leave room for growth, and players enjoy the new features of follow-up games in the series.

You might also consider the possibility of marketing a game as shareware, where you freely give away a limited version of the game (which may, for instance, just provide one character class), and then ask fans to pay for the full version, which would have a full assortment of magic spells and other important features.

Communication

The communication system in the game is important, but not crucial to a hack-and-slash type of game. Granted, such games are popular and have a lot of fans, but I want to provide you with ample opportunity to customize and improve the game. I don't want to fix the game to a specific goal (such as defeating a certain boss character), although that is certainly a goal that might be put into the game as one way to win.

Dialogue in most games can take place at the bottom of the screen, where messages are printed out and where the player can choose what to say to the NPCs. Another way to handle dialogue is to display messages in balloon pop-ups over the players, which is often done in console RPGs. A nice feature to add to the dialogue system is recorded voice acting, although if poorly presented, this can actually take away from the suspension of disbelief. (Always be careful not to do that!) It is sometimes better to just leave the player with his or her imagination, because many RPG fans regularly read fantasy books.

Combat

The combat in Celtic Crusader should take place in real time using the same scrolling map game engine used for walking around. The combat system is more challenging when programming NPCs to react realistically to the dynamic environment than to combat itself. The basis for combat is an engagement of weapons using a custom subset of animated sprite frames showing the swinging of a weapon or the shooting of an arrow. Due to limited time and space, we will only implement melee (hand-to-hand) combat in the version of the game presented in the book, and the idea is for you to continue working on the game, building it to suit your own designs.

When an attack takes place, the player's attack value (which is derived from the player's strength and character levels) is compared to the opponent's defense value (which is based on strength, shield, and armor), and the result is added to a randomly generated number. If the final result is positive, then the attack succeeded; otherwise, the attack missed. On a successful attack, the amount of damage done by the weapon is rolled (usually a range, such as 5 to 12), and that is how much damage the target takes. The damage reduces the health points of the player or NPC, and the target is killed if health drops below zero.

Level Up

Although game design should be considerably more complete than the partial design provided in this chapter, I think you now have a good idea about how to get started with your own RPG design. Drawing what you think each screen should look like and brainstorming gameplay ideas ahead of time makes the game far more interesting when you start writing the source code that actually makes the game work. Without a solid design up front, you are destined to give up on the game before it is finished. In contrast, you will become more and more enthusiastic about the game as you complete the design of each part of the game, because the process opens your mind to the possibilities. This chapter explored just some of the primary aspects of the Celtic Crusader game, giving you a basic idea about how to design a game.

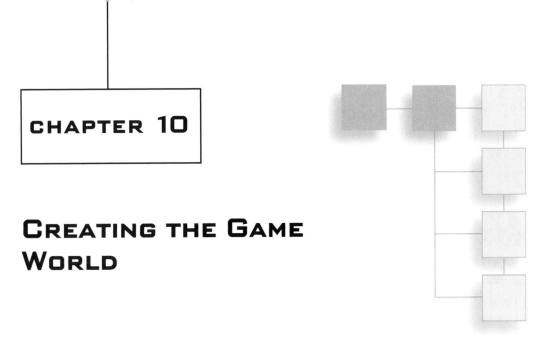

CHAPTER 10

CREATING THE GAME WORLD

The game world defines the rules of the game and presents the player with all of the obstacles that must be overcome to complete the game. Although the world is the most important aspect of a game, it is not always given the proper attention when a game is being designed. This chapter provides an introduction to world building, or more specifically, map editing. You learn to create the game world for Celtic Crusader, as well as levels for your own games, using an excellent program called Mappy. Here is a rundown of the major topics in this chapter:

- Creating the game world

- Importing the source tiles

- Editing the tile map

- Saving the map file as binary

- Saving the map file as text

- Using layers

Creating the Game World

Mappy is a versatile map editing program created by Robin Burrows. Mappy is *freeware*, so you can download it and use it to create maps for your games at no cost, although the pro version has additional features. If you find Mappy as useful as I have, I encourage you to send the author a small donation to express your appreciation for his hard work. The homepage for Mappy is www.tilemap.co.uk.

Why is Mappy so great, you ask? First of all, it's easy to use. In fact, it couldn't be any easier to use without sacrificing features. Mappy supports maps made up of the standard rectangular tiles, as well as isometric and hexagonal tiles. Have you ever played hexagonal games, such as *Panzer General*, or isometric games, such as *Age of Empires?* Well, Mappy lets you create levels similar to the ones used in these games. Mappy has a lot of hidden features that are not obvious at first glance.

Mappy has been used to create many retail (commercial) games, some of which you may have played! I personally know of several developers who have used Mappy to create levels for retail games for Pocket PC, Game Boy Advance, Nokia N-Gage, and wireless (cell phones). If you want to check for a newer version of Mappy, check the homepage. In addition to Mappy, sample games are available for download.

Running Mappy

Mappy is included on the CD-ROM that accompanies this book, in the \tools\mappy folder. You can run Mappy directly without installing it, although I recommend copying the mapwin.exe file to your hard drive. Mappy is so small that it's not unreasonable to copy it to any folder where you may need it. If you copy the executable without the subfolders, INI file, and so on, you miss out on the scripts and settings, so you may want to copy the whole folder containing the executable file to your hard drive.

Creating a New Map

Now let's fire up Mappy and create a new map.

1. Locate mapwin.exe and run it. When first run, Mappy comes up with two blank child windows. See Figure 10.1.

2. Open the File menu and select New Map to bring up the New Map dialog shown in Figure 10.2.

   As the New Map dialog shows, you must enter the size of each tile in your tile image file. The tiles used in Celtic Crusader vary, but most of the ground tiles are 64 × 48 pixels, so I have typed in 64 in the width box and 48 in the height box. (In our actual game, we'll just resize these to 32 × 32, but the original tiles from Reiner's Tileset come in this size.)

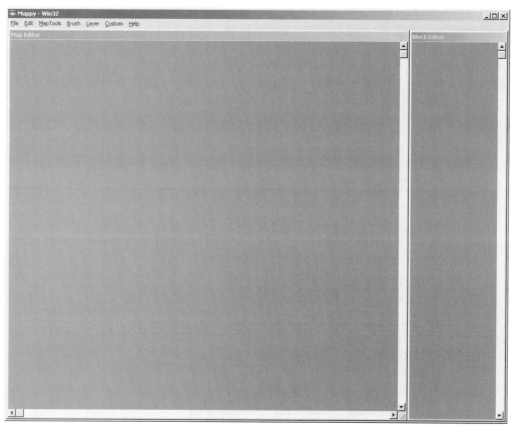

Figure 10.1
Mappy is a simple and unassuming map editor.

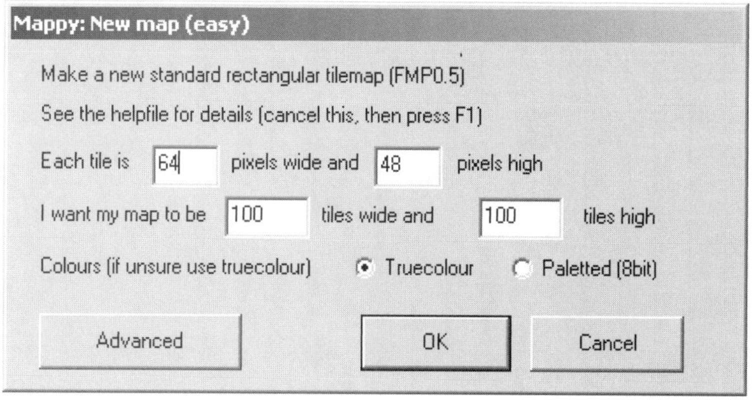

Figure 10.2
The New Map dialog in Mappy is used to configure a new game level.

3. Next you must enter the size of the map. The default 100×100 map is large—probably too large to be useful as a good example at this point, although the entire island of Ireland needs to be much bigger than that. Let's use the default map size for now. Of course, you can use any size you want for the map.

Tip

Mappy allows you to change the map size after it has been created (using MapTools, Resize Map), so if you need more tiles in your map later, it's easy to enlarge. Likewise, you can shrink the map, and Mappy has an option that lets you choose what portion of the map is cropped.

4. If you click the Advanced button on the New Map dialog you see the additional options shown in Figure 10.3. These options allow you to select the exact color depth of the source tiles (8 bit through 32 bit), the map file version to use, and dimensions for nonrectangular map tiles (such as hexagonal and isometric).

5. When you click the OK button, a new map is created and filled with the default black tile (tile #0). At this point, you must import the tile images that you want to use in the map (which is what the next section details). This is where things really get interesting, because you can use multiple image files containing source artwork; Mappy combines all the source tiles into a new image source with correctly positioned tiles. (Saving the tile bitmap file is an option in the Save As dialog.) Mappy looks like Figure 10.4.

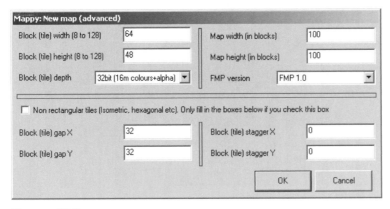

Figure 10.3
The advanced options in the New Map dialog.

Figure 10.4
A new map is ready to be edited, but first some tiles are needed.

Importing the Source Tiles

Here's where you import the tile images that you want to use in the map.

1. Open the File menu and select Import. See Figure 10.5. The Open File dialog appears, allowing you to browse for an image file, which may be BMP, PCX, PNG, or MAR/P (map array file—something that can be exported by Mappy).

   After you choose this file, Mappy imports the tiles into the tile palette shown in Figure 10.6. Recall that you specified the tile size when you created the map file; Mappy used the dimensions provided to read in all of the tiles automatically.

   You must make the image resolution reasonably close to the edges of the tiles, but it doesn't need to be perfect—Mappy is smart enough to account

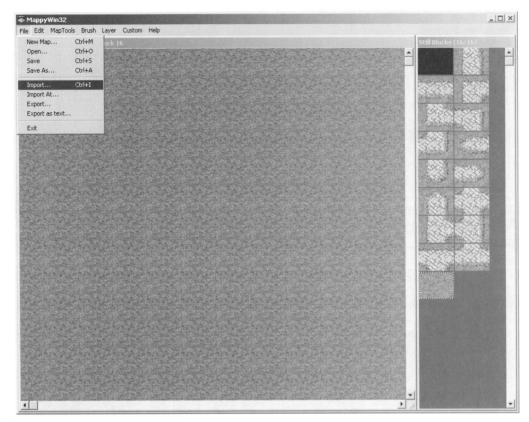

Figure 10.5
The Import option on the File menu.

for a few pixels off the right or bottom edges and move to the next row. In other words, once you create a map with a specified tile size, you *must* use tiles of that size for the entire map, as there is no way to have a tile map with different-sized tiles (which would screw up the drawing process anyway).

Tip

You can import tiles another way that I find even more useful than the Import feature: It is in the MapTools menu under Useful Functions. Look for an option called Create Map from Big Picture and select it, as shown in Figure 10.7.

This brings up the standard Open dialog, which shows the available image files. I have changed the dialog display to show thumbnails rather than a list of files, as shown in Figure 10.8.

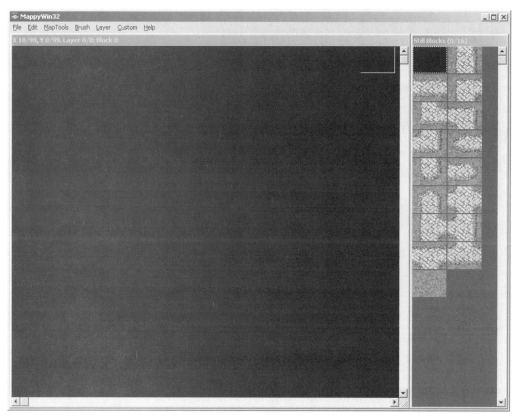

Figure 10.6
The tiles have been imported into Mappy's tile palette.

2. Select the bitmap file to use and click Open. A dialog box appears, asking whether you would like to remove duplicate graphics and blocks. You should *always* do this, because it is the one way I know to clean up the tile palette after several bitmaps have been imported into the palette. There are usually a lot of duplicate tiles in the tile palette after importing large images. This feature optimizes the palette and removes duplicates. After Mappy has imported the image into the tile palette, the result is shown in Figure 10.9. Note how Mappy automatically adds new tiles to the end of the list so the current map is not affected. In contrast, the Import command from the File menu overwrites the palette! You want to use the Create Map from Big Picture option most of the time. This is not a "production" map, obviously; for Celtic Crusader, we'll start over again, so go ahead and mess this one up all you want to get some practice using Mappy.

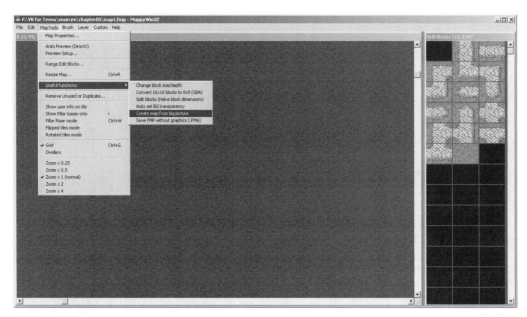

Figure 10.7
Locating the Create Map from Big Picture option.

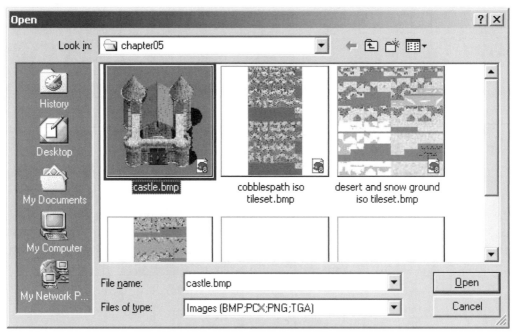

Figure 10.8
Importing an entire bitmap image, which is broken up into tiles.

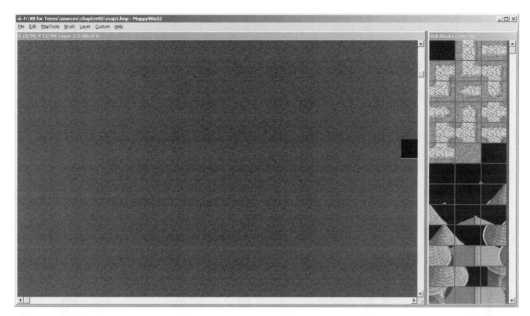

Figure 10.9
The castle image has been imported as a series of tiles.

Editing the Tile Map

You can now create a map with the available tiles. I'd like to show you a convenient feature that I use often. I like to see most of the level on the screen at once to get an overview. Mappy lets you change the zoom level of the map editor display.

1. Open the MapTools menu and select one of the zoom levels to change the zoom.

2. Select a tile from the tile palette and use the mouse to "draw" that tile on the map edit window to see how the chosen zoom level appears.

I frequently use 0.5 (1/2 zoom), shown in Figure 10.10. Until you have added some tiles to the map window, you won't see anything happen after changing the zoom.

Now let me show you a quick shortcut for filling the entire map with a certain tile.

1. Select a neutral tile that is good as a backdrop, such as the grass, dirt, or stone tile.

2. Open the Custom menu. This menu contains scripts that can be run to manipulate a map.

   You can write your own scripts if you learn the Lua language. Visit www.lua.org for more information.

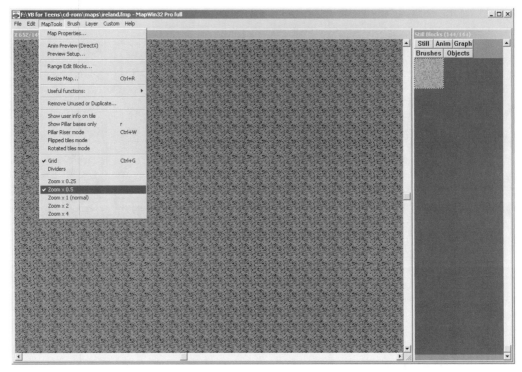

Figure 10.10
Changing the zoom level of the map editor window.

3. Select the script called Solid Rectangle (see Figure 10.11) to bring up the dialog shown in Figure 10.12.

4. Modify the width and height parameters for the rectangle (such as 10,10).

5. Click OK, and the map will be filled with the currently selected tile, as shown in Figure 10.13.

Selecting a different tile and filling in the whole map results in what you see in Figure 10.14.

Go ahead and play around with Mappy to gain familiarity with it. You can erase tiles with the right mouse button and select tiles in the palette with the left button. You can use the keyboard arrow keys to scroll the map in any direction. (This is very handy when you want to keep your other hand on the mouse for quick editing.) Try to create an interesting map; I'll show you how to save the map in two different formats that you'll use in the following sample programs.

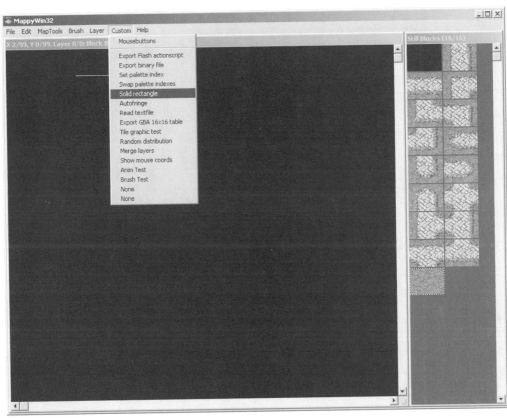

Figure 10.11
Filling a region of the map with a specified tile.

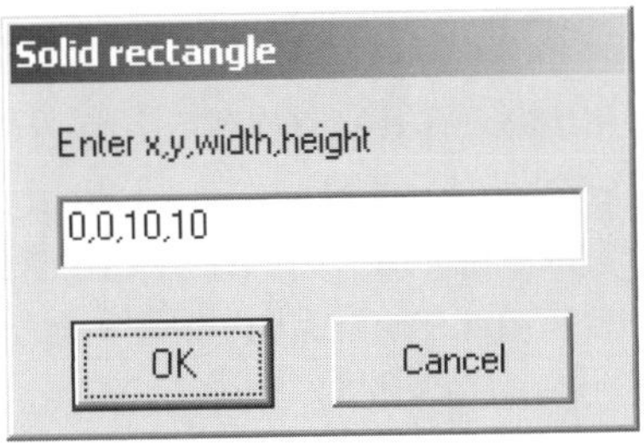

Figure 10.12
Specifying the range of map tiles to be filled in with the selected tile.

Saving the Map File as FMP

Have you created an interesting map to save yet? If not, go ahead and create a map, even if it's just a hodgepodge of tiles. Don't be afraid to save a *lot* of different

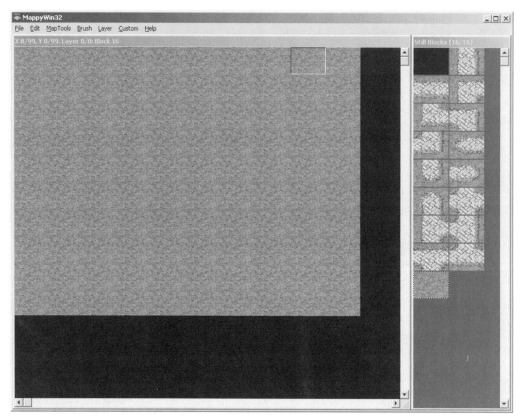

Figure 10.13
The Solid Rectangle script fills a region of the map with a tile.

files. Disk space is cheap, but your imagination is valuable. I'll show you how to save the map file first, and then you'll export the map to a format we can load in VB. For now, open the File menu and select Save As to bring up the Save As dialog shown in Figure 10.15. You want to save your source maps in the default Mappy format for safekeeping, even if you plan to export the file for use in Visual Basic.

Unfortunately, there's no simple way to load a native Mappy file directly in Visual Basic, so use the simpler export format. First, type a filename such as map1.fmp and click Save. FMP is the native format for a Mappy file. Always be sure to save your maps in this format first, and then export them, because you'll want to open up the native file whenever you need to make changes to a level.

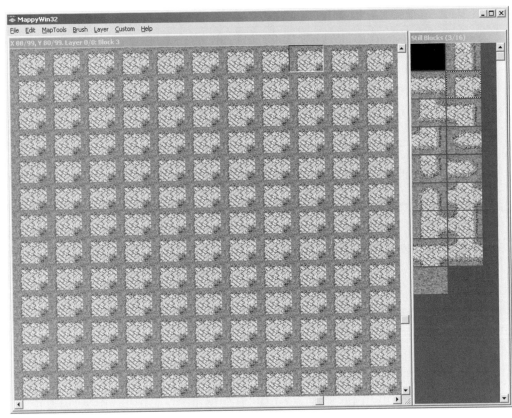

Figure 10.14
Filling in the whole map with a specific tile.

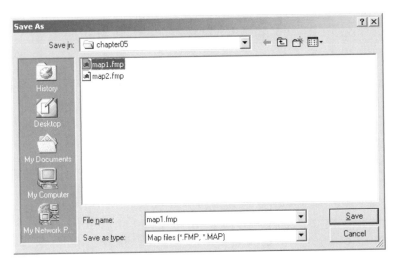

Figure 10.15
The Save As dialog in Mappy is used to save a map file.

Tip

Always keep many backup copies of your original source map files, all of the artwork used in your games, as well as your source code! Make second and third copies and store them on a flash drive or CD-R or on an FTP server. *Always* have a backup location for all of your hard work so it is never left exposed on your single PC, because it's *painful* losing your files.

I use a freeware backup program called Cobian Backup, which is available from http://sourceforge. net/projects/cobianbackup. Cobian lets you specify a regular schedule and it doesn't store files in some weird format, it just copies files to the backup location and keeps track of them for you. Once you've done a complete backup, it will then do incremental updates every day (if you schedule it properly). I use an external hard drive connected to my PC with a USB cable, and this works very well.

Saving the Map File as Text

Now that you have saved the new level in the standard Mappy file format, I'd like to show you how to export the map to a simple text file that can be pasted into a program. The result is an array in text format that can be easily modified to work in Visual Basic.

1. Open the File menu and select Export. Do not select Export As Text at this time. That is an entirely different option used to export a map to accommodate multiple layers. At the moment, start with just a simple map export.

2. Select Export to bring up the Export dialog shown in Figure 10.16.

   You can explore the uses for the various formats in the Export dialog when you have an opportunity; I'll explain the one option you need to export the map data as text.

3. You want to select the third check box from the top: Map Array as Comma Values Only (?.CSV). If you want to build an image containing the tiles in the proper order as they were in Mappy, then you can also select the Graphics Blocks as Picture (?.BMP) check box. I strongly recommend exporting the image. For one thing, Mappy adds the blank tile that you may have used in some parts of the map. Mappy also numbers the tiles consecutively, starting with this blank tile, unless you check the option Skip Block 0. (I suggest leaving it *unchecked*.) Normally, you should be able to just leave the default of 20 in the Blocks a Row input field, but feel free to change it if you wish.

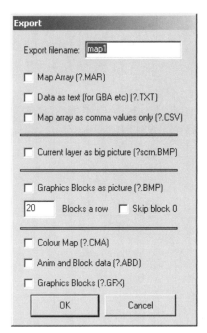

Figure 10.16
The Export dialog in Mappy lets you choose options for exporting the map.

For our purposes, both the CSV and BMP files are needed to properly draw the map in Visual Basic. The CSV file is dumped into a Visual Basic module file, while the bitmap file is loaded at runtime.

4. Click OK to export the map.

The Saved Bitmap File

Mappy outputs the map with the name provided in the Export dialog as two files: map1.BMP and map1.CSV. (Your map name may differ.) Microsoft Excel recognizes the CSV format, but there is no point to loading it into Excel (if you have Microsoft Office installed). Instead, rename the file to map1.txt and then open it with Notepad or another text editor. You can now copy the map data text and paste it into a source code file, and you have the bitmap image handy as well. The resulting bitmap file is shown in Figure 10.17 (with the cobblestone and castle tile sets).

You know, with the ability to export the tiles from Mappy, there's nothing you can't do with this wonderful program. You can import all kinds of weird tiled bitmaps into your world and let Mappy generate one big bitmap file, which you

Figure 10.17
The bitmap file generated by Mappy.

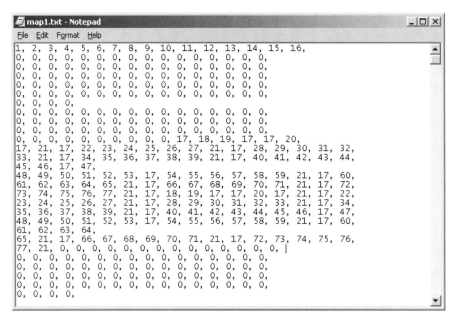

Figure 10.18
The map data file generated by Mappy.

can use in your program. So, you don't need to worry about loading all of your source tiles—just a single bitmap file.

The Saved Data File

Mappy creates a text file filled with tile values separated by commas; it looks something like Figure 10.18.

The real question is how you use this text file in a program. That's a logical question at this point in the chapter. However, I'm going to defer the discussion until the next chapter, which is focused entirely on loading the map and traversing the Celtic Crusader world. My goal here is just to introduce you to Mappy and help you to get familiar with map editing so you can use Mappy to create your own game world.

Advanced Map Editing

I've been holding back, anticipating some advanced techniques while going over the basics. Mappy doesn't look very feature rich by default, but a couple of relatively unknown secrets make it very powerful. One such feature is *layering and onion skinning.* You can set up one of the layers as the background and then do all of your drawing on a "top" layer without affecting the background. You can draw, erase—everything—and the layer underneath remains untouched.

Using Layers

Layering is a powerful feature of Mappy that becomes even more interesting when you load a Mappy data file directly in your game (something that is not possible here, unfortunately, due to there being no Visual Basic library for Mappy). A layer is just another tile map that exists above or below other tile maps in a multilayer fashion. For the purpose of creating an RPG world, layers are helpful when designing the world map; the layering isn't needed after the map has been saved, although it's extremely helpful while working on the map.

1. To add another layer to the map, open the Layer menu and select Add Layer, as shown in Figure 10.19.

2. Next, go back into the Layer menu and check the option called Background Colored so the background layer will be darkened. This makes it easier to identify your foreground layer work.

3. Open Layer again and select the option called Onion Skin to bring up the Onion Skin dialog box, shown in Figure 10.20. This allows you to view the background layer while working on other layers.

Transparency

An important consideration that I should mention is the topic of transparency. Mappy lets you draw transparent layers over the background layer, with some spectacular results. Take a look at Figure 10.21, showing tiles being drawn with Onion Skin enabled on the background; the top layer is being drawn transparently.

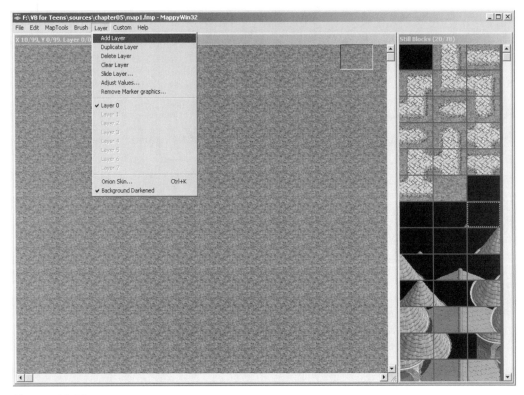

Figure 10.19
Adding another layer to the map in Mappy.

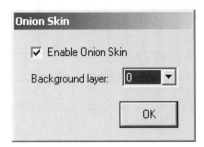

Figure 10.20
Enabling the Onion Skin feature.

Mappy understands the transparency of a source image if you set the transparent color to pink—that is, a color with a Red/Green/Blue combination of (255,0,255). If you are using a graphic editor such as Pro Motion or Paint Shop Pro, you can edit a color's RGB directly. What you want to do is create a pink color with values of (255,0,255) and then perform flood fill anywhere on the

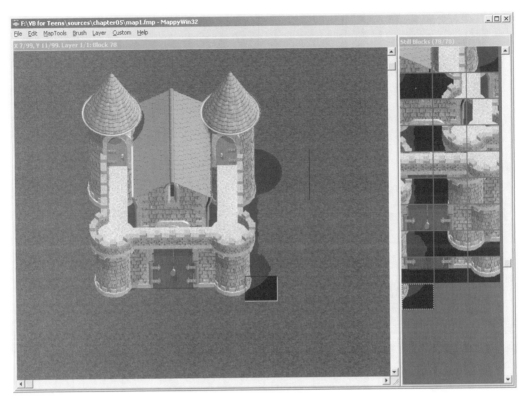

Figure 10.21
The castle re-created in Mappy from the source tiles.

bitmap that you want to have come up transparently in Mappy (and in your game world). It really is irrelevant in the final map file because the tiles do not need to be transparent.

To add the castle to Mappy's tile palette, I cropped the castle bitmap you saw in the previous chapter (with the two extra isometric views of the castle), showing just the single rectangular castle. Then I made the surrounding pixels around the castle pink so it would show up transparently in Mappy. (See Figure 10.22.) Don't worry about blank space around the source bitmaps. Mappy optimizes the tile palette, removing any duplicate blank tiles. (That's a nice feature, isn't it?)

Combining Layers

Using the techniques you've learned here, you should be able to fill the background layer with a common tile and then do the "real work" on another layer so you don't have to constantly go back and fix background tiles that get messed up

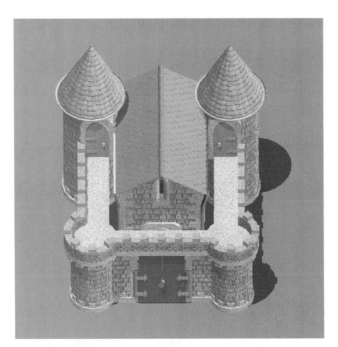

Figure 10.22
The source bitmap for the castle with transparent (pink) color around the edges.

while building your world. In fact, feel free to create several layers if it makes the work easier on you. You might have one layer just for towns and roads, with another layer for mountains and rivers, with yet another layer for roads and bridges. Do whatever works for you.

The time comes when you're finished and you need to export the map for use in your game. What can you do with all the layers? First of all, save the map in the standard Mappy format so you can edit the map at any time. You'll want to export the map when you need to dump it into Visual Basic for use in the game. There is an imperfect option that I want to at least bring to your attention, even if it isn't the ideal solution. The Custom menu contains scripts that you can run to do various things to your map. One such script is called Merge Layers. This script works well for some types of maps, but the only problem is that the additional layers lose their transparency, as shown in Figure 10.23.

The ideal solution to transparency, as it turns out, is only rendering of objects transparently *within your program,* I'm afraid. There is no way to export the entire map with all layers merged together while also retaining transparency. Therefore, a lot of attention is given to drawing the background tiles as well as to

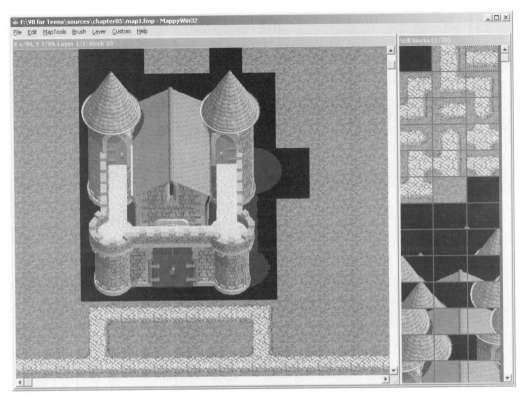

Figure 10.23
Merging the layers results in a loss of transparency.

drawing a transparent layer from a Mappy file in Celtic Crusader (and any other game you plan to write). The castle is a very unusual problem that will not be actually used in the game as a tile set. If we use the castle in the game, it will be loaded as a sprite, but I thought it was an attractive image to use as an illustration.

A simpler option is to modify the tiles used in the upper layers so that rather than being transparent, these tiles have the background tile integrated (and lined up so it appears seamless). This very good approach would certainly make the map editing much smoother, although it requires more up-front work to edit the images. As it turns out, a lot of stuff needs to be drawn transparently in the game anyway, such as trees and of course all of the non-player characters (NPCs) and animals in the game, and we'll just be using sprites, so don't worry about this issue within Mappy; just use Mappy to create a tilemap, and leave everything else to your code.

Level Up

This chapter moved rather quickly through a brief Mappy tutorial, which provided you with a working understanding of how Mappy can be used to create and edit levels and maps. The tilemap is the most important part of Celtic Crusader because it is the foundation—literally, it is *the world* on which our characters will walk. You can create a large, vast desert or a lush green world and populate it with vegetation and roads and even buildings using Mappy. But we'll stick to creating tilemaps with Mappy and add in the details using sprites and source code.

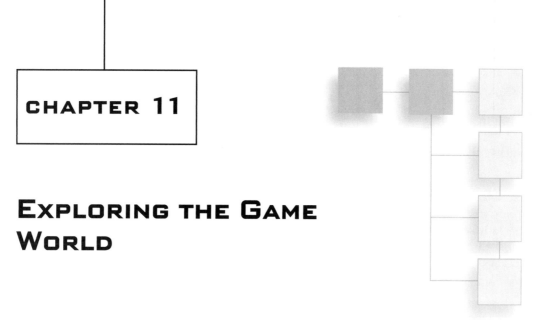

CHAPTER 11

EXPLORING THE GAME WORLD

This chapter combines the tile-based scroller class with the texture-based sprite class to let you explore the game world of Celtic Crusader using an animated character sprite for the first time. This is the first step toward building the RPG engine that is coming together in this book, and it is a significant step forward from the simple example programs you have seen up to this point. This chapter combines the tile scroller, sprite, and input code to allow your character to literally walk around in the actual game world (created in Mappy). Here are the major topics in this chapter:

- Mapping the game world

- Loading a binary Mappy file

- The animated character artwork

- The WalkAbout program

Mapping the Game World

The first thing I discovered when attempting to create ninth-century Ireland using Mappy was that this game world is *huge*. As the WalkAbout program that you develop later in this chapter demonstrates, it takes several minutes to walk clear across the map (including water tiles). From the very top to the very bottom of the map, it takes even longer! What is even more surprising is that the WalkAbout program scrolls at twice the normal speed at which the game should move. Instead of two pixels at a time (per screen update), it scrolls at four pixels, which means that in the realistic version of the running game, the game world is large enough to let the player explore for many *virtual* miles in all directions.

Note

If this map were represented in memory rather than being stored virtually as a tilemap (with the scrolling view generated on the fly), it would be a bitmap image with a resolution of 48,000 × 64,000 pixels and it would require about 100 gigabytes of memory (which is obviously impossible). Instead, the tile engine only requires a couple megabytes.

This is an interesting fact because some data compression algorithms use a similar method to compress data. If you were to display the entire game world for Celtic Crusader on computer monitors, where each tile is 32 × 32, and each monitor was set at a resolution of 1600 × 1200, it would be a grid of 30 monitors across by 53 monitors tall! That's a huge game world indeed.

Refamiliarizing Yourself with the Ireland Map

Why does the game need such a large map? For one thing, it demonstrates clearly that VB is fully capable of handling a large-scale game. Second, it proves that the tile-based scroller engine, in theory as well as in practice, is simply incredible at rendering a huge game world. Take a look at Figure 11.1, which shows the original map of ninth-century Ireland first introduced back in Chapter 9. As you may recall, this map was drawn by hand, scanned, and then cleaned up and enhanced using the GIMP.

Now take a look at Figure 11.2. This figure shows a portion of the map of Ireland as it appears in Mappy (after a half day spent creating the tile map of the game world!).

The huge size of the game world in Celtic Crusader should be very encouraging to you, especially if you have a good imagination and you would like to create a massive RPG with a long, complex storyline and intense, varied character-development features.

Digitizing the Real World

Creating the map of Ireland with Mappy was no small undertaking, as it required many hours of work to make it look right, along with a custom program written

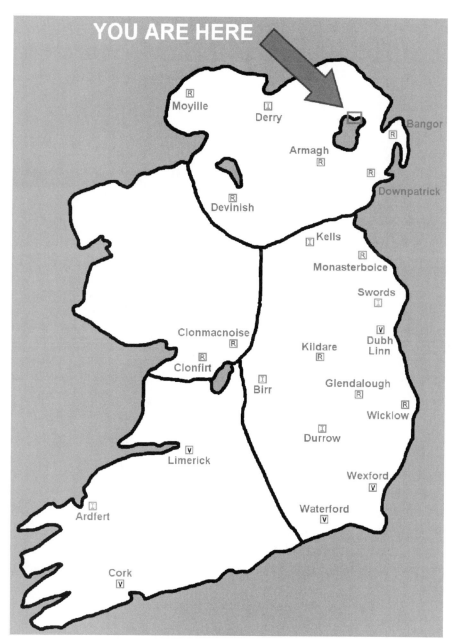

Figure 11.1
The original digitized and enhanced map of ninth-century Ireland.

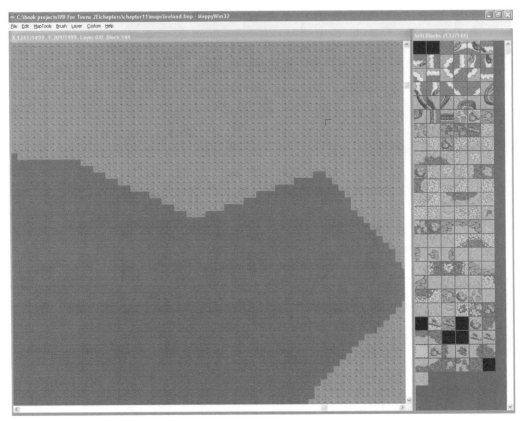

Figure 11.2
The same portion of the map as it appears in Mappy.

just to display the entire map scaled down so that it is visible in its entirety. The ViewMap program is available in the folder for this chapter on the CD-ROM. Figure 11.3 shows the program displaying a *very early version* of the Ireland map with a small border of water tiles and some reference points added to the map to help while editing.

Although ViewMap can view any Mappy map that you create (and saved in the binary .MAR format; more on that later), you need to modify the program if you are using a map with different dimensions, as it is currently configured for Ireland.MAR, which is a huge map of 1,500 tiles across and 2,000 tiles down. Just modify the MAPW and MAPH constants for your own map. (As is often the case, custom-written utility programs are not always versatile because such programs are meant to solve problems quickly. My goal was to view the whole map while I was creating it in Mappy.) I think the ViewMap tool will work just fine for any

Figure 11.3
The ViewMap program draws a very early version of the game world created in Mappy.

map, but you must export it to a MAR file. A MAR file is comprised of two-byte "short" integers with the low- and high-order bytes reversed, so when we read a short integer from the file, the value is inverted by dividing it by 32. Beyond that, it's *very* easy to load. Here's the entire program:

```
Imports System
imports System.Windows.Forms
Imports System.Drawing
Imports Microsoft.VisualBasic

Public Class Form1
    Const TITLE As String = "MAPPY MAR FILE VIEWER"
    Const MAPW As Integer = 1500
    Const MAPH As Integer = 2000
    Private mapdata(MAPW * MAPH) As Short
    Private surface As Graphics
```

```
Private Sub Form1_Load(ByVal sender As System.Object, _
ByVal e As System.EventArgs) Handles MyBase.Load

    'make form slightly bigger than map
    Me.Size = New Size(MAPW / 2.8, MAPH / 2.8)
    Me.Text = TITLE

    'load the map file
    Load_MAR("ireland.mar", MAPW, MAPH)
End Sub

Private Sub Form1_Paint(ByVal sender As Object, _
ByVal e As System.Windows.Forms.PaintEventArgs) Handles Me.Paint

    Dim x, y As Integer
    Dim x1, y1 As Single
    Dim tile As Integer
    Dim g As Graphics = e.Graphics
    Dim c As System.Drawing.Pen = Pens.Black

    g.Clear(Color.White)

    'draw tiny lines (i.e. pixels) for each tile
    For y = 0 To MAPH - 1 Step 3
        For x = 0 To MAPW - 1 Step 3

            'color is grayscale based on tile #
            tile = mapdata(y * MAPW + x)
            c = New Pen(Color.FromArgb(tile Mod 255, tile Mod 255, tile Mod
            255))

            x1 = x / 3
            y1 = y / 3
            g.DrawLine(c, x1, y1, x1 + 1, y1)
        Next x
    Next y
End Sub

Public Sub Load_MAR(ByVal filename As String, ByVal lWidth As Long, _
ByVal lHeight As Long)
    'there's no error handling code here!
    'if file doesn't exit, it'll just crash...
```

```
        Dim n As Long
        Dim i As Short

        'open the binary map file
        FileOpen(1, filename, OpenMode.Binary, OpenAccess.Read, OpenShare.
        Default)

        'prepare the array for the map data
        ReDim mapdata(lWidth * lHeight)

        'read the map data
        For n = 0 To lWidth * lHeight - lWidth - 1
            'read one short integer
            FileGet(1, i)
            'reverse bytes
            mapdata(n) = i / 32
        Next n

        'close the file
        FileClose(1)
    End Sub

    Private Sub Form1_KeyDown(ByVal sender As Object, _
    ByVal e As System.Windows.Forms.KeyEventArgs) Handles Me.KeyDown
        If e.KeyCode = Keys.Escape Then
            Me.Close()
        End If
    End Sub
End Class
```

The Load_MAR routine will be very helpful indeed, so we'll keep it handy for a new class that I have planned for the game world. This new "game world" class will actually serve the role of "game engine" and will handle a lot more of the details of the RPG engine as we build it in upcoming chapters.

Now, if you notice from the tilemap, the reference points are inserted into the bitmap image and in the Mappy file using tiles to help keep track of the map's scale while editing with tiles. Figure 11.4 shows the ireland.bmp file (the original scanned and enhanced image) with some of the reference points visible. The darker dots represent towns.

The map was originally 3,000 × 4,000 tiles, but I quickly realized that this would be utterly daunting to edit and not really necessary, so I settled on 1,500 × 2,000.

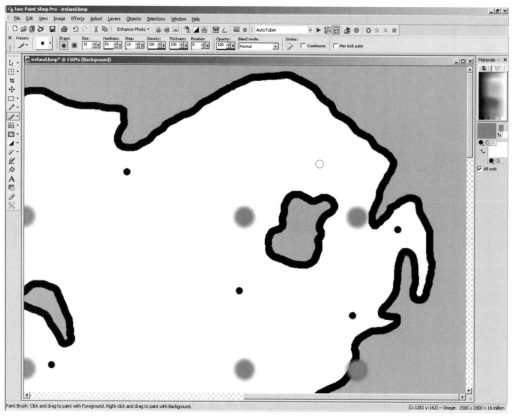

Figure 11.4
The ireland.bmp file has the same dimensions as the Mappy file (1,500 pixels = 1,500 tiles).

I realized that the game world would be very difficult, if not impossible, to create in Mappy without very specific coordinates from the original map image. To be honest, these dimensions are still quite large for an average game, but I was thinking of the huge game worlds in *Ultima* and similar games when designing it. You could create a compelling RPG with much less.

I decided to take the original bitmap and resize it so that it has the same dimensions as the tilemap in Mappy. In other words, if my Mappy map is 1,500 tiles across, then my bitmap image is 1,500 pixels across; likewise for the height of the tilemap and the bitmap image. This makes it possible to model the "real" map with great precision. Using Mappy's line tool, I clicked on a point in the map that corresponds to a point on the border of the island in the bitmap image. Then, locating a new spot, I highlighted the spot with the mouse (I'm still in Mappy here) and pressed the L key to draw a line of tiles from the previous click spot to the current highlighted spot.

By carefully following the contour of the terrain in the bitmap, I painstakingly created a map of Ireland in Mappy. You can see the smaller reference points around the contour of the island in Figure 11.5 as well as around the lakes (which *are* included in the Mappy file). The large dots on the image were only used early on and were not needed once the contour had been digitized. Manually creating a tilemap from a scanned map is challenging, but quite worth it when the result actually resembles the original scan.

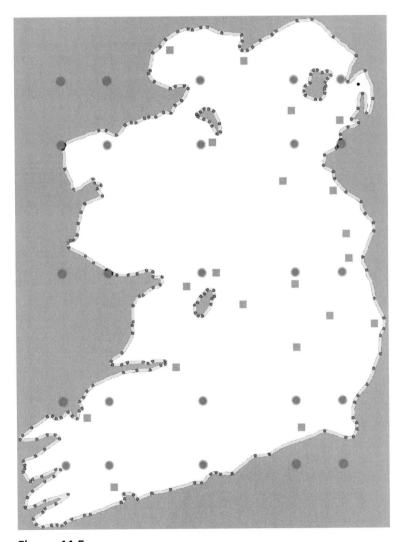

Figure 11.5
Mappy creates an accurate representation of Ireland by breaking down the outline of the island into reference points.

The next screenshot of ViewMap (see Figure 11.6) shows the completed tilemap of Ireland used in the Celtic Crusader game. You can now see why this program was needed; otherwise, it's impossible to see what the tilemap really looks like, because you usually see a small portion of it at a time. It's nearly complete in this version. What remains to be done with the tilemap is a smoothing of the land/ocean transitions, because the beaches are still quite crude. The tile images provided by Reiner Prokein (www.reinerstileset.de) include beach contours, so

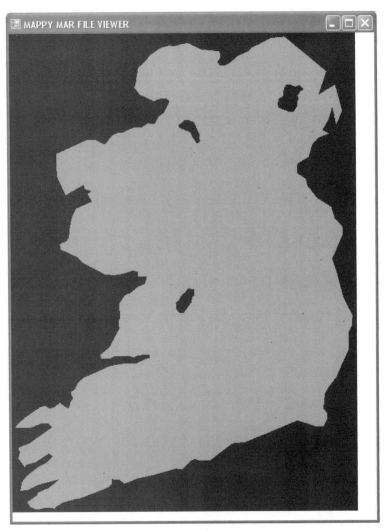

Figure 11.6
The ViewMap program showing the nearly completed tilemap for Celtic Crusader.

I'll be able to add them to the tilemap in Mappy. A lot more work needs to be done with the tilemap beyond the beaches, because this map is *the world*. Although we'll be able to do just about anything with sprites positioned at global coordinates (relative to the entire game world, rather than just the screen), it's usually more convenient to place things such as portals right in the map and then programmatically identify such tiles based on their tile numbers.

Exporting the Tilemap to a Binary File

The ability to load the map back into memory and render it onscreen using the tile engine is the key to this large map being usable. This tilemap is a thousand times bigger than any sample tilemap you have used in previous chapters. Therefore, you must assume that Visual Basic would take a very long time to load this file if it were stored in the same manner—using an exported text file of comma-separated values (a .CSV file). The answer to this very serious problem is to use a binary file format instead of a text file format.

Mappy can export a lot of different files, and this is one of its best features, since you aren't required to use the .FMP format if you don't want to. Mappy can export your tilemap into a very simple binary file that contains *nothing but* the tile numbers, in sequential order, as short integers. This means Mappy writes two bytes into the binary file for every tile numbered in order, just like the text file format but without all the wasted space associated with a text file. In my testing, it took more than 20 seconds to load a text map exported from this map of Ireland. In contrast, the binary version of the file takes only about three seconds to load.

First, you need to know how to export a tilemap to the binary file format. As you have already learned, you can export a file in Mappy using the File, Export option, which brings up the dialog box shown in Figure 11.7.

Just select the first option, Map Array (?.MAR) to save the tilemap as a binary file. The .MAR format (which is short for *map array*) is the format I just described, where each tile is saved as a two-byte short integer, which can be read in VB.NET using a *short integer*. In the older Visual Basic 6.0, an integer was only 16 bits, while a short was 8 bits. Now in VB.NET, a short integer is 16 bits, while an integer is 32 bits. So, we must use a short to read in the map array values. To demonstrate, take a look at the Load_MAR subroutine again and note the type of variable I've used when reading from the file. Likewise, the mapdata array has been defined as an array of short integers.

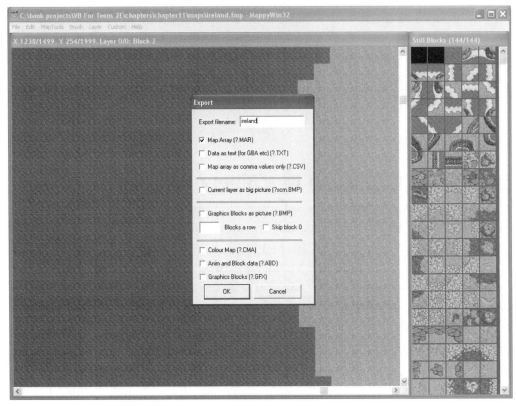

Figure 11.7
The Export dialog box in Mappy is where you can export your tilemap to a binary file.

```
Public Sub Load_MAR(ByVal filename As String, ByVal lWidth As Long, _
ByVal lHeight As Long)
    Dim n As Long
    Dim i As Short

    'open the binary map file
    FileOpen(1, filename, OpenMode.Binary, OpenAccess.Read, OpenShare.
    Default)

    'prepare the array for the map data
    ReDim mapdata(lWidth * lHeight)

    'read the map data
    For n = 0 To lWidth * lHeight - lWidth - 1
        'read one short integer
```

```
        FileGet(1, i)
        'reverse bytes
        mapdata(n) = i / 32
    Next n

    'close the file
    FileClose(1)
End Sub
```

The FileGet subroutine has many overloaded versions available in order to read many different types of data from a binary file. The appropriate overloaded version of FileGet is used depending on the type of variable you use in the second parameter. So, if you change i to a normal integer, it won't work!

The Animated Character Artwork

Now I'd like to discuss how you can prepare a sprite for use in this game. Each sprite is somewhat different in the number of frames it uses for each type of animation, as well as the types of animation available. All of the character sprites that I'm using in Celtic Crusader have the full eight-direction walking animation sequences, as well as frames for attacking with a weapon. Some sprites have a death animation, and some have running and falling. To keep the game as uniform as possible, you should use character sprites that have the exact same number of animation frames for the key animation that takes place in the game. That way you can switch character classes (Warrior, Paladin, Scout, and Wizard) without changing any source code.

I have based my work in the WalkAbout program on the Paladin version of the hero sprite, and it is shown in Figure 11.8.

The source artwork from Reiner's Tilesets does not come in this format, but it comes with each frame of animation stored in a separate bitmap file. The easiest way to combine these frames into a sprite animation sheet is with Cosmigo's Pro Motion sprite editor and animation program. Because Pro Motion works best with single animation strips, I decided to import each group of bitmaps for the character's walking animation in all eight directions. Using Pro Motion, I exported all into individual bitmap files and combined them into a single, large file using the GIMP. Figure 11.9 shows the individual animation strips for the Paladin Hero character.

Nothing beats experimentation, so it is up to you to use the freely available sprites provided by Reiner's Tilesets to enhance Celtic Crusader to suit your own

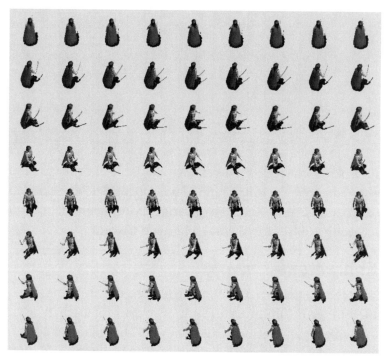

Figure 11.8
The sword-wielding Paladin sprite is the hero figure in the WalkAbout program.

imagination. We can only accomplish so much in this book, so I want to give you as many tools, tips, and tricks as I can possibly squeeze in at this time. All you need are Pro Motion, Mappy, and the GIMP to create the artwork for your own RPG. There are so many sprites and tiles available at www.reinerstilesets.de that it would take a whole book just to list them all! There is a sprite for everything you can possibly imagine adding to an RPG, including fireballs and other types of magic spells, with both casting animation and the projectile animation of the fireball itself!

The WalkAbout Program

You have already received a complete tutorial on how to use tile-based scrolling as well as how to draw transparent, animated sprites. The only thing left to do is combine these two techniques into a single program that animates the hero character at the center of the window while scrolling in the appropriate direction. Sounds easy, doesn't it? As a matter of fact, once the map is actually ready to go, it

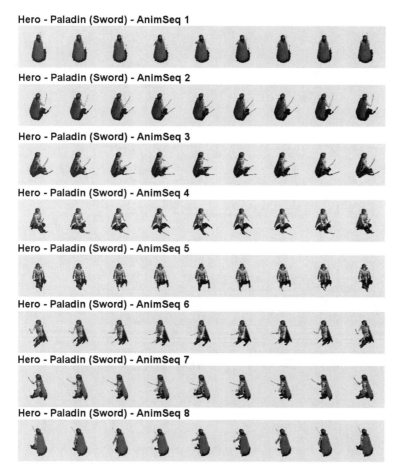

Figure 11.9
There are eight animation strips to give the Paladin Hero full eight-way movement.

is rather easy to get this program going. Figure 11.10 shows the WalkAbout program running. Note that the player sprite has all eight directions of travel. The WalkAbout program is a fully functional prototype of the player walking around on the actual Celtic Crusader tilemap.

In addition, this program displays the current ScrollX and ScrollY values on the screen along with the current tile that the player is standing on. This is a helpful thing to know, because the character will be walking on all sorts of tiles, and depending on the tile number, different things may be triggered (such as a portal or door heading into a dungeon). This screenshot also shows how the player remains stationary at the center of the screen. The sense of movement is just simulated by scrolling the ground underneath the player, which adds to the effect

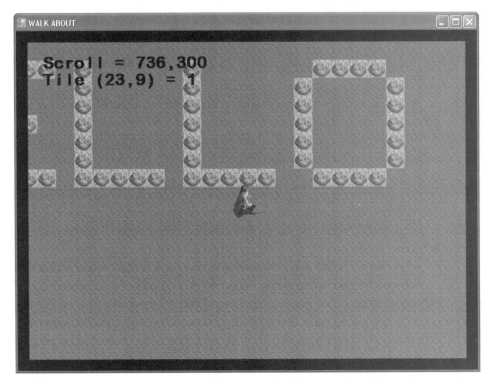

Figure 11.10
The upper-left corner of the tilemap contains a "HELLO" message for testing purposes.

by using a walking animation. Figure 11.11 shows another screenshot of the program. As you can see, much work remains to be done on the terrain tiles to improve their appearance.

Notice how the tile number changed from the previous screenshot. Tile #1 contains water, while tile #143 contains grass. You can locate these tiles in the ireland.bmp image, which contains the tile images.

The WalkAbout program needs the following classes:

- CDirect3D

- CSprite

- CBitmapFont

- CTileScroller

- CKeyboard

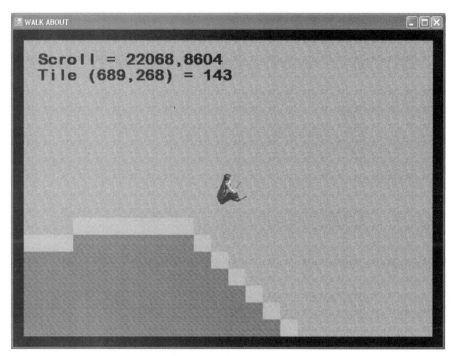

Figure 11.11
Another portion of the Celtic Crusader tilemap.

There are several resources you will also obviously need to run this program, such as the ireland.mar and ireland.bmp files for the tilemap, the arial18.png bit-mapped font, and the hero_sword_walk.png file containing the hero sprite.

Let's go over the source code for the WalkAbout program. Let's start with the global constants and variables:

```
Imports Microsoft.DirectX
Imports Microsoft.DirectX.Direct3D
Imports Microsoft.DirectX.DirectInput

Public Class Form1
    Const TITLE As String = "WALK ABOUT"
    Const SCREENW As Integer = 800
    Const SCREENH As Integer = 600

    'scroller constants
    Const MAPW As Integer = 1500
    Const MAPH As Integer = 2000
```

```
    Const TILEW As Integer = 32
    Const TILEH As Integer = 32
    Const COLUMNS As Integer = 16

    'scrolling values
    Public SpeedX As Integer
    Public SpeedY As Integer

    Private d3d As CDirect3D
    Private keyboard As CKeyboard
    Private WithEvents clock As Timer
    Private font1 As CBitmapFont

    Private scroller As CTileScroller
    Private mapdata() As Byte
    Private tiles As CSprite

    Const HEROSPEED As Integer = 4
    Dim hero As CSprite
    Dim SuperHero As Boolean
```

Next up is the Form1_Load subroutine, which is where all of our initialization code goes, including the loading of all sprites and creation of the tilemap.

```
Private Sub Form1_Load(ByVal sender As System.Object, _
ByVal e As System.EventArgs) Handles MyBase.Load
    Dim time As Integer
    Dim start As Integer = time = System.DateTime.Now.Millisecond()
    Me.Size = New Size(SCREENW, SCREENH)
    Me.Text = TITLE

    'initialize directx
    d3d = New CDirect3D(Me)
    d3d.Init(SCREENW, SCREENH, True)
    keyboard = New CKeyboard(Me)

    'load font
    font1 = New CBitmapFont(d3d)
    font1.Load("arial18.png")
    font1.SetColumns(16)
    font1.SetLetterSize(32, 32)
    font1.SetStartFrame(128)
    font1.SpacingModifier = 14
```

```
    'create the tile scroller
    scroller = New CTileScroller(d3d, SCREENW, SCREENH, TILEW, TILEH,
    COLUMNS)
    scroller.MapWidthInTiles = MAPW
    scroller.MapHeightInTiles = MAPH
    scroller.ScrollX = 0
    scroller.ScrollY = 0

    'load the tiles
    scroller.LoadTiles("ireland.bmp", 512, 512)

    'load tilemap
    Load_MAR("ireland.mar", MAPW, MAPH)

    'load hero sprite
    hero = New CSprite(d3d)
    hero.Load("hero_sword_walk.png")
    hero.Columns = 9
    hero.StartFrame = 0
    hero.EndFrame = 8
    hero.FrameThreshold = 3
    hero.FrameWidth = 96
    hero.FrameHeight = 96
    hero.SetPosition((SCREENW - 96) / 2, (SCREENH - 96) / 2)

    'initialize timer
    clock = New Timer()
    clock.Interval = 20
    clock.Start()
End Sub
```

The next routine is clock_Tick, which is our de facto game loop until a better solution presents itself. (I have some ideas about that, which I'll share with you in the next chapter.) This routine calls some helper routines, such as UpdateScrollPosition, PrintScrollData, and CheckInput, to bring the demo to life.

```
Private Sub clock_Tick(ByVal sender As Object, ByVal e As System.EventArgs)_
Handles clock.Tick
    Static scrollRect As New Rectangle(20, 20, 760, 560)

    UpdateScrollPosition()
    scroller.UpdateTilemap(mapdata)
```

```
        d3d.StartRendering(Color.Black)
        d3d.StartSprites()

        scroller.Draw(scrollRect)
        hero.Animate()
        hero.DrawFrame()
        PrintScrollData()

        d3d.StopSprites()
        d3d.StopRendering()

        'get input
        CheckInput()
End Sub
```

The next two routines are `PrintScrollData` and `Load_MAR`. `PrintScrollData` calculates the current tile number under the player character's sprite at the center of the window and prints out that tile number. This crucial piece of information will be automatically calculated next chapter when we begin building the game engine.

```
Public Sub PrintScrollData()
        Dim player As Point
        Dim tile As Point
        Dim tilenum As Long

        player.X = scroller.ScrollX + SCREENW / 2
        player.Y = scroller.ScrollY + SCREENH / 2
        tile.X = player.X \ TILEW
        tile.Y = player.Y \ TILEH

        tilenum = mapdata(tile.Y * MAPW + tile.X)

        font1.Print(40, 40, Color.Black, _
            "Scroll = " + player.X.ToString + "," + player.Y.ToString)

        font1.Print(40, 70, Color.Black, _
            "Tile (" + tile.X.ToString + "," + tile.Y.ToString + ") = " _
            + tilenum.ToString)
End Sub

Public Sub Load_MAR(ByVal filename As String, ByVal lWidth As Long, _
ByVal lHeight As Long)
```

```
Dim n As Long
Dim i As Short

'open the binary map file
FileOpen(1, filename, OpenMode.Binary, OpenAccess.Read, OpenShare.
Default)

'prepare the array for the map data
ReDim mapdata(lWidth * lHeight)

'read the map data
For n = 0 To lWidth * lHeight - 1
    'read one short integer
    FileGet(1, i)
    'reverse bytes
    mapdata(n) = i / 32 - 1
Next n

'close the file
FileClose(1)
End Sub
```

CheckInput is quite a lengthy subroutine, not because it's complex but rather because it handles the player character's movement and the velocity of the scroller. Depending on the direction the character sprite is facing, the scroller will be adjusted to move in the appropriate direction via a helper routine called SetScroll. Depending on the direction, the sprite's StartFrame, EndFrame, and CurrentFrame properties are set so that the sprite will "walk" in that direction. There is a feature in this program that is helpful when testing a large map: When you are holding the Shift key while walking, the scroller will move faster than normal so you can quickly zoom across the map if you wish.

```
Public Sub CheckInput()
    keyboard.Poll()

    If keyboard.KeyState(Key.Up) Or keyboard.KeyState(Key.NumPad8) Then 'N
        hero.StartFrame = 0
        hero.EndFrame = 8
        hero.CurrentFrame = 0
        SetScroll(0, -HEROSPEED)
    End If
    If keyboard.KeyState(Key.NumPad9) Then 'NE
```

```
    hero.StartFrame = 9 * 1
    hero.EndFrame = hero.StartFrame + 8
    hero.CurrentFrame = hero.StartFrame
    SetScroll(HEROSPEED, -HEROSPEED)
End If
If keyboard.KeyState(Key.NumPad6) Or keyboard.KeyState(Key.Right)
Then 'E
    hero.StartFrame = 9 * 2
    hero.EndFrame = hero.StartFrame + 8
    hero.CurrentFrame = hero.StartFrame
    SetScroll(HEROSPEED, 0)
End If
If keyboard.KeyState(Key.NumPad3) Then 'SE
    hero.StartFrame = 9 * 3
    hero.EndFrame = hero.StartFrame + 8
    hero.CurrentFrame = hero.StartFrame
    SetScroll(HEROSPEED, HEROSPEED)
End If
If keyboard.KeyState(Key.NumPad2) Or keyboard.KeyState(Key.Down)
Then 'S
    hero.StartFrame = 9 * 4
    hero.EndFrame = hero.StartFrame + 8
    hero.CurrentFrame = hero.StartFrame
    SetScroll(0, HEROSPEED)
End If
If keyboard.KeyState(Key.NumPad1) Then 'SW
    hero.StartFrame = 9 * 5
    hero.EndFrame = hero.StartFrame + 8
    hero.CurrentFrame = hero.StartFrame
    SetScroll(-HEROSPEED, HEROSPEED)
End If
If keyboard.KeyState(Key.NumPad4) Or keyboard.KeyState(Key.Left)
Then 'W
    hero.StartFrame = 9 * 6
    hero.EndFrame = hero.StartFrame + 8
    hero.CurrentFrame = hero.StartFrame
    SetScroll(-HEROSPEED, 0)
End If
If keyboard.KeyState(Key.NumPad7) Then 'NW
    hero.StartFrame = 9 * 7
    hero.EndFrame = hero.StartFrame + 8
    hero.CurrentFrame = hero.StartFrame
    SetScroll(-HEROSPEED, -HEROSPEED)
End If
```

```
    If keyboard.KeyState(Key.LeftShift) Or keyboard.KeyState(Key.
    RightShift) Then
        SuperHero = True
    End If

    If keyboard.KeyState(Key.Escape) Then
        clock.Stop()
        Me.Close()
    End If

End Sub

Public Sub SetScroll(ByVal horiz As Long, ByVal vert As Long)
    SpeedX = horiz
    SpeedY = vert

    If SuperHero Then
        SpeedX = SpeedX * 4
        SpeedY = SpeedY * 4
    End If
End Sub
```

The last two subroutines in the WalkAbout program are UpdateScrollPosition and Form1_Closing. The UpdateScrollPosition routine is called from the game loop to move the scrolling position based on the SpeedX and SpeedY variables, which determine the direction the scroller moves, and these variables are set by the SetScroll routine based on user input.

```
Public Sub UpdateScrollPosition()
    Dim GameWorldW As Long = MAPW * TILEW
    Dim GameWorldH As Long = MAPH * TILEH

    'update horizontal scrolling position and speed
    scroller.ScrollX = scroller.ScrollX + SpeedX
    If (scroller.ScrollX < 0) Then
        scroller.ScrollX = 0
        SpeedX = 0
    ElseIf scroller.ScrollX > GameWorldW - SCREENW Then
        scroller.ScrollX = GameWorldH - SCREENW
        SpeedX = 0
    End If
    'update vertical scrolling position and speed
    scroller.ScrollY = scroller.ScrollY + SpeedY
```

```
        If scroller.ScrollY < 0 Then
            scroller.ScrollY = 0
            SpeedY = 0
        ElseIf scroller.ScrollY > GameWorldW - SCREENH Then
            scroller.ScrollY = GameWorldH - SCREENH
            SpeedY = 0
        End If
    End Sub

    Private Sub Form1_FormClosing(ByVal sender As Object, _
    ByVal e As System.Windows.Forms.FormClosingEventArgs) _
    Handles Me.FormClosing
        d3d = Nothing
        keyboard = Nothing
    End Sub

End Class
```

Level Up

This chapter produced the first real prototype of the game that you have seen so far, by pulling together the tile-based scroller, the texture-based sprite code, and keyboard input. These classes work in tandem to produce a scroller with an animated sprite at the center, which moves in a direction specified using the arrow keys and the numeric keypad for motion. You can literally walk anywhere in the map now using a fully animated sprite for the player's character. Although the map of Ireland is sparse at this point, that was intentional because now you have a large game world that you can customize to suit your own imagination.

Although this island resembles Ireland, your game players need not know that detail, as you could just as easily call it by another name. Without seeing the entire game world, the player has no real sense of the shape of the world because it is so immense (unless you provide a map). Furthermore, you could build several games out of the single map by using different parts of it. As you'll learn in the coming chapters, adding scenery and inanimate objects, as well as NPCs, make an otherwise spartan world come to life.

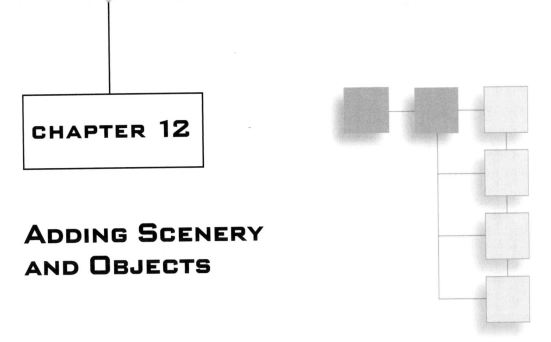

CHAPTER 12

ADDING SCENERY AND OBJECTS

This chapter shows you how to fill the world with scenery and keep the player from walking through solid objects. This scenery is added to the game world in such a way that does not require you to edit the map file. Instead, objects such as trees can be added to the game using sprites to make it a livelier place in which to host the overall storyline and gameplay. You learn how to add inanimate objects, such as trees, bushes, buildings, and other objects, to fill the mostly empty terrain in the game. These inanimate objects are solid so that the player's character (PC) cannot walk through them (similar to solid tiles that are impassable). Here are the major topics in this chapter:

- Inserting random scenery

- The scenery container lists

- Loading the scenery graphics

- Modifying the game loop

- Keeping the player out of the scenery

- Drawing the scenery sprites

The World Is a Desert

The current game world is a big, empty, barren, desolate, boring place considering that it's supposed to be the home for the characters in the game—not to mention that the game is supposed to be fun! To liven up the world, you need to add some scenery. I'll show you how to add some random trees to the world—with collision detection—and you can adapt this code to just about any cosmetic graphic image that you want to add to the game world. There are a lot of sprites in the graphic collection of Reiner's Tilesets that liven up the world, including 3D renderings of houses, buildings, castles, towers, windmills, and many different types of trees! You can access these renderings at www.reinerstileset.de.

There are some great pieces of artwork available that you can use to beautify this game world. I focus on planting a few dozen random trees on the landscape near where the player's character starts off in the game, to show you how such objects are added to the game. You can add any other type of graphic to the game, and it is included in the collision detection routine (so the player can't walk through these solid objects).

The artwork for the scenery in this chapter includes four very highly detailed trees that have been modeled and rendered (like all of Reiner's artwork). You can see the four trees used to spruce up the game world in Figure 12.1. The effect of the trees is even greater when you notice that there are many small transparent regions among the tree leaves, which increases the realism.

Although we could really go all out by adding many items of scenery to the game world, I just want to give you an example in this chapter of *how* to add scenery items, rather than actually filling the world with items. However, there is a performance penalty if you use too many scenery items added randomly across the game world. Although it's important to have scenery in the game world, make your scenery important and relevant and put it in locations that are likely to be seen by the player. The game engine is smart enough to ignore objects that are nowhere near the player, but the game must still go through all of the scenery

Figure 12.1
These four trees help improve the appearance of the game world.

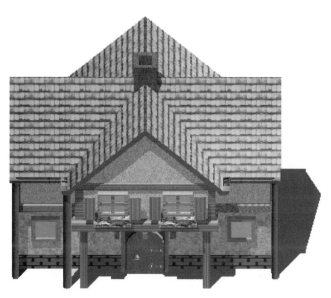

Figure 12.2
This house is used as a scenery object in the game.

objects in a list and evaluate each one. So, go ahead and add several hundred scenery objects. In fact, the game can probably handle a few thousand objects. But note that there will be a performance hit because all of those objects must be "looked at" by the game's logic even if those objects are not visible on the screen.

In addition to the trees, I've added one house to each of the towns in the game. All of the towns have been added to a list of locations that includes the town's name and coordinates in the game world. So, by iterating through the list of locations, you can add scenery items near the town. This is exactly what is done in the example Scenery Collision program in this chapter. Figure 12.2 shows the house artwork. This is just one house of many available in Reiner's Tileset collection, and I've reduced its size by half. Although the house is not to scale with the player, it is less obtrusive this way, and besides, we aren't going for too much realism with this game. You may use this as a basis for building up the towns according to your own design. Reiner provides castles, keeps, houses, walls, fences, wells, roads, signs, and other real-world items that would make the game interesting.

Inserting Random Scenery

What I want to do is use these four trees and house artwork to add random scenery to the game world. The sprites are represented using the CSprite class and randomly placed in the game world—although that placement is close to each town, rather than just sprinkled randomly throughout the world, so the player is more likely to see them. It's unusual to find a lone tree out in the middle of nowhere without any other trees nearby, so when adding random trees and other scenery objects, I recommend adding them in groves or small bunches. Remember how huge this game world is? Well, even a few hundred trees is rather spartan for this large world, so placing them all near the towns makes them more likely to be seen, which makes the game a little more interesting.

When you turn this into a complete game, you can easily change the code that places the trees and have it scatter the trees throughout the entire countryside. And remember that you can adapt this code to include inanimate objects other than trees; you can randomly place huts, shacks, houses, windmills, rocks, and even small mountains (all of which are available in Reiner's Tilesets). Figure 12.3 shows the new version of Celtic Crusader with scenery added.

Figure 12.3
The new version of the game now features solid trees and houses.

The Scenery List

Let's get started working on the new code for the scenery. For starters, I'm just using four pieces of artwork to represent the trees, and currently just a single house image. These sprites are randomly placed near each of the towns in the game world. You can modify these values if you want to add scenery or increase the total number of scenery items that are placed on the map.

The town locations are made available using a custom structure and a list called locations:

```
Structure LocationType
    Dim name As String
    Dim x As Integer
    Dim y As Integer
    Dim radius As Integer
 End Structure

 Dim locations As List(Of LocationType)
```

The locations list is filled with town information manually. I didn't use any fancy constant array or anything. Instead, the towns are just added to the list one at a time in the LoadLocations subroutine, although a helper called CreateLocation cleans up the code a bit.

```
Private Sub LoadLocations()
    'all locations are referenced by tile #, not pixels
    locations = New List(Of LocationType)

    'Leinster Region
    CreateLocation("Dubh Linn", 1350, 950, 10)
    CreateLocation("Swords", 1340, 860, 10)
    CreateLocation("Monasterboice", 1280, 690, 10)
    CreateLocation("Kells", 1080, 645, 10)
    CreateLocation("Kildare", 1125, 1050, 10)
    CreateLocation("Glendalough", 1265, 1175, 10)
    CreateLocation("Durrow", 1135, 1295, 10)
    CreateLocation("Wicklow", 1446, 1209, 10)
    CreateLocation("Birr", 915, 1126, 10)
    CreateLocation("Wexford", 1336, 1503, 10)
    CreateLocation("Waterford", 1147, 1610, 10)

    'Connaught Region
    CreateLocation("Clonmacnoise", 808, 1006, 10)
    CreateLocation("Clonfirt", 700, 1050, 10)
```

```
'Munster Region
CreateLocation("Limerick", 645, 1370, 10)
CreateLocation("Ardfert", 288, 1564, 10)
CreateLocation("Cork", 397, 1840, 10)

'Ulster Region
CreateLocation("Devinish", 802, 500, 10)
CreateLocation("Moyille", 630, 135, 10)
CreateLocation("Derry", 928, 180, 0)
CreateLocation("Armagh", 1120, 375, 10)
CreateLocation("Downpatrick", 1312, 412, 10)
CreateLocation("Bangor", 1390, 270, 10)

End Sub

Public Sub CreateLocation(ByVal name As String, ByVal x As Integer, _
ByVal y As Integer, ByVal radius As Integer)
    Dim loc As LocationType
    loc.name = name
    loc.x = x
    loc.y = y
    loc.radius = radius
    locations.Add(loc)
End Sub
```

Finally we come to the scenery list definition. This is a linked list of CSprite objects called sceneryList. As a dynamically sized list, it has essentially unlimited room for scenery objects (limited only by available memory). This is a far superior solution than using an array with for loops to access it (as was done in the first edition of this book!).

```
Private sceneryList As List(Of CSprite)
```

Loading the Scenery Graphics

A subroutine called LoadScenery, called from Form1_Load, loads all of the scenery objects and places them in the game world. Important disclaimer: I've chosen to write simple code here in order to get scenery into the game world, but it takes up a *ton* of memory doing it this way. That's the usual tradeoff for simplicity—a lack of efficiency. But we'll rectify the problem next chapter by causing scenery to share artwork. Basically, each scenery image is loaded for each item, without any image sharing. If you load 100 trees, you will get 100 individual tree images in memory, even though they are duplicated.

Anyway, this LoadScenery routine adds a single house and 10 random trees to each town. There are no controls that keep the objects from overlapping each other this early in the game's development (another item for the to-do list!).

```
Public Sub LoadScenery()
    Dim loc As LocationType
    Dim spr As CSprite
    Dim n As Integer

    'create scenery list
    sceneryList = New List(Of CSprite)

    'iterate through the towns
    For Each loc In locations

        'add 10 trees to each town
        For n = 1 To 10
            spr = New CSprite(d3d)
            spr.Identifier = 901
            spr.Load("trees.png")
            spr.FrameWidth = 128
            spr.FrameHeight = 128
            spr.Columns = 4
            spr.CurrentFrame = rand.Next(4)
            spr.SetPosition(loc.x + rand.Next(500), loc.y + rand.Next(500))
            sceneryList.Add(spr)
        Next

        'add 1 building to each town
        spr = New CSprite(d3d)
        spr.Identifier = 900
        spr.Load("house2.png")
        spr.FrameWidth = 192
        spr.FrameHeight = 192
        spr.Columns = 1
        spr.SetPosition(loc.x + 6, loc.y + 2)
        sceneryList.Add(spr)
    Next
End Sub
```

Modifying the Game Loop

Now I'd like to show the complete game loop so you can see how everything is being handled by the game. The various update and drawing routines are called from here inside the game loop and generally must be in the order that you see here. For instance, the tile and scenery collision code must come before the tile scroller is updated because the collision routines modify ScrollX and ScrollY. You know ScrollX and ScrollY are directly responsible for the current view of the game world on the screen. Within a timed code block section in the game loop are the drawing routines that display everything on the screen.

The game loop here has some new state-based code that helps when loading the large game world tilemap from the ireland_map.mar file. Because this file is large and we are only reading it sequentially, it takes time to load. Rather than just show a frozen window, I've added some code here that displays the progress on the screen. Figure 12.4 shows this progress screen.

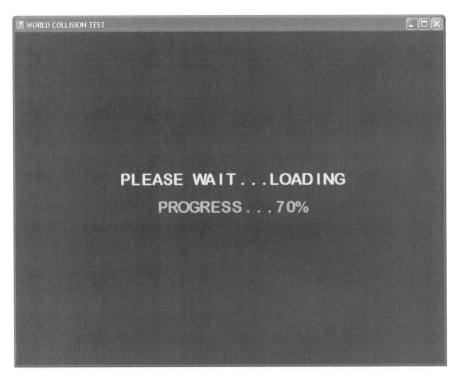

Figure 12.4
This screen displays the progress while the large tilemap file is loaded.

```
Private Sub clock_Tick(ByVal sender As Object, ByVal e As System.EventArgs) _
    Handles clock.Tick
        Static scrollRect As New Rectangle(0, 0, 800, 576)
        Static start As Integer = System.DateTime.Now.Millisecond()

        If gameover Then
            clock.Stop()
            Me.Close()
            Return
        End If

        If mapState = mapStates.NOTLOADED Then
            mapState = mapStates.LOADING
            Load_MAR(MAPDATAFILE, MAPW, MAPH)

        ElseIf mapState = mapStates.LOADING Then
            d3d.StartRendering(Color.DarkBlue)
            d3d.StartSprites()
            font1.Print(190, 250, Color.Yellow, "PLEASE WAIT...LOADING")
            font1.Print(260, 300, Color.Orange, "PROGRESS..." + _
                mapLoadProgress.ToString("NO") + "%")
            d3d.StopSprites()
            d3d.StopRendering()

        ElseIf mapState = mapStates.LOADED Then
            CheckInput()
            UpdateScrollPosition()
            CheckSceneryCollisions()
            scroller.UpdateTilemap(mapdata)
            CheckLocations()
            hero.Animate()

            If DateTime.Now.Millisecond() > start + 20 Then
                start = DateTime.Now.Millisecond()

                d3d.StartRendering(Color.Black)
                d3d.StartSprites()

                scroller.Draw(scrollRect)
                DrawScenery()
                hero.DrawFrame()
                PrintScrollData()
```

```
            d3d.StopSprites()
            d3d.StopRendering()
        End If
    End If
End Sub
```

Keeping the Player Out of the Scenery

Scenery is one thing, but realistic scenery is quite another. In my opinion, everything in the game should react to the solid tiles and scenery, so eventually when we add non-player characters to the game, they will need to avoid obstacles in the game too. But let's start with preventing the player from walking through scenery objects. The CheckSceneryCollisions subroutine first checks to see whether a scenery sprite is visible in the current viewport. If so, then the routine checks for a collision with the player's sprite and adjusts ScrollX and ScrollY if necessary. Because this occurs before the tile scroller is updated, it appears as if the player simply cannot pass through (when in fact, the player's sprite is being moved back a few pixels after a collision).

```
Public Sub CheckSceneryCollisions()
    Dim spr As CSprite
    Dim pos As Point
    Dim objectRect As Rectangle
    Dim adjust As Integer

    'grab a zone around the player slightly larger than the screen
    Dim screenArea As New Rectangle(player.locationPixels.X - 200, _
        player.locationPixels.Y - 200, SCREENW + 400, SCREENH + 400)

    'surround player with a rectangle (reduced to improve collision)
    Dim playerRect As New Rectangle(SCREENW / 2 - 24, SCREENH / 2 - 24, 48, 48)

    'check all scenery objects
    For Each spr In sceneryList
        'find scenery object's global pixel position
        pos.X = (spr.GetX * 32) + spr.FrameWidth / 2
        pos.Y = (spr.GetY * 32) + spr.FrameHeight / 2

        'is this scenery object visible on the screen?
        If screenArea.Contains(pos.X, pos.Y) Then
            pos.X = spr.GetX * 32 - player.locationPixels.X
            pos.Y = spr.GetY * 32 - player.locationPixels.Y
```

```
            'surround scenery object in a rectangle
            adjust = spr.FrameWidth / 4
            objectRect = New Rectangle(pos.X + adjust, pos.Y + adjust, _
                spr.FrameWidth - adjust * 2, spr.FrameHeight - adjust * 2)

            If objectRect.IntersectsWith(playerRect) Then
                scroller.ScrollX -= SpeedX
                scroller.ScrollY -= SpeedY
                SpeedX = 0
                SpeedY = 0
            End If
        End If
    Next
End Sub
```

Drawing the Scenery Sprites

Assuming that a scenery sprite is visible in the current viewport (which represents the visible portion of the game world, centered around the player's sprite),
then the scenery sprites are drawn in the viewport at an adjusted position that
corresponds to the player's position. One good feature of this routine is that it
draws the scenery sprites even when they are outside the bounds of the screen,
so they will appear to slowly come into view (rather than "popping" into the
viewport, as our previous edition used to do!). We gain this attractive means of
drawing sprites using Direct3D's camera view, which becomes a virtual clipping
region. (In reality, Direct3D.Sprite renders sprites onto a 3D surface, not actually
to the video buffer.)

```
Public Sub DrawScenery()
    Dim spr As CSprite
    Dim pos As Point

    Dim screenArea As New Rectangle(player.locationPixels.X - 200, _
        player.locationPixels.Y - 200, SCREENW + 400, SCREENH + 400)

    For Each spr In sceneryList
        'is this scenery object near the player?
        pos.X = (spr.GetX * 32) + spr.FrameWidth / 2
        pos.Y = (spr.GetY * 32) + spr.FrameHeight / 2

        If screenArea.Contains(pos.X, pos.Y) Then
            pos.X = spr.GetX * 32 - player.locationPixels.X
```

```
            pos.Y = spr.GetY * 32 - player.locationPixels.Y
            spr.DrawFrame(pos)
        End If
    Next
End Sub
```

New Character Animations

I have converted the animation strips for the Paladin wielding a sword for the version of Celtic Crusader presented in this chapter.

New Hero Animations

Figure 12.5 shows the hero character's walking animation sequences, and he is wielding a sword. We will continue to use this bitmap as the primary sprite sheet for the player's character for the upcoming new versions of the game, although in the next chapter we'll add a new character creation screen that will allow the player to choose a character class for use in the game!

Figure 12.5
The Paladin's walking animation frames.

The Latest Code

I have intentionally left out much of the code for the example provided for this chapter and have chosen to just focus on the key code. I recommend you open the example project provided on the CD-ROM to examine the complete source code. The project is called Scenery Collision and can be considered the first "alpha" version of Celtic Crusader! The game is beginning to take shape. The chapters in the upcoming Part III, "The Characters," will give us an opportunity to put all of the code we've developed in this chapter into a new class that will function as our RPG engine.

Level Up

This chapter provided the ability to add cosmetic improvements to the game in the form of solid scenery. These items of scenery currently include four trees and a house, which are tested for collision with the player to give them a realistic feel in the game. You can add your own scenery objects to the game world using the same basic code provided in this chapter, as the list of objects can easily accommodate new artwork. Just remember that your texture files must be stored with a standard texture resolution, such as 256×256, 512×512, or 1024×1024. If you get strange errors when loading an image for the game, be sure to double check the resolution, because it may be an oddly sized image that Direct3D can't convert up to one of the standard formats.

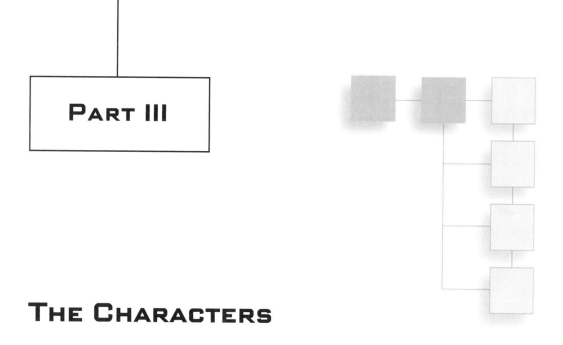

PART III

THE CHARACTERS

Part III starts off with a chapter on creating the player character and a chapter on items and a player inventory system. The next chapter focuses on non-player characters (NPCs) and monsters that make good fodder for the player to use for gaining experience and leveling up. Just getting NPCs into the game world is the first issue; following that, you expand on the idea by making it possible to interact with the NPCs by communicating with them. By the time you have finished with this part of the book, you will have a much more playable game in Celtic Crusader, and the only thing left to do will be to add a combat system, which you'll do in the final chapter.

- Chapter 13: Creating the Player Character

- Chapter 14: Building the Celtic Crusader Engine

- Chapter 15: Keeping Track of Inventory

- Chapter 16: Adding NPCs and Monsters

- Chapter 17: Engaging in Combat

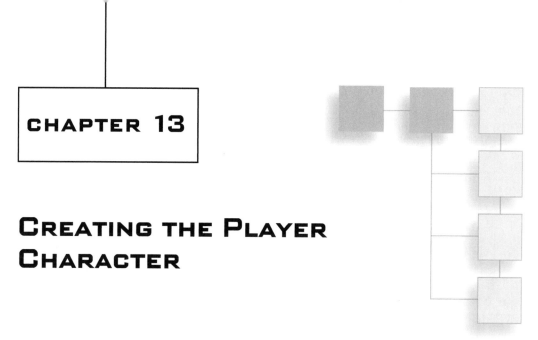

CHAPTER 13

CREATING THE PLAYER CHARACTER

This chapter provides a discussion of player character creation with the usual base and player-selectable attributes and skills from a selection of character classes (Warrior, Paladin, Scout, and Wizard). You will learn how to take the designs of the character classes and make use of them in the game by applying the player character's attributes to the combat system and other aspects of any traditional RPG, such as gaining experience and leveling up. Here is a breakdown of the major topics in this chapter:

- Character classes and attributes

- Gaining experience and leveling up

- The base character classes

- The character class data type

Character Classes and Attributes

All of the previous chapters have focused on the difficult task of getting a player, fully animated, to walk around in the game world. Both the animation and the movement should be realistic, and tile-collision detection should prevent the player from walking through solid and impassable tiles (which still requires some work but is coming together). Now that these basic problems have been solved, you can get more into the game's design and into the nuances of combat and NPC interaction. The player attributes are as follows:

- **Strength** represents the character's ability to carry a weight and swing a weapon. It is generally good for the warrior and knight classes, which carry blunt weapons. Strength is used to calculate the attack value for the character.

- **Dexterity** represents the agility of the character, the ability to manipulate objects (such as a weapon), and the skill with which the player uses his or her hands in general. A very low dexterity means the character is clumsy, while a very high dexterity means the character can perform complex actions.

- **Stamina** represents a character's *endurance,* the ability to continue performing an activity for a long period of time. Very high stamina provides a character with the ability to engage in lengthy battles without rest, while a character with low stamina tires quickly (and is likely to fall in battle).

- **Intellect** represents the character's ability to learn, remember things, and solve problems. A very high intellect is required by the mage class, while relatively low intellect is common in fighter classes, where brute force is more important than mental faculties. This trait affects the amount of experience gained for performing actions.

- **Charisma** represents the character's attractiveness and generally affects how others respond to the character. A character with very high charisma attracts others, while very low charisma repels others. Charisma may also reflect the scariness of a monster.

Gaining Experience and Leveling Up

One of the most rewarding aspects of a role-playing game (RPG) is gaining experience by performing actions in the game (usually combat) and leveling up your character. When you start the game, the character is also just starting out as a level 1 with no experience. This reflects the player's own skill level with the game, and that is the appeal of an RPG: *You,* the player, gain experience with the game while your PC gains experience at the same time.

Both you and your character improve as you play the game, so you transfer some of your own identity to the character. In some cases, younger players even assume some of the identity of their inspiring characters. This fascinating give-and-take relationship can really draw someone into your game if you design it well! Like I have said, cut back on the magic and let players really get out in the game world and experience some good, solid combat to make the whole experience feel more real.

The Base Character Classes

The standard, or *base,* classes can be used for the player as well as for the NPCs. You should feel free to create as many classes as you want to make your game world diversified and interesting. The classes I have described here are just the usual classes you find in an RPG, which you might consider the stock classes. Each class also has subclasses, or specialties within that class. For instance, Paladins are really just a subclass of the Knight, which may include Teutonic Knight, Crusader, and so on.

When you are designing a game, you can make it as historically accurate or as fictional as you want; don't feel compelled to make every class realistic or historically based. You might make up a completely fictional type of Knight subclass, such as a Dark Knight or a Gothic Knight, with some dark magic abilities. However, I want to encourage you to shy away from overdoing the magic system in a game. Many RPGs I have played use character classes that might be thought of as wizards on steroids, because the whole game boils down to upgrading spells and magic, with little emphasis on "realistic" combat.

You would be surprised by how effective an RPG can be with just a *few* magic abilities. You can really go overboard with the hocus pocus, and that tends to trivialize a well-designed storyline and render interesting characters into fireball targets. No warrior should be able to do *any* magic whatsoever. Think about it: The warriors are basically barbarians—massive, hulking fighters who use brute force to bash skulls on the battlefield (think Arnold Schwarzenegger in the *Conan* movies). This type of character can become civilized and educated, but so many games blur the line here and allow any class to develop magical abilities. I'm just pointing out some obvious design concerns with characters. If you really want a world of magic, then go ahead and create magical characters; that sounds like a really fun game, as a matter of fact! If you are designing a traditional RPG, then be realistic with your classes and keep the magic reasonable. Think about *The Lords of the Rings;* these stories are the sole source of inspiration for every RPG ever made. Everything since J.R.R. Tolkien has been derivative!

Tables 13.1 through 13.5 present my idea of a character class structure that you can use in the game for character class modifiers. The usual base value is 10 points

Table 13.1 Warrior

Attribute	Modifiers
Strength	+8
Dexterity	+4
Stamina	+6
Intellect	−3
Charisma	0

Table 13.2 Knight/Paladin

Attribute	Modifiers
Strength	+6
Dexterity	+4
Stamina	+3
Intellect	−3
Charisma	+5

Table 13.3 Rogue/Thief

Attribute	Modifiers
Strength	−1
Dexterity	+7
Stamina	+5
Intellect	+3
Charisma	+1

Table 13.4 Scout/Archer

Attribute	Modifiers
Strength	+3
Dexterity	+8
Stamina	+5
Intellect	−2
Charisma	+1

Table 13.5 Mage/Wizard

Attribute	Modifiers
Strength	−6
Dexterity	+3
Stamina	+5
Intellect	+9
Charisma	+4

Table 13.6 Peasant

Attribute	Modifiers
Strength	+2
Dexterity	+2
Stamina	+2
Intellect	0
Charisma	+1

for each attribute, so you'll want to keep that in mind when setting negative values. (You don't want to go below 1 point on any attribute.)

In addition to these combat classes, you might want to create some base classes for some of the regular people in the world, such as townsfolk, peasants, farmers, and so on. These non-combat NPCs might all just share the same character class (with weak combat skills, poor experience, and so on). See Table 13.6.

One design consideration that you might use is the concept of *class modifiers.* Say you have a set of stock classes like those listed in the preceding tables. Instead of re-creating a class from scratch using similar values, you can create a subclass based on the parent class, but that modifies the attributes by a small amount to produce the new class with custom attributes.

Say, for instance, that you want to create a new type of Warrior called the Berserker, which is an extremely stupid and ugly character with immense strength and stamina. Sounds a little bit scary, doesn't it? By setting the base class of the Berserker to Warrior, you can then modify the base class at any time, and the Berserker automatically is changed along with the base class (Warrior). This works great for balancing the gameplay without requiring that you modify *every single* subclass that you have used in the game. Since our character class system in

Celtic Crusader will be based on classes, we can easily subclass the base character classes to create new types of characters in this manner.

The Enemy and Monster Classes

We can also create fantasy creatures and monsters described in Tables 13.7 to 13.14. These creatures are unprecedented because they have no equal on the "good side." But you will not want to make all of the bad guys too powerful—save that for the unusual monsters that are rarely encountered, or the game will be way too hard to

Table 13.7 Dragon

Attribute	Modifiers
Strength	+30
Dexterity	+40
Stamina	+20
Intellect	0
Charisma	−9

Table 13.8 Orc

Attribute	Modifiers
Strength	+8
Dexterity	+2
Stamina	+7
Intellect	−6
Charisma	−8

Table 13.9 Ogre

Attribute	Modifiers
Strength	+6
Dexterity	+3
Stamina	−2
Intellect	−8
Charisma	−7

Table 13.10   Mummy

Attribute	Modifiers
Strength	+2
Dexterity	+3
Stamina	+3
Intellect	−6
Charisma	−2

Table 13.11   Skeleton

Attribute	Modifiers
Strength	+4
Dexterity	+5
Stamina	+1
Intellect	−8
Charisma	−6

Table 13.12   Zombie

Attribute	Modifiers
Strength	+2
Dexterity	+8
Stamina	+7
Intellect	−4
Charisma	−9

Table 13.13   Giant Spider

Attribute	Modifiers
Strength	+16
Dexterity	+18
Stamina	+15
Intellect	+5
Charisma	−9

Table 13.14 Crocodilian

Attribute	Modifiers
Strength	+12
Dexterity	+10
Stamina	+10
Intellect	+8
Charisma	−3

play. You will generally want to have at least one type of *bad guy* for each type of *character class* available to the player, and duplicate that character all over the game world. In addition, you must add weaker enemy characters that make good fodder for the player to help with leveling up. Because the human but otherwise *bad* characters share the same stats as the human *good guys,* we don't need to define them separately. Remember, these are generic class types, or races, not individuals.

Using Character Types in the Game

You know what type of data you want to use in the game based on the descriptions of the various classes. How, then, do you make use of those classes in the game? Among the many ways that you could approach this problem, two solutions immediately come to mind:

- Hard coded in source code

- Loaded from data files

The first option seems to be more reasonable, especially when you are just getting started. It does help to have a character class ready for use before deciding which method you would prefer to use in the game. Although a data file for each type of character or monster would make the game more data driven and expandable, our first goal is to *finish the game,* not to be overly concerned about what will happen *after* the game is finished. That's another important rule of game development: *Feature creep will ruin a game, not make it better.*

Managing the Character Stats

The base character class is the same for all types of characters (and even monsters) in the game, and all of the named classes (such as Warrior) are derived from this base class. This class includes the character's name, class, experience, and level, as well as the five attributes, and can be extended with any additional information you want to use. The Stats structure contains the properties that will make it possible to differentiate the various character and monster classes in the game. A constructor is included to make it easier to create new instances of the structure in code. This code is found in the Character module found in the Character.vb source file.

```
Public Structure Stats
    Dim STR As Short
    Dim DEX As Short
    Dim STA As Short
    Dim INT As Short
    Dim CHA As Short
    Dim Experience As Short
    Dim Level As Short
    Dim Name As String
    Dim ClassType As String

    Public Sub New(ByVal str As Short, ByVal dex As Short, _
    ByVal sta As Short, ByVal int As Short, ByVal cha As Short)
        Me.STR = str
        Me.DEX = dex
        Me.STA = sta
        Me.INT = int
        Me.CHA = cha
        Me.Experience = 0
        Me.Level = 1
    End Sub
End Type
```

Now let's use this character structure to define the characters we've discussed so far. Some of these might or might not make it into the game, but the artwork for them is available on the CD-ROM should you wish to use them.

```
'hero characters
Public Warrior As New Stats(8, 4, 6, -3, 0)
Public Paladin As New Stats(6, 4, 3, -3, 5)
Public Rogue As New Stats(-1, 7, 5, 3, 1)
Public Scout As New Stats(3, 8, 5, -2, 1)
Public Wizard As New Stats(-6, 3, 5, 9, 4)

'neutral characters
Public Peasant As New Stats(2, 2, 2, 0, 1)
'enemy characters and monsters
Public Dragon As New Stats(30, 40, 20, 0, -9)
```

```
Public Orc As New Stats(8, 2, 7, -6, -8)
Public Ogre As New Stats(6, 3, -2, -8, -7)
Public Mummy As New Stats(2, 3, 3, -6, -2)
Public Skeleton As New Stats(4, 5, 1, -10, -6)
Public Zombie As New Stats(2, 8, 7, -4, -9)
Public Spider As New Stats(16, 18, 15, 5, -9)
Public Crocodilian As New Stats(12, 10, 10, 8, -3)
```

The Characters Module

Let's put this code all together into a single module file so it can be added to the main game project in the next chapter and used for character stats. The Characters.vb file should contain the code provided a moment ago, in addition to the CreatePlayer subroutine, which is called when the player chooses a character. We'll develop the player selection screen in the next chapter.

```
Public Sub CreatePlayer(ByVal classname As String)
    'load sprite image specific to chosen class
    Select Case classname
        Case "WARRIOR"
            PlayerSprite.Load("warrior_walk.png")
        Case "PALADIN"
            PlayerSprite.Load("paladin_walk.png")
        Case "SCOUT"
            PlayerSprite.Load("scout_walk.png")
        Case "WIZARD"
            PlayerSprite.Load("wizard_walk.png")
    End Select

    'set additional properties
    PlayerClass = classname
    PlayerSprite.FrameThreshold = 2
    PlayerSprite.FrameWidth = 96
    PlayerSprite.FrameHeight = 96
    PlayerSprite.Columns = 8
    PlayerSprite.StartFrame = 0
    PlayerSprite.EndFrame = 7
    PlayerSprite.X = (800 - 96) / 2
    PlayerSprite.Y = (600 - 96) / 2
End Sub
```

We will make *extensive* modifications to the Characters module while continuing to develop the game.

Character Artwork

All of the characters and monsters discussed in this chapter have been chosen very carefully because we have artwork available for them. Generally, when a game is being designed from the ground up, the game designer will not limit himself to what artwork is available, because none exists before the game goes into development. But in our case, we have all of this fantastic artwork provided by Reiner Prokein (www.reinerstileset.de). I've defined characters based on the available artwork. Thanks to Reiner, we have a *lot* of characters!

I'm just going to show you a few of the character sprite sheets available for the game, but note that there are three sprite sheets for every character mentioned in this chapter:

- Walk animation

- Attack animation

- Die animation

Believe it or not, we have even *more* animations than these available (such as talking, getting hit, and running), but they are not universally available for *every* character. The additional animations can be found on Reiner's website. Figure 13.1 shows the three sprite sheets for the warrior character.

All of the sprite sheets used in Celtic Crusader were significantly manipulated from their original sources provided by Reiner Prokein. All of the sprites arranged in columns and rows in a sprite sheet and transparent regions have been converted to an alpha channel in each file, which is saved in the Portable Network Graphics (PNG) file format. When you visit Reiner's website, you will not find sprite sheets like these, as they are provided in individual bitmaps. Just be aware that additional work will be required on your part to add new characters or animations to your game.

In the Character Module folder on the CD-ROM under this chapter is the Characters.vb module file and the four character walk animations that are available at this point:

- Warrior Walking (warrior_walk.png)

- Paladin Walking (paladin_walk.png)

- Scout Walking (scout_walk.png)

- Wizard Walking (wizard_walk.png)

WALKING ANIMATION   **ATTACKING ANIMATION**

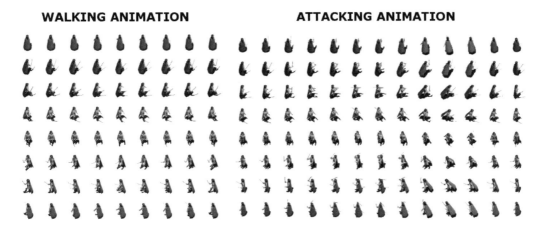

DYING ANIMATION

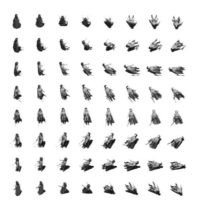

Figure 13.1
The warrior sprite sheets for walking, attacking, and dying.

Level Up

This chapter filled in the details of character attributes and classes. Now that things are looking pretty good in the game department, you can focus some attention again on character design. The last few chapters have focused on designing the game world and interacting with the world in general. After having read this chapter, I'm sure you are eager to add some characters to the world and give the player something to do! Stay tuned, because the next chapter gets into that subject while we create a title screen and a character selection screen, and gather all of the miscellaneous code developed thus far into a game engine class. The character selection screen in the next chapter will let you choose the character class and then play with that particular sprite animation and associated class stats.

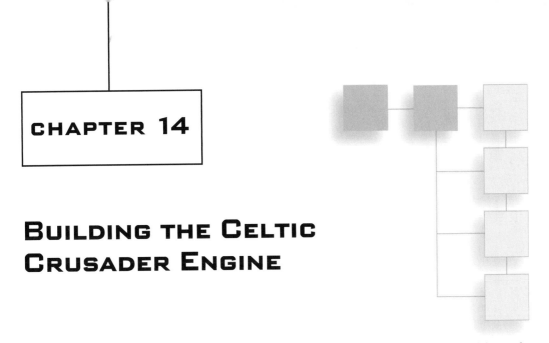

CHAPTER 14

BUILDING THE CELTIC CRUSADER ENGINE

In this chapter we'll create the core engine by putting all of the reusable code we've developed up to this point into a class that manages all of it, providing the most common objects and functions through one convenient "engine" class. Here is the plan:

- Assemble the game engine

- Add a title screen

- Choose a character class

Assembling the Game Engine

I've mentioned before that Celtic Crusader is too large to provide complete source code listings in the book, so I'll rely again on the files that come with the book on the CD-ROM. However, there have been *dramatic* changes made to the example project from the previous chapter in order to shift the development of Celtic Crusader from a demo program to a complete game based on a full-blown engine for handling all of our reusable code. Due to all of these changes, I'll provide the core engine code here and then, from this point forward in each chapter, we will simply modify it to customize the gameplay. You might think of this as our first "RPG engine."

Note

The source code in this book was meant to be studied, not necessarily typed in manually, because not every line of code for the featured game has been provided in print. The reason for this is length and the limitations of the *For Teens* book series. However, the RPGEngine and Form1 code listings that follow are provided in their entirety as a base starting point for the game engine.

You've already seen some of the code for the Characters.vb file, and we've built up a good assortment of classes into a game library that handles most of the heavy lifting regarding drawing a tilemap and sprites with Direct3D. Here are all of the files in the project at this point:

- CBitmapFont

- CDirect3D

- Characters

- CKeyboard

- CMouse

- CSprite

- CSoundDevice

- CSound

- CTileScroller

Up to this point we've been writing a lot of duplicate code for various mundane things, such as initializing Direct3D, the bitmapped fonts, the keyboard and mouse, and the tile scroller. These things will not really change during the development of the game so it would be helpful to move these common object definitions, constants, and variables into a reusable engine class. Having a single class handle all of these various details will allow us to simply create a new engine object in our main form code and call upon the engine's properties and methods to perform tasks such as rendering the scroll buffer.

The RPGEngine Class

Open the Celtic Crusader project from the CD-ROM in the folder for this chapter so you can follow along as we examine the code. A new class has been added to the project: "RPGEngine." The RPGEngine.vb file is quite lengthy, but it is divided up into regions using the #region…#end region feature of Visual Studio editor, so that huge portions of code are separated and kept distinct. I felt this was better than creating numerous helper classes. Now let's get started on the RPGEngine class.

RPGEngine Class Definition

First up is the class definition for Engine, which includes the variable definitions too.

```
'-------------------------------------------------------------
' Visual Basic Game Programming For Teens, Second Edition
' Chapter 13 - RPG ENGINE CORE
'-------------------------------------------------------------

Imports System
Imports System.Drawing
Imports Microsoft.DirectX
Imports Microsoft.DirectX.Direct3D
Imports Microsoft.DirectX.DirectInput

Public Class RPGEngine

#Region "ENGINE VARIABLES"
    Structure LocationType
        Dim name As String
        Dim x As Integer
        Dim y As Integer
        Dim radius As Integer
    End Structure

    Private p_d3d As CDirect3D
    Private p_keyboard As CKeyboard
    Private p_mouse As CMouse
    Private p_scroller As CTileScroller
    Private p_tiles As CSprite
    Private p_screenw As Integer
    Private p_screenh As Integer
    Private p_mapdata() As Byte
    Private p_bigfont As CBitmapFont
    Private p_smallfont As CBitmapFont
    Private ref_form As Windows.Forms.Control
    Private p_scrollRect As Rectangle
```

```
            Private p_mousepos As Point
            Private p_sceneryList As List(Of CSprite)
            Private p_locations As List(Of LocationType)

            Public SpeedX As Integer
            Public SpeedY As Integer
            Public MapLoadProgress As Single = 0.0
    #End Region
```

Core RPGEngine Routines

The following core engine routines include the constructor (the New subroutine), which first runs when the engine object is created by the main program. Also in this core code is a reference to the Direct3D object, scroll position (in other words, the player's location), and other global values that will be needed by the game.

```
#Region "CORE ENGINE"
    Public Sub New(ByRef frm As Windows.Forms.Control, ByVal title As String, _
    ByVal screenw As Integer, ByVal screenh As Integer)
        p_screenw = screenw
        p_screenh = screenh
        MousePos = New Point(400, 300)

        'initialize window
        ref_form = frm
        ref_form.Size = New Size(screenw + 8, screenh + 34)
        ref_form.Text = title

        'initialize directx
        p_d3d = New CDirect3D(ref_form)
        p_d3d.Init(screenw, screenh, True)
        p_keyboard = New CKeyboard(ref_form)
        p_mouse = New CMouse(ref_form)

        'load large font
        p_bigfont = New CBitmapFont(p_d3d)
        p_bigfont.Load("arial18.png")
        p_bigfont.SetColumns(16)
        p_bigfont.SetLetterSize(32, 32)
        p_bigfont.SetStartFrame(128)
        p_bigfont.SpacingModifier = 12
```

```
        'load small font
        p_smallfont = New CBitmapFont(p_d3d)
        p_smallfont.Load("trebuchet_verdana_10.png")
        p_smallfont.SetColumns(16)
        p_smallfont.SetLetterSize(16, 16)
        p_smallfont.SetStartFrame(0)
        p_smallfont.SpacingModifier = 6

        'create scenery manager
        p_sceneryList = New List(Of CSprite)

        'create locations manager
        p_locations = New List(Of LocationType)
    End Sub

    Public ReadOnly Property Direct3D() As CDirect3D
        Get
            Return p_d3d
        End Get
    End Property

    Public Sub Update()
        p_mouse.Poll()
        p_keyboard.Poll()
    End Sub

    Public Sub RenderStart()
        p_d3d.StartRendering(Color.DarkBlue)
        p_d3d.StartSprites()
    End Sub

    Public Sub RenderStop()
        p_d3d.StopSprites()
        p_d3d.StopRendering()
    End Sub

    Public Property ScrollX() As Integer
        Get
            Return p_scroller.ScrollX
        End Get
        Set(ByVal value As Integer)
            p_scroller.ScrollX = value
```

```
            End Set
        End Property

        Public Property ScrollY() As Integer
            Get
                    Return p_scroller.ScrollY
            End Get
            Set(ByVal value As Integer)
                p_scroller.ScrollY = value
            End Set
        End Property

        Public Function KeyDown(ByVal key As DirectInput.Key) As Boolean
            Return p_keyboard.KeyState(key)
        End Function

        Public Function MouseMove() As Point
            Return New Point(p_mouse.X, p_mouse.Y)
        End Function

        Public Function MouseWheel() As Integer
            Return p_mouse.Wheel
        End Function

        Public Property MousePos() As Point
            Get
                    Return p_mousepos
            End Get
            Set(ByVal value As Point)
                p_mousepos = value
            End Set
        End Property

        Public Function MouseClick(ByVal button As Integer) As Boolean
            If p_mouse.Button() > 0 Then
                Return True
            Else
                Return False
            End If
        End Function

        Public Sub Print(ByVal x As Integer, ByVal y As Integer, ByVal col As Color, _
        ByVal text As String, Optional ByVal shadow As Boolean = False)
```

```
        If shadow Then
            p_smallfont.Print(x + 1, y + 1, Color.Black, text)
        End If
        p_smallfont.Print(x, y, col, text)
    End Sub

    Public Sub PrintLarge(ByVal x As Integer, ByVal y As Integer, _
    ByVal col As Color, ByVal text As String, _
    Optional ByVal shadow As Boolean = False)
        If shadow Then
            p_bigfont.Print(x + 1, y + 1, Color.Black, text)
        End If
        p_bigfont.Print(x, y, col, text)
    End Sub
#End Region
```

Game World (Tile Scroller) Code

The game world code includes all of the reusable routines developed in the last few chapters and some new ones for a modified version of the old Load_MAR routine. Remember that it used to load up a map file within a while loop? That is not very user friendly, and I don't want the player to sit there staring at a blank screen for several seconds while it loads, so I made some changes. Now, from the main game loop, you can call the new LoadMapTiles routine incrementally, and it will keep the file open until the map has been completely loaded. This is more of a *passive* way to load the file, and it allows you to engage the player while the map is loading (essentially in the background).

Figure 14.1 shows the new title screen for the game. Note the message in the bottom-left corner, printing the map loading progress. When you click the screen, the title screen is replaced by the character selection screen, shown in Figure 14.2. The map loading progress continues to print out on this screen as well, while the player chooses a character. This is all handled by the ChooseCharacter routine in the main Form1 source code file.

```
' - - - - - - - - - - - - - - - - - - - - - - - - - - - - - - - - - - - - -
' GAME WORLD (TILE SCROLLER) RELATED CODE
' - - - - - - - - - - - - - - - - - - - - - - - - - - - - - - - - - - - - -
#Region "GAME WORLD"
    Public Sub CreateScroller(ByVal mapw As Integer, ByVal maph As Integer, _
```

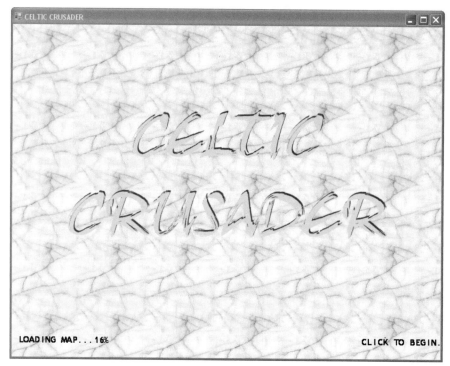

Figure 14.1
The title screen is shown to the player while the map loads.

```
        ByVal tilew As Integer, ByVal tileh As Integer, ByVal columns As Integer)

        'create the tile scroller
        p_scroller = New CTileScroller(p_d3d, p_screenw, p_screenh, _
            tilew, tileh, columns)
        p_scroller.MapWidthInTiles = mapw
        p_scroller.MapHeightInTiles = maph
    End Sub

    Public Sub OpenMapFile(ByVal mapfile As String)
        'round off scroll buffer height to nearest whole tile
        Dim scrollheight As Integer = CInt(p_screenh \ p_scroller.TileWidth) _
            * p_scroller.TileWidth
        p_scrollRect = New Rectangle(0, 0, p_screenw, scrollheight)

        'open the binary map file
        FileOpen(1, mapfile, OpenMode.Binary, OpenAccess.Read, OpenShare.
        Default)
```

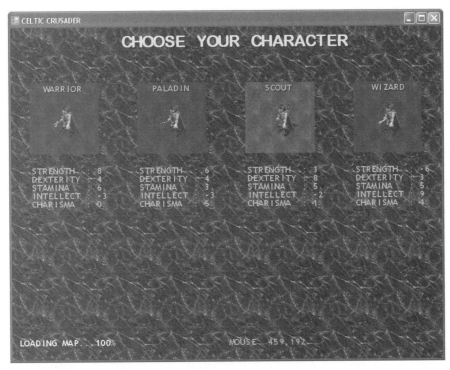

Figure 14.2
The character selection screen (with map loading progress).

```
        'prepare the array for the map data
        ReDim p_mapdata(p_scroller.MapWidthInTiles * p_scroller.MapHeight
        InTiles)
End Sub

Public Sub LoadMapTiles(ByVal tilesfile As String, _
ByVal tilefilewidth As Integer, ByVal tilefileheight As Integer)

        p_scroller.LoadTiles(tilesfile, tilefilewidth, tilefileheight)

End Sub

Public Sub MapLoadUpdate()
        Static position As Integer = 0
        Static tile As Short
        Static width As Integer = p_scroller.MapWidthInTiles
        Static height As Integer = p_scroller.MapHeightInTiles
```

```
            'passive map loading--note there is no loop
            If position < width * height - 1 Then
                'read one short integer
                FileGet(1, tile)

                'reverse bytes
                p_mapdata(position) = tile / 32 - 1

                'update progress
                MapLoadProgress = position / (width * height) * 100.0

                'move to the next tile #
                position += 1
            Else
                MapLoadProgress = 100.0
                FileClose(1)
            End If

    End Sub

    Public ReadOnly Property GetTileAt(ByVal location As Point)
        Get
            Return p_mapdata(location.Y * p_scroller.MapWidthInTiles +
            location.X)
        End Get
    End Property

    Public Sub SetScrollSpeed(ByVal horiz As Long, ByVal vert As Long)
        SpeedX = horiz
        SpeedY = vert
    End Sub

    Public Sub UpdateScroller()
        UpdateScrollPosition()
        p_scroller.UpdateTilemap(p_mapdata)
    End Sub

    Public Sub DrawScroller()
        p_scroller.Draw(p_scrollRect)
    End Sub

    Public Sub UpdateScrollPosition()
```

```
        Dim GameWorldW As Long = p_scroller.MapWidthInTiles * p_scroller.
        TileWidth
        Dim GameWorldH As Long = p_scroller.MapHeightInTiles * p_scroller.
        TileHeight

        'update horizontal scrolling position and speed
        p_scroller.ScrollX = p_scroller.ScrollX + SpeedX
        If (p_scroller.ScrollX < 0) Then
            p_scroller.ScrollX = 0
            SpeedX = 0
        ElseIf p_scroller.ScrollX > GameWorldW - p_screenw Then
            p_scroller.ScrollX = GameWorldH - p_screenw
            SpeedX = 0
        End If

        'update vertical scrolling position and speed
        p_scroller.ScrollY = p_scroller.ScrollY + SpeedY
        If p_scroller.ScrollY < 0 Then
            p_scroller.ScrollY = 0
            SpeedY = 0
        ElseIf p_scroller.ScrollY > GameWorldW - p_screenh Then
            p_scroller.ScrollY = GameWorldH - p_screenh
            SpeedY = 0
        End If

    End Sub
#End Region
```

Scenery-Related Code

The next section of code handles the scenery, which was originally added to the
game in Chapter 12. Now all of the scenery routines are located in the RPGEngine
class file.

```
'-------------------------------------------------------------------
' SCENERY RELATED CODE
'-------------------------------------------------------------------
#Region "SCENERY"
    Public Sub AddScenery(ByRef sprite As CSprite)
        p_sceneryList.Add(sprite)
    End Sub

    Public Sub DrawScenery(ByVal location As Point)
```

```
        Dim spr As CSprite
        Dim pos As Point

        Dim screenArea As New Rectangle(location.X - 200, location.Y - 200, _
            800 + 400, 600 + 400)

        For Each spr In p_sceneryList
            'is this scenery object near the player?
            pos.X = (spr.X * 32) + spr.FrameWidth / 2
            pos.Y = (spr.Y * 32) + spr.FrameHeight / 2

            If screenArea.Contains(pos.X, pos.Y) Then
                pos.X = spr.X * 32 - location.X
                pos.Y = spr.Y * 32 - location.Y
                spr.DrawFrame(pos)
            End If
        Next
    End Sub

    Public Sub CheckSceneryCollisions(ByVal location As Point)
        Dim spr As CSprite
        Dim pos As Point
        Dim objectRect As Rectangle
        Dim adjust As Integer

        'grab a zone around the player slightly larger than the screen
        Dim screenArea As New Rectangle(location.X - 200, _
            location.Y - 200, 800 + 400, 600 + 400)

        'surround player with a rectangle (reduced to improve collision)
        Dim playerRect As New Rectangle(400 - 24, 300 - 24, 48, 48)

        'check all scenery objects
        For Each spr In p_sceneryList

            'find scenery object's global pixel position
            pos.X = (spr.X * 32) + spr.FrameWidth / 2
            pos.Y = (spr.Y * 32) + spr.FrameHeight / 2

            'is this scenery object visible on the screen?
            If screenArea.Contains(pos.X, pos.Y) Then
                pos.X = spr.X * 32 - location.X
                pos.Y = spr.Y * 32 - location.Y
```

```
                    'surround scenery object in a rectangle
                    adjust = spr.FrameWidth / 5
                    objectRect = New Rectangle(pos.X + adjust, pos.Y + adjust, _
                        spr.FrameWidth - adjust * 2, spr.FrameHeight - adjust * 2)

                    If objectRect.IntersectsWith(playerRect) Then
                        ScrollX -= SpeedX
                        ScrollY -= SpeedY
                        SpeedX = 0
                        SpeedY = 0
                    End If

                End If
            Next
        End Sub
#End Region
```

Location-Related Code

The location-related routines provide functionality for the locations list, which was added in the previous chapter as well. Recall that a location can be anyplace on the map that you identify with a name and a global coordinate. I have thus far only defined the locations of all of the towns in Celtic Crusader, but new locations can easily be added. For instance, you might define locations on the game world where certain types of monsters reside, and when the monsters are killed they will respawn from that single location. How about a Dragon hatchery or an Orc nest?

```
'--------------------------------------------------------------
' LOCATION RELATED CODE
'--------------------------------------------------------------
#Region "LOCATIONS"

    Public ReadOnly Property Locations() As List(Of LocationType)
        Get
            Return p_locations
        End Get
    End Property

    Public Sub CreateLocation(ByVal name As String, ByVal x As Integer, _
    ByVal y As Integer, ByVal radius As Integer)
```

```
        Dim loc As LocationType
        loc.name = name
        loc.x = x
        loc.y = y
        loc.radius = radius
        p_locations.Add(loc)
    End Sub

    Public Sub LoadLocations()
        'Leinster Region
        CreateLocation("Dubh Linn", 1350, 950, 10)
        CreateLocation("Swords", 1340, 860, 10)
        CreateLocation("Monasterboice", 1280, 690, 10)
        CreateLocation("Kells", 1080, 645, 10)
        CreateLocation("Kildare", 1125, 1050, 10)
        CreateLocation("Glendalough", 1265, 1175, 10)
        CreateLocation("Durrow", 1135, 1295, 10)
        CreateLocation("Wicklow", 1446, 1209, 10)
        CreateLocation("Birr", 915, 1126, 10)
        CreateLocation("Wexford", 1336, 1503, 10)
        CreateLocation("Waterford", 1147, 1610, 10)

        'Connaught Region
        CreateLocation("Clonmacnoise", 808, 1006, 10)
        CreateLocation("Clonfirt", 700, 1050, 10)

        'Munster Region
        CreateLocation("Limerick", 645, 1370, 10)
        CreateLocation("Ardfert", 288, 1564, 10)
        CreateLocation("Cork", 397, 1840, 10)

        'Ulster Region
        CreateLocation("Devinish", 802, 500, 10)
        CreateLocation("Moyille", 630, 135, 10)
        CreateLocation("Derry", 928, 180, 0)
        CreateLocation("Armagh", 1120, 375, 10)
        CreateLocation("Downpatrick", 1312, 412, 10)
        CreateLocation("Bangor", 1390, 270, 10)
    End Sub

    Public Sub GotoLocation(ByVal town As Integer)
        Dim loc As LocationType
        loc = p_locations(town)
```

```
            ScrollX = (loc.x - 8) * 32
            ScrollY = (loc.y - 8) * 32
        End Sub
#End Region
```

Miscellaneous Engine Code

The last portion of code for the Engine class includes the destructor (Finalize), which performs cleanup duties, and some helper routines that have already come in handy in the main game's code.

```
'----------------------------------------------------------------------
' MISCELLANEOUS CODE
'----------------------------------------------------------------------
#Region "MISCELLANEOUS"
    Public Function Contains(ByVal p As Point, ByVal r As Rectangle)
        Return r.Contains(p)
    End Function

    Public Function Contains(ByVal x As Integer, ByVal y As Integer, _
    ByVal r As Rectangle)

        Return r.Contains(x, y)

    End Function

    Public Function ScreenRect() As Rectangle

        Return New Rectangle(0, 0, 800, 600)

    End Function

    Protected Overrides Sub Finalize()
        MyBase.Finalize()
        p_d3d = Nothing
        p_keyboard = Nothing
        p_mouse = Nothing
    End Sub
#End Region

End Class
```

The Main Source Code File

Now that we have gone through the complete code listing for the game engine class, we'll explore the main source code file contained in Form1.vb. The main code is dramatically shortened due to the bulk of the game code being moved into the engine. For the sake of clarity, I will provide the complete code listing here, but this will not become a practice. This project will need the following library references added:

- Microsoft.DirectX

- Microsoft.DirectX.Direct3D

- Microsoft.DirectX.DirectInput

- Microsoft.DirectX.DirectSound

- Microsoft.DirectX.AudioVideoPlayback

The main code for the game is now under the control of a true game loop, and the old timer has been abandoned. The structure of the startup code and the loop follows professional game programming practices, and this code resembles true game engine code now. Let's take a look at the definitions for our program:

```
' - - - - - - - - - - - - - - - - - - - - - - - - - - - - - - - - - - - - - - - - - - - - - - - -
' Visual Basic Game Programming For Teens, Second Edition
' Chapter 13 - Celtic Crusader
' - - - - - - - - - - - - - - - - - - - - - - - - - - - - - - - - - - - - - - - - - - - - - - - -
Imports System
Imports System.Drawing
Imports Microsoft.DirectX
Imports Microsoft.DirectX.Direct3D
Imports Microsoft.DirectX.DirectInput
Imports Microsoft.DirectX.DirectSound
Imports Microsoft.DirectX.AudioVideoPlayback

Public Class Form1

    Public Enum GameStates
        STARTUP = 0
        MAPLOADING = 1
        MAPLOADED = 2
    End Enum
```

```
Private engine As Engine
Private GameOver As Boolean = False
Private rand As Random
Public GameState As GameStates
Private locationName As String
Private locationPixels As Point
Private locationTiles As Point
```

Take a look at that small variables list—that's a far cry from what it looked like previously, with nearly a full page of definitions. It is *wonderful* how much an engine (or even just a game library) cleans up the code and allows you to focus on the truly important stuff—designing and building the game and making it *fun*. Now let's take a look at the startup subroutine. Note how the major objects being created and helper routines being called are described in very high-level terms, such as "location manager." This type of terminology is appropriate for the front end of the game now, since all of the real work is being done behind the scenes in the Engine class. After everything is loaded and ready to go, the Start() routine is called.

```
Private Sub Form1_Load(ByVal sender As System.Object, _
ByVal e As System.EventArgs) Handles MyBase.Load
    GameState = GameStates.STARTUP
    rand = New Random(My.Computer.Clock.TickCount())

    'init the game engine
    engine = New RPGEngine(Me, "CELTIC CRUSADER", 800, 600)

    'init player manager
    PlayerSprite = New CSprite(engine.Direct3D)

    'init location manager
    locationName = ""
    locationPixels = New Point(0, 0)
    locationTiles = New Point(0, 0)
    engine.LoadLocations()

    'init scenery manager
    LoadScenery()

    'init tilemap manager
    engine.CreateScroller(1500, 2000, 32, 32, 16)
    engine.LoadMapTiles("ireland_tiles.bmp", 512, 512)
```

```
        engine.ScrollX = 1345 * 32
        engine.ScrollY = 945 * 32
        engine.OpenMapFile("ireland_map.mar")

        Me.Show()
        Application.DoEvents()
        Start()
    End Sub
```

The Start subroutine contains a real game loop! Finally! This routine performs several calls to support routines in order to make the game function properly. The first thing you should notice is that there is some timing inside the while loop, with some routines being called from within the timed portion, and some being called outside of the timing. This is a vitally important issue! The game must be allowed to update itself as *quickly as possible*, without timing code bogging it down. At the same time, we *do* want some things to function consistently, such as the screen refresh and user input.

The update routine that is called outside of any timing, and therefore runs without limitation, is called InsaneUpdate. The update routine that is called from within the timed portion of the loop is called CivilizedUpdate. Both routines receive the current tick count value as a parameter, should you wish to use it for any additional fine-tuning of your game with sub-millisecond timing. The CivilizedUpdate call is sandwiched between the engine's RenderStart and RenderStop routines, which handle both the 3D rendering, 2D sprite drawing, and screen refreshing. As a result, you could not use this engine for any 3D graphics. To provide 3D support again, you would need to detach the 2D sprite call. Just remember that CivilizedUpdate does all of the drawing!

```
Public Sub Start()
    Dim time As Integer = 0

    'start up the game loop
    While Not GameOver

        'updates run as fast as possible
        engine.Update()
        InsaneUpdate(time)

        'render at a consistent framerate
        If My.Computer.Clock.TickCount() > time + 20 Then
            time = My.Computer.Clock.TickCount()
```

```
            engine.RenderStart()
            CivilizedUpdate(time)
            engine.RenderStop()

            Application.DoEvents()

            If engine.KeyDown(Key.Escape) Then GameOver = True

        End If

    End While

    Application.Exit()

End Sub
```

The `InsaneUpdate` subroutine runs as fast as the game loop can call it, without any timing of any kind. This works great for time-critical game code, such as the scroller update. We don't want to draw the scroller this fast, but we do want to update the scroll buffer as quickly as possible to keep the display looking smooth. The `GameState` variable is used here to break up the game loop into parts, which makes it possible to display the title screen, character selection, and main game screen all from the same routine, simply based on the state of the game.

```
Public Sub InsaneUpdate(ByVal time As Integer)
    Select Case GameState

        'keep updating mapload regardless of what we're doing on the screen
        Case GameStates.STARTUP, GameStates.MAPLOADING

            'update passive map loading process
            If engine.MapLoadProgress < 100.0 Then
                engine.MapLoadUpdate()
            Else
                'don't move on until player chooses a class
                If PlayerClass <> "" Then
                    GameState = GameStates.MAPLOADED
                End If
            End If

        Case GameStates.MAPLOADED

            'update scroll position and scroll buffer
            engine.UpdateScroller()
```

```
            engine.CheckSceneryCollisions(locationPixels)
            CheckLocations()

            'update player's position based on scroll location
            locationPixels = New Point(engine.ScrollX + 400 - 48, _
                engine.ScrollY + 300 - 48)
            locationTiles.X = locationPixels.X / 32
            locationTiles.Y = locationPixels.Y / 32

        End Select
    End Sub
```

The `CivilizedUpdate` routine is next, providing all of the graphics output of the game in a timely fashion. With a 20-millisecond delay, the game screen will refresh at about 50 frames per second (FPS).

```
Public Sub CivilizedUpdate(ByVal time As Integer)
    Select Case GameState
        Case GameStates.STARTUP
            TitleScreen()
            engine.Print(10, 560, Color.Black, "LOADING MAP..." + _
                engine.MapLoadProgress.ToString("N0") + "%")

        Case GameStates.MAPLOADING

            ChooseCharacter()
            engine.Print(10, 560, Color.White, "LOADING MAP..." + _
                engine.MapLoadProgress.ToString("N0") + "%")

        Case GameStates.MAPLOADED

            CheckInput()

            engine.DrawScroller()
            engine.DrawScenery(locationPixels)
            PlayerSprite.Animate()
            PlayerSprite.DrawFrame()

            Dim tilenum As Long
            tilenum = engine.GetTileAt(locationTiles)

            engine.Print(20, 20, Color.Black, _
                "Scroll = " + locationPixels.X.ToString + "," + _
                locationPixels.Y.ToString)
```

```
        engine.Print(20, 35, Color.Black, _
            "Tile (" + locationTiles.X.ToString + "," + _
            locationTiles.Y.ToString + ") = " + tilenum.ToString)

        engine.Print(650, 20, Color.White, "LOCATION:")
        engine.Print(650, 35, Color.White, locationName)


    End Select
End Sub
```

The `TitleScreen` subroutine is called by `CivilizedUpdate` to draw the title screen and look for a mouse click before switching control over to the character selection screen.

```
Public Sub TitleScreen()
    Static title As New CSprite(engine.Direct3D)
    Static clicked As Boolean = False
    Static rect As New Rectangle(10, 300, 800, 300)

    If Not clicked Then
        If title.Image Is Nothing Then
            title.Load("title.bmp")
            title.FrameSize = New Point(800, 600)
            title.Columns = 1
        End If

        title.DrawFrame()
        engine.Print(650, 560, Color.Black, "CLICK TO BEGIN...")

        'limit mouse click to bottom half of screen
        If rect.Contains(engine.MousePos) Then
            If engine.MouseClick(1) Then
                clicked = True
            End If
        End If

    Else
        title = Nothing
        GameState = GameStates.MAPLOADING
    End If
End Sub
```

The `ChooseCharacter` subroutine is a monster because it's so huge. But it does have one redeeming quality: It is completely self-contained, using static variables for all images, and it runs fast as a result. This routine displays the four character classes and allows the player to choose a class to use for his or her character in the game. I wanted this routine to be self-contained because it required so many sprites that would have cluttered the main program with globals. This routine demonstrates the Character module for the first time, using the stats for the Warrior, Paladin, Scout, and Wizard characters created in the Character module.

```
Public Sub ChooseCharacter()
    Static marble As New CSprite(engine.Direct3D)
    Static warrior As New CSprite(engine.Direct3D)
    Static knight As New CSprite(engine.Direct3D)
    Static archer As New CSprite(engine.Direct3D)
    Static wizard As New CSprite(engine.Direct3D)
    Static selection1 As New CSprite(engine.Direct3D)
    Static selection2 As New CSprite(engine.Direct3D)
    Static selection3 As New CSprite(engine.Direct3D)
    Static selection4 As New CSprite(engine.Direct3D)
    Static selection_normal As New CSprite(engine.Direct3D)
    Static selection_highlight As New CSprite(engine.Direct3D)
    Static spriteChosen As Boolean = False
    Static mousePos As New CSprite(engine.Direct3D)
    Static screenBounds As New Rectangle(0, 0, 800, 600)
    Dim pos As PointF

    If Not spriteChosen Then

        'load the marble background
        If marble.Image Is Nothing Then
            marble.Load("marble.bmp")
        End If

        'load normal and highlight selection boxes
        If selection_normal.Image() Is Nothing Then
            selection_normal.Load("selection_normal.png")
        End If
        If selection_highlight.Image Is Nothing Then
            selection_highlight.Load("selection_highlight.png")
        End If

        ' load the warrior sprite and selection box
        If selection1.Image Is Nothing Then
            selection1.Image = selection_normal.Image
```

```
        selection1.Columns = 1
        selection1.Position = New Point(35, 100)
        selection1.FrameSize = New Point(128, 128)
    End If

    If warrior.Image() Is Nothing Then
        warrior.Load("warrior_walk.png")
        warrior.Columns = 8
        warrior.FrameSize = New Point(96, 96)
        warrior.StartFrame = 40
        warrior.EndFrame = 40 + 7
        warrior.FrameThreshold = 4
        warrior.CurrentFrame = warrior.StartFrame
        warrior.X = selection1.X + 20
        warrior.Y = selection1.Y + 20
    End If

    'load the knight sprite and selection box
    If selection2.Image() Is Nothing Then
        selection2.Image = selection_normal.Image
        selection2.Columns = 1
        selection2.Position = New Point(235, 100)
        selection2.FrameSize = New Point(128, 128)
    End If
    If knight.Image Is Nothing Then
        knight.Load("paladin_walk.png")
        knight.Columns = 8
        knight.FrameSize = New Point(96, 96)
        knight.StartFrame = 40
        knight.EndFrame = 40 + 7
        knight.FrameThreshold = 4
        knight.CurrentFrame = knight.StartFrame
        knight.X = selection2.X + 20
        knight.Y = selection2.Y + 20
    End If

    'load the archer sprite and selection box
    If selection3.Image() Is Nothing Then
        selection3.Image = selection_normal.Image
        selection3.Columns = 1
        selection3.Position = New Point(435, 100)
        selection3.FrameSize = New Point(128, 128)
    End If
```

```
If archer.Image() Is Nothing Then
    archer.Load("scout_walk.png")
    archer.Columns = 8
    archer.FrameSize = New Point(96, 96)
    archer.StartFrame = 40
    archer.EndFrame = 40 + 7
    archer.FrameThreshold = 4
    archer.CurrentFrame = archer.StartFrame
    archer.X = selection3.X + 20
    archer.Y = selection3.Y + 20
End If

'load the wizard sprite and selection box
If selection4.Image() Is Nothing Then
    selection4.Image = selection_normal.Image
    selection4.Columns = 1
    selection4.Position = New Point(635, 100)
    selection4.FrameSize = New Point(128, 128)
End If
If wizard.Image() Is Nothing Then
    wizard.Load("wizard_walk.png")
    wizard.Columns = 8
    wizard.FrameSize = New Point(96, 96)
    wizard.StartFrame = 40
    wizard.EndFrame = 40 + 7
    wizard.FrameThreshold = 4
    wizard.CurrentFrame = wizard.StartFrame
    wizard.X = selection4.X + 20
    wizard.Y = selection4.Y + 20
End If

'draw background
marble.Draw(engine.ScreenRect, engine.ScreenRect)
engine.PrintLarge(200, 10, Color.Yellow, "CHOOSE YOUR CHARACTER", True)

'draw characters and selection boxes
selection1.DrawFrame()
warrior.Animate()
warrior.DrawFrame()

selection2.DrawFrame()
knight.Animate()
knight.DrawFrame()
```

```
selection3.DrawFrame()
archer.Animate()
archer.DrawFrame()

selection4.DrawFrame()
wizard.Animate()
wizard.DrawFrame()

'print character class names
pos = selection1.Position
engine.Print(pos.X + 24, pos.Y + 2, Color.Orange, "WARRIOR", True)
engine.Print(pos.X, pos.Y + 150, Color.Orange, "STRENGTH  : " + _
    Character.Warrior.STR.ToString)
engine.Print(pos.X, pos.Y + 165, Color.Orange, "DEXTERITY : " + _
    Character.Warrior.DEX.ToString)
engine.Print(pos.X, pos.Y + 180, Color.Orange, "STAMINA   : " + _
    Character.Warrior.STA.ToString)
engine.Print(pos.X, pos.Y + 195, Color.Orange, "INTELLECT : " + _
    Character.Warrior.INT.ToString)
engine.Print(pos.X, pos.Y + 210, Color.Orange, "CHARISMA  : " + _
    Character.Warrior.CHA.ToString)

pos = selection2.Position
engine.Print(pos.X + 24, pos.Y + 2, Color.Orange, "PALADIN", True)
engine.Print(pos.X, pos.Y + 150, Color.Orange, "STRENGTH  : " + _
    Character.Paladin.STR.ToString)
engine.Print(pos.X, pos.Y + 165, Color.Orange, "DEXTERITY : " + _
    Character.Paladin.DEX.ToString)
engine.Print(pos.X, pos.Y + 180, Color.Orange, "STAMINA   : " + _
    Character.Paladin.STA.ToString)
engine.Print(pos.X, pos.Y + 195, Color.Orange, "INTELLECT : " + _
    Character.Paladin.INT.ToString)
engine.Print(pos.X, pos.Y + 210, Color.Orange, "CHARISMA  : " + _
    Character.Paladin.CHA.ToString)

pos = selection3.Position
engine.Print(pos.X + 33, pos.Y + 2, Color.Orange, "SCOUT", True)
engine.Print(pos.X, pos.Y + 150, Color.Orange, "STRENGTH  : " + _
    Character.Scout.STR.ToString)
engine.Print(pos.X, pos.Y + 165, Color.Orange, "DEXTERITY : " + _
    Character.Scout.DEX.ToString)
engine.Print(pos.X, pos.Y + 180, Color.Orange, "STAMINA   : " + _
    Character.Scout.STA.ToString)
```

```
engine.Print(pos.X, pos.Y + 195, Color.Orange, "INTELLECT : " + _
    Character.Scout.INT.ToString)
engine.Print(pos.X, pos.Y + 210, Color.Orange, "CHARISMA  : " + _
    Character.Scout.CHA.ToString)

pos = selection4.Position
engine.Print(pos.X + 33, pos.Y + 2, Color.Orange, "WIZARD", True)
engine.Print(pos.X, pos.Y + 150, Color.Orange, "STRENGTH  : " + _
    Character.Wizard.STR.ToString)
engine.Print(pos.X, pos.Y + 165, Color.Orange, "DEXTERITY : " + _
    Character.Wizard.DEX.ToString)
engine.Print(pos.X, pos.Y + 180, Color.Orange, "STAMINA   : " + _
    Character.Wizard.STA.ToString)
engine.Print(pos.X, pos.Y + 195, Color.Orange, "INTELLECT : " + _
    Character.Wizard.INT.ToString)
engine.Print(pos.X, pos.Y + 210, Color.Orange, "CHARISMA  : " + _
    Character.Wizard.CHA.ToString)

'update mouse movement
mousePos.Position = engine.MousePos
mousePos.FrameSize = New Point(8, 8)
engine.Print(400, 560, Color.DarkGray, "MOUSE: " + _
    mousePos.X.ToString + "," + mousePos.Y.ToString)

'highlight selection boxes when mouse moves over
If selection1.CollidesWith(mousePos) Then
    selection1.Image = selection_highlight.Image
    If engine.MouseClick(1) Then
        spriteChosen = True
        CreatePlayer("WARRIOR")
    End If
Else
    selection1.Image = selection_normal.Image
End If

If selection2.CollidesWith(mousePos) Then
    selection2.Image = selection_highlight.Image
    If engine.MouseClick(1) Then
        spriteChosen = True
        CreatePlayer("PALADIN")
    End If
Else
    selection2.Image = selection_normal.Image
```

```
        End If

        If selection3.CollidesWith(mousePos) Then
            selection3.Image = selection_highlight.Image
            If engine.MouseClick(1) Then
                spriteChosen = True
                CreatePlayer("SCOUT")
            End If
        Else
            selection3.Image = selection_normal.Image
        End If

        If selection4.CollidesWith(mousePos) Then
            selection4.Image = selection_highlight.Image
            If engine.MouseClick(1) Then
                spriteChosen = True
                CreatePlayer("WIZARD")
            End If
        Else
            selection4.Image = selection_normal.Image
        End If

    Else
        'character has been chosen; destroy static resources
        warrior = Nothing
        knight = Nothing
        archer = Nothing
        wizard = Nothing
        selection1 = Nothing
        selection2 = Nothing
        selection3 = Nothing
        selection4 = Nothing
        mousePos = Nothing
    End If
End Sub
```

For the sake of completeness I'll provide the last few routines here to make the program in this chapter even though you've seen these before. (They were developed in the previous chapter.) Once again, this is the one and only time I'll provide complete listings, so this chapter is a keystone point in the book.

```
Public Sub LoadScenery()
    Dim loc As Engine.LocationType
```

```
        Dim spr As CSprite
        Dim n As Integer

        'iterate through the towns
        For Each loc In engine.locations

            'add 10 trees to each town
            For n = 1 To 10
                spr = New CSprite(engine.Direct3D)
                spr.Identifier = 901
                spr.Load("trees.png")
                spr.FrameSize = New Point(128, 128)
                spr.Columns = 4
                spr.CurrentFrame = rand.Next(4)
                spr.Position = New Point(loc.x + rand.Next(20), loc.y + rand.Next(20))
                engine.AddScenery(spr)
            Next

            'add 1 building to each town
            spr = New CSprite(engine.Direct3D)
            spr.Identifier = 900
            spr.Load("house2.png")
            spr.FrameWidth = 192
            spr.FrameHeight = 192
            spr.Columns = 1
            spr.Position = New Point(loc.x + 6, loc.y + 2)
            engine.AddScenery(spr)
        Next
End Sub

Public Sub CheckLocations()
    Dim tilex, tiley As Integer
    Dim loc As Engine.LocationType
    Dim rect As Rectangle

    tilex = (engine.ScrollX + 400) / 32
    tiley = (engine.ScrollY + 300) / 32

    For Each loc In engine.Locations
        rect = New Rectangle(loc.x - loc.radius, loc.y - loc.radius, _
            loc.radius * 2, loc.radius * 2)
```

```
            If rect.Contains(tilex, tiley) Then
                locationName = loc.name
                Return
            End If
        Next

    locationName = "Wandering"
End Sub

Public Sub CheckInput()
    engine.SetScrollSpeed(0, 0)
    PlayerSprite.AnimationFlag = False

    'numeric keypad moves character
    If engine.KeyDown(Key.Up) Or engine.KeyDown(Key.NumPad8) Then 'N
        PlayerSprite.StartFrame = 0
        PlayerSprite.EndFrame = 7
        PlayerSprite.AnimationFlag = True
        engine.SetScrollSpeed(0, -1)

    ElseIf engine.KeyDown(Key.NumPad9) Then 'NE
        PlayerSprite.StartFrame = 8 * 1
        PlayerSprite.EndFrame = PlayerSprite.StartFrame + 7
        PlayerSprite.AnimationFlag = True
        engine.SetScrollSpeed(1, -1)

    ElseIf engine.KeyDown(Key.NumPad6) Or engine.KeyDown(Key.Right) Then 'E
        PlayerSprite.StartFrame = 8 * 2
        PlayerSprite.EndFrame = PlayerSprite.StartFrame + 7
        PlayerSprite.AnimationFlag = True
        engine.SetScrollSpeed(1, 0)

    ElseIf engine.KeyDown(Key.NumPad3) Then 'SE
        PlayerSprite.StartFrame = 8 * 3
        PlayerSprite.EndFrame = PlayerSprite.StartFrame + 7
        PlayerSprite.AnimationFlag = True
        engine.SetScrollSpeed(1, 1)

    ElseIf engine.KeyDown(Key.NumPad2) Or engine.KeyDown(Key.Down) Then 'S
        PlayerSprite.StartFrame = 8 * 4
        PlayerSprite.EndFrame = PlayerSprite.StartFrame + 7
        PlayerSprite.AnimationFlag = True
        engine.SetScrollSpeed(0, 1)
```

```
    ElseIf engine.KeyDown(Key.NumPad1) Then 'SW
        PlayerSprite.StartFrame = 8 * 5
        PlayerSprite.EndFrame = PlayerSprite.StartFrame + 7
        PlayerSprite.AnimationFlag = True
        engine.SetScrollSpeed(-1, 1)

    ElseIf engine.KeyDown(Key.NumPad4) Or engine.KeyDown(Key.Left) Then 'W
        PlayerSprite.StartFrame = 8 * 6
        PlayerSprite.EndFrame = PlayerSprite.StartFrame + 7
        PlayerSprite.AnimationFlag = True
        engine.SetScrollSpeed(-1, 0)

    ElseIf engine.KeyDown(Key.NumPad7) Then 'NW
        PlayerSprite.StartFrame = 8 * 7
        PlayerSprite.EndFrame = PlayerSprite.StartFrame + 7
        PlayerSprite.AnimationFlag = True
        engine.SetScrollSpeed(-1, -1)
    End If

    'function keys F1-F12 quick jump to towns
    If engine.KeyDown(Key.F1) Then engine.GotoLocation(0)
    If engine.KeyDown(Key.F2) Then engine.GotoLocation(1)
    If engine.KeyDown(Key.F3) Then engine.GotoLocation(2)
    If engine.KeyDown(Key.F4) Then engine.GotoLocation(3)
    If engine.KeyDown(Key.F5) Then engine.GotoLocation(4)
    If engine.KeyDown(Key.F6) Then engine.GotoLocation(5)
    If engine.KeyDown(Key.F7) Then engine.GotoLocation(6)
    If engine.KeyDown(Key.F8) Then engine.GotoLocation(7)
    If engine.KeyDown(Key.F9) Then engine.GotoLocation(8)
    If engine.KeyDown(Key.F10) Then engine.GotoLocation(9)
    If engine.KeyDown(Key.F11) Then engine.GotoLocation(10)
    If engine.KeyDown(Key.F12) Then engine.GotoLocation(11)
End Sub

Private Sub Form1_MouseMove(ByVal sender As Object, _
ByVal e As System.Windows.Forms.MouseEventArgs) Handles Me.MouseMove

    engine.MousePos = New Point(e.X, e.Y)

End Sub
End Class
```

Test Run

With the new character selection screen now available, the game takes on a whole new dimension of playability (even though we haven't added combat or character interaction yet). Figure 14.3 shows the main game after the Paladin character has been selected. Likewise, Figure 14.4 shows the game now with the Scout character chosen. Since the sprite sheets for these characters are configured in the same way, we can rely on the sprites drawing correctly after simply changing the filename depending on the chosen character class. As you can clearly see, not a thing has changed in the way the game functions, but we have moved about three-fourths of the code out of the main code file and into a support class. From this point forward, working on the game will be dramatically easier. (Now if we can just get the darned trees to stop growing up through the houses!)

Figure 14.3
The Paladin character wields a sword and performs good deeds (at least, in theory).

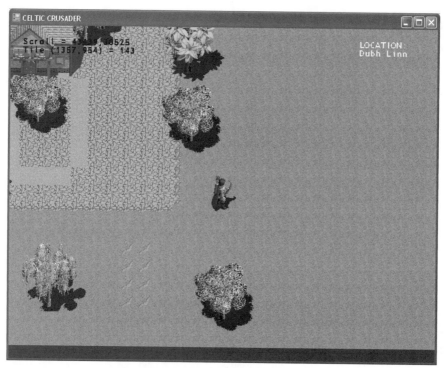

Figure 14.4
The Scout character bears a bow.

Level Up

This chapter pulled together all of the concepts and code developed up to this point and developed a comprehensive game engine for use by Celtic Crusader (and any future games you may have planned). We aren't finished with the engine by any means! On the contrary, there is much work still needed before this will be a true RPG.

CHAPTER 15

KEEPING TRACK OF INVENTORY

Some role-playing games are so focused on inventory micromanagement that they lose track of the fun factor and replace real gameplay with inventory management! I've seen some RPGs allow the player to carry around *tons* of inventory items. (I mean literally *thousands* of pounds of items!) This is, of course, completely ridiculous. But some players like micromanagement. I guess there's room for those types of games, as long as there are players for them. I've always been a fan of the simpler approach—giving the player simple weapon, armor, and modifier items. Why should the player want to spend hours of game time swapping armor items when a single suit of armor would be easier to deal with? (Some games allow you to configure chest plate, leggings, helmet, bracers, and so on individually.) There's certainly some realism in this, but does it make a game more *fun*? We'll discuss this subject and the approach we'll be taking in Celtic Crusader in this chapter. Here are the key topics:

- Managing inventory

- Creating the player

- Creating items

Managing Inventory

Isn't it great that the game engine has been developed up to the point where we can begin discussing higher-level topics, such as character creation and inventory management? It feels as if all the hard work getting to this point was justified. Now I'll explain the approach I've decided to take with Celtic Crusader when it comes to managing inventory.

There are many different approaches or possible directions we could take with an inventory system. One possibility is to give the player a "backpack" in which all inventory items are stored. (This is used in a lot of games.) Another approach is to display a list of inventory items by name (popular in online MUDs [*multi-user dungeons*]). We could limit the player to a fixed number of inventory items or base the limit on weight, in which case every item in the game would need to have a weight property.

Another approach is to follow more of an *arcade*-style inventory system in which the player only possesses what he or she needs. In other words, the player has a weapon, armor, and modifiers, such as rings and amulets. The player wields a single weapon, based on the character's class (such as axe, sword, bow, or staff), wears a complete suit of armor (such as leather, studded, scale, or chain), and then has the option of wearing rings or amulets. I call the latter items *modifiers* because they are worn merely to modify the player's capabilities (such as strength or intelligence). This is the approach I've taken with the game.

A full-blown global inventory system would require a *lot* of source code that we simply don't have time or space to cover in this short book. Adding inventory items to the world is a distinct possibility with all of the existing code, but I have not gone that far with the current version of Celtic Crusader presented in this chapter. It's simply too much work, and we haven't even gotten to combat yet. If you would like to add items to the game world and make it possible for the player to pick them up, that is *definitely* doable with the existing engine. You would need to add an item somewhere in the world, and then duplicate the code in the DrawScenery subroutine to have the game draw inventory items on the screen when they're in range of the player. Rather than colliding with items, the player would walk over them and have an opportunity to pick up such items. You could use some of Reiner's treasure chest sprites throughout the world for the player to find, and then give the player a random amount of gold for finding each one!

For a simple inventory system like the one used in our game, you would simply display the new item and ask the player whether he or she would like to replace the current item with the new one. It's as simple as that. There are no armories or blacksmiths in this game; you simply replace gear with better stuff as you find it, and earn gold by defeating enemies, not by selling gear. (This model somewhat resembles *Gauntlet Legends* and the follow-ups in the series.)

Creating the Player

We need to add support for basic items to the game engine. The most logical place to add this code is in the Characters module, where the character and player structures are already located (because the player will be equipping these items). I'm assuming that you're building on the Celtic Crusader project from the previous chapter. Let's open up the Characters file in the editor. Here is the `PlayerType` structure definition and variable declaration:

```
Structure PlayerType
    Dim Name As String
    Dim CharClass As String
    Dim Experience As Short
    Dim MaxHealth As Short
    Dim Health As Short
    Dim Level As Short
    Dim Gold As Integer
    Dim Attack As Integer
    Dim Defense As Integer
    Dim STR As Short
    Dim DEX As Short
    Dim STA As Short
    Dim INT As Short
    Dim CHA As Short
    Dim sprite As CSprite
    Dim weapon As ItemType
    Dim armor As ItemType
    Dim ring As ItemType
End Structure

Public Player As PlayerType
```

This player structure can be expanded as needed to accommodate more properties and attributes for the player character. You may also modify the `Stats` structure used to define monsters in the game world. A helper subroutine called `CreatePlayer` is also added to the Characters module. This routine fills the `Player` structure variable with values for the type of character desired, whether that is Warrior, Paladin, Scout, or Wizard. Also included in this routine are calls to an as-yet-unknown function called CreateItem. We'll get to that in a minute. But take notice of how the player's weapon, armor, and ring objects receive the return value of CreateItem. This must be a very versatile function! At a certain point, we'll merge the player character and NPC structures, but let's take it one step at a time.

```
Public Sub CreatePlayer(ByVal classname As String)
    Const BASE As Short = 10
    Player.Name = "HERO"
    Player.MaxHealth = 100
    Player.Health = 100
    Player.Experience = 0
    Player.Level = 1
    Player.Gold = 100

        Select Case classname
            Case "WARRIOR"
                Player.sprite.Load("warrior_walk.png")
                Player.STR = BASE + Warrior.STR
                Player.DEX = BASE + Warrior.DEX
                Player.STA = BASE + Warrior.STA
                Player.INT = BASE + Warrior.INT
                Player.CHA = BASE + Warrior.CHA
                Player.weapon = CreateItem("axe", 1)
                Player.armor = CreateItem("armor", 1)
                Player.ring = CreateItem("ring", 1)

            Case "PALADIN"
                Player.sprite.Load("paladin_walk.png")
                Player.STR = BASE + Paladin.STR
                Player.DEX = BASE + Paladin.DEX
                Player.STA = BASE + Paladin.STA
                Player.INT = BASE + Paladin.INT
                Player.CHA = BASE + Paladin.CHA
                Player.weapon = CreateItem("sword", 1)
                Player.armor = CreateItem("armor", 1)
                Player.ring = CreateItem("ring", 1)

            Case "SCOUT"
                Player.sprite.Load("scout_walk.png")
                Player.STR = BASE + Scout.STR
```

```
            Player.DEX = BASE + Scout.DEX
            Player.STA = BASE + Scout.STA
            Player.INT = BASE + Scout.INT
            Player.CHA = BASE + Scout.CHA
            Player.weapon = CreateItem("bow", 1)
            Player.armor = CreateItem("armor", 1)
            Player.ring = CreateItem("ring", 1)

        Case "WIZARD"
            Player.sprite.Load("wizard_walk.png")
            Player.STR = BASE + Wizard.STR
            Player.DEX = BASE + Wizard.DEX
            Player.STA = BASE + Wizard.STA
            Player.INT = BASE + Wizard.INT
            Player.CHA = BASE + Wizard.CHA
            Player.weapon = CreateItem("staff", 1)
            Player.armor = CreateItem("armor", 1)
            Player.ring = CreateItem("ring", 1)
    End Select

    'set additional properties
    Player.CharClass = classname
    Player.sprite.FrameThreshold = 2
    Player.sprite.FrameWidth = 96
    Player.sprite.FrameHeight = 96
    Player.sprite.Columns = 8
    Player.sprite.StartFrame = 0
    Player.sprite.EndFrame = 7
    Player.sprite.X = (800 - 96) / 2
    Player.sprite.Y = (600 - 96) / 2
    Player.Attack = (Player.weapon.attack + Player.STR) / 2 + Player.Level
    Player.Defense = (Player.armor.defend + Player.STA) / 2 + Player.Level
End Sub
```

Creating Items

Although Celtic Crusader does not include a fully featured inventory system, the ItemType structure provides support for large-scale inventory management via its properties. For example, individual items can be created with a unique name using the name property, or a generic class of item can be created using the type property. A short constructor accepts a value for the item's name, type, attack, and defend properties (because weapons and armor will be the most common types of items).

```
Structure ItemType
    Dim name As String
    Dim type As String
    Dim attack As Short
    Dim defend As Short
    Dim ranged As Boolean
    Dim tohit As Short
    Dim str_mod As Short
    Dim dex_mod As Short
    Dim sta_mod As Short
    Dim int_mod As Short
    Dim cha_mod As Short
    Dim sprite As CSprite
    Dim position As Point

    Public Sub New(ByVal name As String, ByVal type As String, _
    ByVal attack As Short, ByVal defend As Short)
        Me.name = name
        Me.attack = attack
        Me.defend = defend
        Me.ranged = False
        Me.tohit = 0
        Me.str_mod = 0
        Me.dex_mod = 0
        Me.sta_mod = 0
        Me.int_mod = 0
        Me.cha_mod = 0
        Me.sprite = Nothing
    End Sub
End Structure
```

To assist with item creation, here is a helper routine called CreateItem. This routine is actually quite versatile, capable of producing *random* items of various types with attribute modifiers. For instance, by passing "sword" as the type and 2 as the level, CreateItem can create a wide variety of swords for you, such as "Short Sword +1" and "Holy Sword +2" or just a simple "Long Sword." If you provide a higher level and a type of "bow", the function may create a "Compound Bow +20", for instance. Similarly, you can create armor items and rings as well (anyone want a "Ring of Damage +15" that adds 15 damages to all attack rolls?). The code for a "ring" will be particularly interesting, so I recommend you study it to see how advanced modifiers are created. You can create *any* type of weapon or armor item you wish using custom modifiers (via the modifier properties, such as str_mod, which modifies strength).

```
Public Function CreateItem(ByVal type As String, _
Optional ByVal level As Short = 0) As ItemType
    Dim rand As New Random()
    Dim item As New ItemType("", "", 0, 0)

    Dim axePrefixes() As String = {"Small", "Large", "Heavy", "Battle"}
    Dim swordPrefixes() As String = {"Short", "Long", "Gnarly", "Holy"}
    Dim bowPrefixes() As String = {"Light", "Compound", "Long", "Hunter's"}
    Dim staffPrefixes() As String = {"Wooden", "Mage", "Quarter", "Magic"}
    Dim armorPrefixes() As String = {"Leather", "Studded", "Scale", "Chain"}

    Select Case type
        Case "axe"
            item = New ItemType("Axe", "axe", 0, 0)
            item.name = axePrefixes(rand.Next(axePrefixes.Length)) + _
                " " + item.name
            item.attack = rand.Next(level * 2) + 1
            If level > 0 Then
                item.tohit = rand.Next(level) + 1
                If item.tohit > 0 Then item.name += " +" + item.tohit.ToString
            End If

        Case "sword"
            item = New ItemType("Sword", "sword", 0, 0)
            item.name = swordPrefixes(rand.Next(swordPrefixes.Length)) + _
                " " + item.name
            item.attack = rand.Next(level * 2) + 1
            If level > 0 Then
                item.tohit = rand.Next(level) + 1
                If item.tohit > 0 Then item.name += " +" + item.tohit.ToString
            End If

        Case "bow"
            item = New ItemType("Bow", "bow", 0, 0)
            item.name = bowPrefixes(rand.Next(bowPrefixes.Length)) + _
                " " + item.name
            item.attack = rand.Next(level * 2) + 1
            If level > 0 Then
                item.ranged = True
                item.attack = level
```

```
            item.tohit = rand.Next(level) + 1
            If item.tohit > 0 Then item.name += " +" + item.tohit.ToString
        End If

    Case "staff"
        item = New ItemType("Staff", "staff", 0, 0)
        item.name = staffPrefixes(rand.Next(staffPrefixes.Length)) + _
            " " + item.name
        item.attack = rand.Next(level * 2) + 1
        If level > 0 Then
            item.ranged = True
            item.tohit = rand.Next(level) + 1
            If item.tohit > 0 Then item.name += " +" + item.tohit.ToString
        End If

    Case "armor"
        item = New ItemType("Armor", "armor", 0, 0)
        item.name = armorPrefixes(rand.Next(armorPrefixes.Length)) + _
            " " + item.name
        item.defend = rand.Next(level * 2) + 1

    Case "ring"
        item = New ItemType("Ring", "ring", 0, 0)
        Select Case rand.Next(8)
            Case 0
                item.attack = rand.Next(level) + 1
                item.name += " of Att +" + item.attack.ToString
            Case 1
                item.defend = rand.Next(level) + 1
                item.name += " of Def +" + item.defend.ToString
            Case 2
                item.str_mod = rand.Next(level) + 1
                item.name += " of Str +" + item.str_mod.ToString
            Case 3
                item.dex_mod = rand.Next(level) + 1
                item.name += " of Dex +" + item.dex_mod.ToString
            Case 4
                item.sta_mod = rand.Next(level) + 1
                item.name += " of Sta +" + item.sta_mod.ToString
            Case 5
                item.int_mod = rand.Next(level) + 1
                item.name += " of Int +" + item.int_mod.ToString
```

```
            Case 6
                item.cha_mod = rand.Next(level) + 1
                item.name += " of Cha +" + item.cha_mod.ToString
            Case 7
                item.tohit = rand.Next(level) + 1
                item.name += " of Dmg +" + item.tohit.ToString
        End Select
    End Select

    Return item

End Function
```

Main Code Modifications

The only routine in the Form1 source code file that I've modified in this chapter is `PrintPlayerStats`. Now that we have all of these statistics and items and whatnot, it's time to add all of this data to the game screen so the player can become *emotionally involved* with his or her character. I guess that is really what the appeal of RPGs is all about—creating a character to whom you relate, and then guiding that character through a fantasy world.

I've made significant changes to `PrintPlayerStats` in order to print out the player's vital stats (strength, dexterity, and so on), along with the weapon, armor, and ring objects that the player has been given (via the `CreatePlayer` routine). Take a look at Figure 15.1 for a screenshot of the game at this point, with all of the stats printed out. It's starting to look like a real RPG!

Now listen up. This might seem a limited way to handle inventory, but you can swap the weapon, armor, and ring *at any time* with *any other object!* These object holders in the `Player` structure are merely *holders* for the objects. You can create a hundred different weapons, stored in an array or linked list, and give one at random to the player when the game starts up. You don't have to keep the `CreateItem` function if you don't want to! Do you see the potential? The three items displayed on the screen are *just the beginning.* Imagine besting a very tough foe—let's say a dragon—and claiming a hot new Battle Axe with +20 to hit and +10 to all stats! As the game master, you have the freedom to create weapons like this. All it takes is a few lines of source code. When the player acquires the new weapon, just set `player.weapon` equal to the new object . . . literally . . . and that object will be displayed instead of the old one. Most importantly, that new weapon's properties are stored with the player as well.

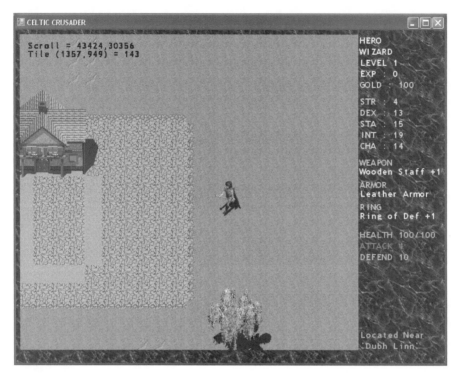

Figure 15.1
The new version of Celtic Crusader now displays the player's stats and inventory items.

```
Public Sub PrintPlayerStats()
    Dim x As Integer = 640

    engine.Print(x, 10, Color.Ivory, Player.Name)
    engine.Print(x, 30, Color.Ivory, Player.CharClass)
    engine.Print(x, 50, Color.Ivory, "LEVEL " + Player.Level.ToString)
    engine.Print(x, 70, Color.Ivory, "EXP : " + Player.Experience.ToString)
    engine.Print(x, 90, Color.Gold, "GOLD : " + Player.gold.tostring)

    engine.Print(x, 120, Color.Yellow, "STR : " + Player.STR.ToString)
    engine.Print(x, 140, Color.Yellow, "DEX : " + Player.DEX.ToString)
    engine.Print(x, 160, Color.Yellow, "STA : " + Player.STA.ToString)
    engine.Print(x, 180, Color.Yellow, "INT : " + Player.INT.ToString)
    engine.Print(x, 200, Color.Yellow, "CHA : " + Player.CHA.ToString)

    engine.Print(x, 230, Color.LightBlue, "WEAPON")
    engine.Print(x, 246, Color.Azure, Player.weapon.name)
    engine.Print(x, 270, Color.LightBlue, "ARMOR")
    engine.Print(x, 286, Color.Azure, Player.armor.name)
    engine.Print(x, 310, Color.LightBlue, "RING")
```

```
engine.Print(x, 326, Color.Azure, Player.ring.name)

engine.Print(x, 360, Color.LightGreen, "HEALTH " + _
    Player.Health.ToString + "/" + Player.MaxHealth.ToString)
engine.Print(x, 380, Color.OrangeRed, "ATTACK " + Player.Attack.ToString)
engine.Print(x, 400, Color.OrangeRed, "DEFEND " + Player.Defense.ToString)

engine.Print(x, 540, Color.YellowGreen, "Located Near")
engine.Print(x, 560, Color.YellowGreen, "'" + locationName + "'")

'display ring's stat modifiers
If Player.ring.str_mod > 0 Then
    engine.Print(x + 180, 120, Color.LightGreen, "+ " + _
        Player.ring.str_mod.ToString)
End If
If Player.ring.dex_mod > 0 Then
    engine.Print(x + 180, 120, Color.LightGreen, "+ " + _
        Player.ring.dex_mod.ToString)
End If
If Player.ring.sta_mod > 0 Then
    engine.Print(x + 180, 120, Color.LightGreen, "+ " + _
        Player.ring.sta_mod.ToString)
End If
If Player.ring.int_mod > 0 Then
    engine.Print(x + 180, 120, Color.LightGreen, "+ " + _
        Player.ring.int_mod.ToString)
End If
If Player.ring.cha_mod > 0 Then
    engine.Print(x + 180, 120, Color.LightGreen, "+ " + _
        Player.ring.cha_mod.ToString)
End If
End Sub
```

Level Up

This chapter provided a new inventory system to Celtic Crusader. Although the inventory system is simplistic, it has great potential because any type of special weapon or modifying item (such as a magic amulet or ring) can be added to the player to modify the player's attributes. We discussed the possibility of adding more inventory items to the game and the potential for creating droppable items when monsters are felled, as well as including random treasure chests in the world.

CHAPTER 16

ADDING NPCs AND MONSTERS

A role-playing game is only fun if the game world is sufficiently populated to allow interaction and fighting with computer-controlled players. These *non-player characters,* or *NPCs* for short, are a vital element of a *role-playing game (RPG)*. Although some types of RPGs prefer to reserve NPCs for human characters, I simplify the issue and define an NPC as any type of character in the game other than the *player's character (PC)* and animals. Animals are defined as the native fauna of the game world and do not necessarily have to be recognizable creatures. You might have alien-type animals in your game, but the difference is that fauna do not engage in combat, and therefore should not be grouped with NPCs.

This chapter fills the role of explaining how to add NPCs to the game world, and also squeezes in a sorely needed discussion of player attributes and the entire player-creation process. Although I am unable to provide a complete tutorial on constructing a player-generation system for this game, I point you in the right direction and provide the essentials for creating each of the five character classes. Through this chapter, you have NPCs with which the player may engage in battle; therefore, the discussion of player attributes (and NPC attributes) is called for.

Here is a breakdown of the major topics in this chapter:

- Introduction to NPCs

- Creating reusable "people"

- Initializing the list of characters

- Moving the characters

- Drawing the characters

Introduction to NPCs

I focus all of my remaining attention on building up the Leinster region of the game world. (You may recall that Leinster is one of the four regions in ninth-century Ireland and consists of the most towns and ruins on the map.) As you might imagine, the creation of an entire game world is a daunting task that requires attention to detail and an investment of time, and it should be directed toward your game's overall storyline. Because I'm limited by the scope of this book, I have to give you the tools you need to take this game to the level you want, according to your own imagination. In essence, I am giving you the game engine and the tools, rather than a completely polished game—without apology, because this is how it should be. I do not want to limit your creative potential with my particular vision for a game. Take this as far and wide as you possibly can! Figure 16.1 shows the new version of Celtic Crusader that you will develop in this chapter.

Starting Position and Range of Movement

The most important thing to consider (after loading the NPC's images, that is) is the starting position. Where does the NPC start off in the game? After this, the next most important thing to consider is this NPC's behavior: What does this character do in the game world? The starting position is an actual pixel X,Y location in the game world. Depending on the behavioral subroutine being used by each NPC, you may want to set the starting position in the middle of a town, so that when the NPC reaches a new destination after walking around for a while, it is basically centered on a town. (Most of the population should be near towns.)

The starting position also specifies where NPCs respawn after being killed (with additional randomness applied along with, perhaps, a different name). The

Figure 16.1
Hero: "Help, I'm surrounded by Viking warriors!"

NPC's range should keep that character relatively close to his or her starting point, and the character's behavior is then based on the movement state (which might be stopped, walking, running, and so on). By respawning an NPC, perhaps at the other side of the game world, you can keep the game flowing smoothly without allowing a rampaging player to decimate your plans for challenging gameplay! Indeed, one thing you might consider is increasing the experience and level of each NPC that is killed, so that over time the game world gets more and more challenging for the player.

If you want to know where a specific town is located, in order to add some characters to the game world near that town, just look at the Locations list in the game engine, since all 22 towns are found in this list. If you just want to refer to these towns, check the LoadLocations subroutine.

A Simple State Engine

I have created a very simple subroutine that is called a *state engine* because it reacts to the character's current state. This subroutine directs the behavior of the

NPCs. You can add behavioral subroutines and states to the game as you learn how to control the NPCs. For starters, I have an enumerated list called `ANIMSTATES` that the gamewill use to keep track of an NPC's location and behavioral properties (such as the starting, current, and destination points in the game world).

```
'keeps track of animation state
Public Enum ANIMSTATES
    NPC_STOPPED = 0
    NPC_WALKING = 1
End Enum
```

The `ANIMSTATES` enumeration will be used in the next chapter to add attack and death animations to each character!

Benevolent versus Malevolent NPCs

You want to use basically two types of NPC in the game (in addition to animals, perhaps, for scenery). *Benevolent NPCs* are harmless people such as villagers, townsfolk, peasants, and perhaps even local law enforcement. (Have you considered the possibility of having local guards attack the player if you harm any local peasants? That would be interesting.) The other type of NPC is *malevolent* in nature—these include characters opposed to the player, including evil creatures, outlaws, bandits, and, of course in the context of this game, Vikings (which should be particularly tough to fight, given the theme of the game). We'll use a list called `Persons` to keep track of characters (friendly or otherwise) in the game.

Creating Reusable "People"

The characters are based on the standard *character classes* (not to be confused with a VB.NET Class) in the Characters module, but a little bit of randomness applied to the characters makes them interesting. The randomness might affect the attributes if you want, but I prefer to just give each character a random experience and level to make him more or less powerful than the player (but not beyond reason). Keep the random characters within a certain range of the player's experience and level to keep the game interesting. The characters will also need to walk around. The simplest form of character movement simply has characters walk toward a destination; when that destination is reached, another destination is determined randomly.

The Data Types and List

The custom data type that tracks each individual NPC is called Person. This structure allows you to keep tabs on every character in the game, with properties that track each character's state, starting position, current position, destination, sprite image, and so on.

```
Structure Person
      Dim name As String
      Dim type As String
      Dim state As NPCSTATES
      Dim homepos As Point
      Dim curpos As Point
      Dim destpos As Point
      Dim direction As Integer
      Dim range As Integer
      Dim SpeedDelay As Integer
      Dim SpeedCount As Integer
      Dim Facing As Integer
      Dim sprite As CSprite

      Public Sub New(ByVal name As String, ByVal type As String)
          Me.name = name
          Me.type = type
      End Sub

End Structure
```

The game actually uses a LinkedList called Persons to manage the characters (that is, to move, animate, and draw them on the screen). This list will handle all characters in the game: NPCs, monsters, and animals. The LinkedList class is part of the System.Collections.Generic namespace.

```
Public Persons As Generic.LinkedList(Of Person)
```

Initializing the List of Characters

I have written a subroutine called LoadCharacters that initializes all of the NPCs in the game. This subroutine is what you modify when you want to add new characters. The subroutine is somewhat hard-coded at present because the game is using just a single class of NPC (Vikings), but you can modify this routine to add more characters to the game world—in any location you wish, based on any character class. Want to add a dragon out in the wilderness of the Connaught region? Fine, go ahead and do it here! I have another idea: How about characters that travel all over the world, from town to town? Wouldn't that be interesting? You can automate the process of causing a character to walk between two towns, back and forth, by simply setting the startpos and destpos positions to the center of two towns.

```
Public Sub LoadCharacters()
    Dim start As Point
    Dim dest As Point
    Dim n As Long

    Persons = New Generic.LinkedList(Of Person)

    For n = 0 To 10
        'set starting location on world map
        start.X = engine.ScrollX + 400 + rand.Next(500)
        start.Y = engine.ScrollY + 300 + rand.Next(500)

        'destination will auto-reset in game loop
        dest.X = start.X
        dest.Y = start.Y

        'create the new person
        Dim viking As New Person("Viking", "person")
        viking.state = NPCSTATES.WALKING
        viking.homepos = start
        viking.curpos = start
        viking.destpos = dest
        viking.direction = 0
        viking.sprite = New CSprite(engine.Direct3D)
        viking.sprite.Load("viking_axe_walk.png")
        viking.sprite.Identifier = n
        viking.sprite.Columns = 8
        viking.sprite.StartFrame = 0
        viking.sprite.EndFrame = 7
        viking.sprite.FrameThreshold = 4
        viking.sprite.FrameSize = New Point(96, 96)
```

```
            Persons.AddLast(viking)

      Next n
End Sub
```

Moving the Characters

The UpdateCharacters subroutine is shown next. This routine goes through the entire list of characters in the Persons list and updates their movements, animations, and collision testing. One thing this routine does not take into account (yet) is the state of each character. You'll want the characters to walk only if the state is set to "walking," and you will want to add new behaviors to the state enumeration as well, at which point this UpdateCharacters routine will be modified to update each character based on state.

```
Public Sub UpdateCharacters()
      Dim peep As Person
      Dim node As LinkedListNode(Of Person)
      Dim n As Integer

      'create a line of all persons
      For n = 0 To Persons.Count - 1
          'grab the next person in line
          node = Persons.First
          peep = node.Value
          Persons.RemoveFirst()

          MovePerson(peep)
          AnimatePerson(peep)

          If (engine.CheckSceneryCollision(locationPixels, peep.sprite
          .FrameSize)) Then
              peep.destpos = peep.curpos
          End If

          'save changes to this person
          node.Value = peep

          'save the person at the end of the line
          Persons.AddLast(node)
      Next
End Sub
```

If all you had to do is move a sprite, it would require a few lines of code at most! However, because these sprites have 64 frames each (*at least*), with eight directions of travel, this requires some forethought. When you see Celtic Crusader from this chapter running, I think you may be floored by how cool it is! If you are expecting a full-featured game at this point, I just want to help you tone down your expectations, because the game *is* coming along. You have to realize the limited amount of space in this book prevents a thorough treatment of the subject, so what you see here is hardcore RPG action! Here's the `MovePerson` routine called by the `UpdateCharacter` routine you saw a moment ago.

```
Private Sub MovePerson(ByRef peep As Person)

    'start character walking to a new location
    If peep.curpos = peep.destpos Then
        peep.destpos.X = peep.homepos.X + rand.Next(1000) - 500
        peep.destpos.Y = peep.homepos.Y + rand.Next(1000) - 500
    End If

    If peep.curpos.X < peep.destpos.X Then
        peep.curpos.X += 1

        'facing south east?
        If peep.curpos.Y < peep.destpos.Y Then
            peep.curpos.Y += 1
            peep.direction = 3

        'facing north east?
        ElseIf peep.curpos.Y > peep.destpos.Y Then
            peep.curpos.Y -= 1
            peep.direction = 1

        'facing east
        Else
            peep.direction = 1
        End If

    ElseIf peep.curpos.X > peep.destpos.X Then
        'needs to walk eastward
        peep.curpos.X = peep.curpos.X - 1

        If peep.curpos.Y < peep.destpos.Y Then
```

```
            'facing SW
            peep.curpos.Y = peep.curpos.Y + 1
            peep.direction = 5
        ElseIf peep.curpos.Y > peep.destpos.Y Then
            'facing NW
            peep.curpos.Y = peep.curpos.Y - 1
            peep.direction = 7
        Else
            'facing WEST
            peep.direction = 6
        End If

    Else 'facing due NORTH or SOUTH
        If peep.curpos.Y < peep.destpos.Y Then
            'facing SOUTH
            peep.curpos.Y = peep.curpos.Y + 1
            peep.direction = 4
        ElseIf peep.curpos.Y > peep.destpos.Y Then
            'facint NORTH
            peep.curpos.Y = peep.curpos.Y - 1
            peep.direction = 0
        End If
    End If
End Sub
```

Also required is the `AnimatePerson` subroutine, also called from `UpdateCharacter`.

```
Private Sub AnimatePerson(ByRef peep As Person)
    peep.sprite.StartFrame = peep.direction * peep.sprite.Columns
    peep.sprite.EndFrame = peep.sprite.StartFrame + 7
    peep.sprite.Animate()
End Sub
```

Drawing the Characters

The `DrawCharacters` subroutine is called by the `UpdateCharacters` routine. It goes through the list of characters in the `Persons` list and draws each character if it is visible on the screen (within the range of the player's global position in the game world).

```
Public Sub DrawCharacters(ByVal location As Point)
    Dim pos As Point
    Dim peep As Person
```

```
      Dim screenArea As New Rectangle( _
          location.X - 200, location.Y - 200, 800 + 400, 600 + 400)

      For Each peep In Persons
          'is this scenery object near the player?
          pos.X = peep.curpos.X + peep.sprite.FrameWidth / 2
          pos.Y = peep.curpos.Y + peep.sprite.FrameHeight / 2

          If screenArea.Contains(pos.X, pos.Y) Then
              pos.X = peep.curpos.X - location.X
              pos.Y = peep.curpos.Y - location.Y
              peep.sprite.DrawFrame(pos)
              engine.Print(pos.X, pos.Y, Color.White, peep.sprite.Identifier
              .ToString)
          End If

      Next
  End Sub
```

The New and Improved Game

This new version of Celtic Crusader is located on the CD-ROM. I encourage you to load up the project and run it, because I don't include complete source code listings in this chapter. Although all of the new subroutines have been covered here, the overall game engine is becoming a bit large, so you'll want to have the project open in its entirety as it exists now, rather than typing in this code.

Now let's talk about the artwork for this new Viking character. Fortunately, as you have seen in previous chapters, we have these wonderful 3D modeled sprites from Reiner. Figure 16.2 shows the Viking sprite loaded into Pro Motion and ready to be exported as a sprite sheet containing eight rows of animation, with eight frames per row (for a total of 64 frames). Each row contains an animation sequence for one of the directions of travel. For easy reference, all of the artwork for the entire game is available on the CD-ROM in the \artwork folder, as well as in each project folder.

After saving the animation strips into a single bitmap file, you can create the alpha channel transparency using the GIMP. Of course, all of the artwork on the

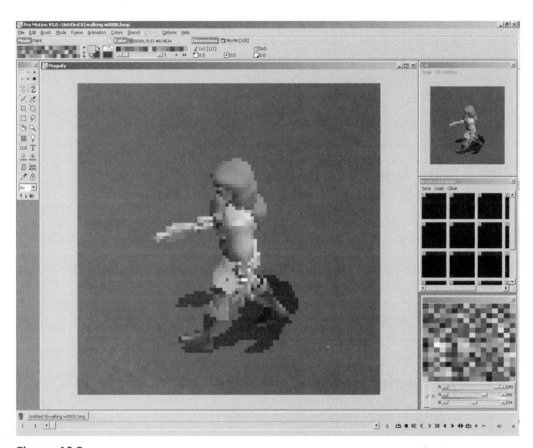

Figure 16.2
The individual Viking Warrior sprites are saved as a sprite sheet by Pro Motion.

CD-ROM has been prepared in advance, but should you wish to add new characters to the game, you will need to become familiar with these tools.

Level Up

This chapter introduced you to the rather complex issues involved in adding NPCs to the game. Although an RPG is playable without a big population of NPCs, it is a good idea to have a large variety of people with whom the player can interact (and fight). Otherwise, the game becomes slow and boring. This chapter gave you the logistical code to get an NPC up on the screen, moving around, and realistically facing in the right direction when walking. The final step, covered in the next chapter, adds a combat system to the game so that the player and NPCs will be able to engage in combat!

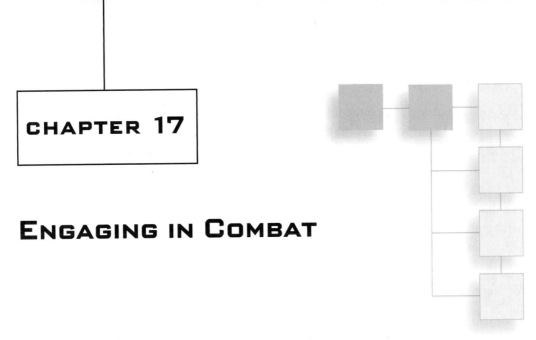

CHAPTER 17

ENGAGING IN COMBAT

Melee combat occurs when opponents fight each other with handheld weapons (whereas unarmed combat occurs when no weapons are used, as in a martial art). The game engine already has support for melee combat, but it is not yet implemented, so that is what we'll do in this chapter. First we must determine when the player is near an enemy, then cause the enemy to turn toward the player, and then allow combat to ensue. Fortunately, the sprites available from Reiner's Tilesets (www.reinerstilesets.de) also include the attack and falling animations. Combat requires another layer of logic added to the state engine that controls the characters. Although higher-level interaction with characters would make the game more realistic, we'll just be treating this like an old-style hack-and-slash game where the goal is not to follow some sort of complex storyline, but rather to gain experience and explore the world. A simple state-based system will be used to cause enemies to attack the player when in close range. Here are the key topics:

- Contemplating the combat system

- Dealing with the player's death

- Combat animations

- Engaging in combat

- Managing the player's state

- Managing the NPC states

Contemplating the Combat System

The Celtic Crusader project, as of the last chapter, is basically a template game that has most of the functionality you need to actually create a *role-playing game (RPG)*, but is lacking most of the finer details. There is just an enormous amount of detail that must be put into even the simplest of RPGs. Although the size and scope of this book are insufficient to completely build the game, we can create a fun hack-and-slash game where the goal is to gain experience and go up levels, with the corresponding new abilities and skills. But this is *your* game to make, not mine! I want to see what you can do with it, not merely have you run *my game*. The final version of Celtic Crusader presented in this chapter is still very much a template that is begging for new content—from *you!* How will you finish the game? Let me explain the combat system.

The previous chapter developed the ability for the player to have encounters with NPCs. From this point, you can engage the NPCs in combat and the game responds appropriately. A higher level of behavior over the NPCs is also needed to turn this template of a game into a finished game—a system of behavior that causes NPCs to seek out and engage the player, rather than always *responding* to the player. At the very least, you can add the ability for NPCs to respond to the player when they "see" you.

Fighting Back

The goal of this chapter is to add combat animations in such a way that it is easy for you to add new characters to the game without requiring much extra work. The hostile NPCs need attack animations, while the peasantry do not, so if the player attacks a peasant or any other nonfighting NPC, then you have to add behavior that causes the character to run away or die, depending on your style. (I recommend adding a state that causes civilians to flee.)

Respawning NPCs

When you are fighting with an NPC and you kill that character, there should be a death animation. These are not always possible in every case, due to a limited number of sprites. You are limited overall by the availability of artwork, without which you have to get creative with your sprites. If you don't have a lot of animations, particularly a character's death animation, you might consider using the fade effect, where a character blinks out of existence or fades away. You might use the alpha color parameter in the sprite class to cause a character to fade out of existence after dying, rather than using a death animation. I have formatted the walk, attack, and death sprite sheets for all four player character classes and the major NPCs featured in the game, but it is such a time-consuming process that I have not prepared all of the artwork in advance. I include all of the artwork suitable for the game (courtesy of Reiner's Tilesets) on the CD-ROM in the \artwork folder. If you tire of editing sprite sheets, the fade effect is a good alternative to death animations, in which case you will only need walk and attack animations. The game is configured at this point to use all three types of animation, so if you are using Reiner's sprites, as I have used extensively in this game, then all three (and more!) are already available.

The important thing is that you recycle your sprites in the game, which means recycling the NPCs. You don't want the NPCs to just respawn at the same place every time, because then the player can see the spawning taking place (which seriously ruins the realism of the game). In addition, if a player learns where some of the NPCs are respawning on the map, he or she will be able to *spawn camp* (which refers to hiding out near a spawn point and killing new players that appear) and rack up a ridiculous amount of experience, which also ruins the game.

Simulating Damage

One aspect of combat you need is some sort of status display showing the hero's health and other attributes. I think it is a good idea to use the main game window for chatting and combat. Figure 17.1 shows the combat sequence featured in the version of Celtic Crusader developed in this chapter, with the enemy Viking character attacking.

Although a combat-focused game might benefit from showing the carnage of bodies on the ground, it requires a lot of extra work on your part. You basically have to keep all of those sprites in memory just to draw their dead bodies, and then create new sprites to respawn the NPCs. This is all just a lot of unnecessary work; the player is plowing through a lot of enemies in the game, anyway. The flicker/fade technique works well overall and can be done by simply changing the color value when drawing a sprite (with the Draw2D subroutine). But perhaps you will show fallen enemy bodies for a short time, after which they will disappear.

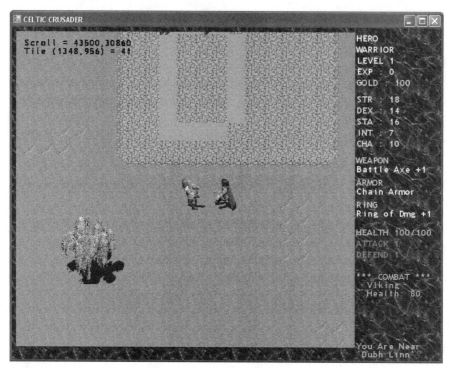

Figure 17.1
An enemy Viking character is attacking the player.

Attack Rolled against Defense

What really happens when you attack another character in the game? That is the basis of the game's combat system, and it has to do with each player's attributes, including weapon and armor class. Usually, the defender's defensive value is compared to the attacker's attack value, and a simulated "roll" of dice is made to determine whether the attack even succeeded (before calculating damage). All of the attributes are available already from the `Person` structure. See Figure 17.2.

If the attack value is less than the defense value, then basically you can do no damage to your opponent! So, say you are a new Warrior with an axe that does +10 damage and you attack a level-10 Viking Berserker with 93 defense points. What happens in this situation? You can stand there and bang against this fellow's armor all day long with your pathetic little axe and do *no damage* to him whatsoever! In a situation like this, you are helplessly outclassed by this character, who swiftly and easily kills you with a single blow.

This is called the *to-hit roll* and it adds a nice layer of realism to the game (as opposed to some games where just swinging your sword kills enemies nearby).

Figure 17.2
The player is attacking the enemy character.

Knowing that not every swing does damage requires you to use some tactics in your fighting method, and this gives players the ability to be somewhat creative in how they fight enemies. You can swing and run or swing several times in a row, hoping to get a hit. But in general, it's a hit-or-miss situation (sorry, bad pun). Figure 17.3 shows the enemy character falling in the death animation.

Many RPGs allow the player to equip modifiers, such as rings and special weapons, with bonuses for the to-hit value. These modifiers increase your chances of scoring a hit when you attack. Not only is it essential for a good RPG, but working with miscellaneous items as well as different types of swords, shields, armor, helmets, and so on is an extremely fun part of the game! Our Person structure (from which all NPCs and the player character are derived) has support for a custom weapon, armor, and ring that the player or NPC may equip, and you have an opportunity to use these special items to customize characters. You may even allow the player to pick up items found in the world and equip them.

The Viking characters in the game start with 100 hit points, but that is *way* too much for an average character. Don't think of hit points as a percentage, but

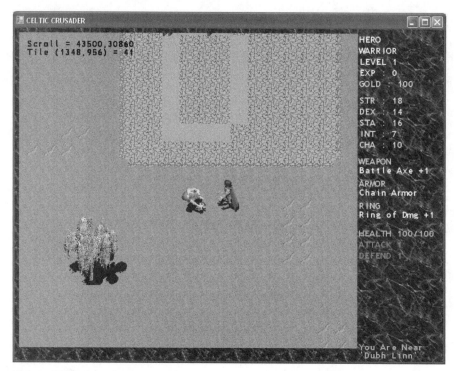

Figure 17.3
This enemy Viking character has been dealt a fatal blow and is falling down.

merely the total health that the character can have when fully healed. The Viking character should start with about 30 hit points, while a *dragon* or other dangerous foe should have upwards of 100 points. With the stock weapon the player is carrying, it takes a very long time to whittle down 100 points of health, and you want the game to move along at a brisk pace so the player doesn't become bored.

Factoring Weapon Values

After the to-hit roll determines that the player did hit his target, determine how much damage was done to the target. This is where the weapon attributes come into play. If the game features real items that you can give your character to use in combat, it makes a big difference in the gameplay. For one thing, you can scatter treasure chests around the game world that contain unique quest items (such as magical swords, shields, and armor), as well as valuable jewels and gold. These types of items are all modeled and available in the sprites provided by Reiner's Tilesets. The artwork department is finished, and it's just a matter of adding this feature to the game. The player's attack and defense properties will need to be recalculated every time his equipment is changed.

Dealing with the Player's Death

One drawback to combat is that you can die. It's a cold, hard, truth, I realize, but it can happen. What should you do, as the game's designer and programmer, when the *player's character (PC)* dies? That is a tough decision that requires some thought and should be based on the overall design of your game. You might let the player save and load the game, but that takes away from the suspension of disbelief. You want the player to be completely immersed in the game and unaware of a file system, an operating system, or even the computer. You want your players to be mesmerized by the content on the screen, and something as cheesy as a load/save feature takes away from that. I'll admit, though, most players abuse the save/load game feature and complain if you don't have one. After all, you want the player to be able to quit at a moment's notice without going through any hassle. Let's face it: Sometimes the real world inserts itself into the reverie you are experiencing in the game, and you have to quit playing.

But just for the sake of gameplay, what is the best way to deal with the player character's death, aside from having a save/load feature? I recommend just respawning the PC at a nearby town at this point. You don't want the player to get too frustrated with having to walk clear across the world again after dying, so respawning at the starting point is a *bad* idea. (Remember how big this world is!)

Implementing the Combat System

I have made some changes to the Celtic Crusader project that you find on the CD-ROM. Before you can engage in combat, one might argue that you need a weapon first. Granted, the hero in this game has been carrying an axe (and at times, a sword) for quite a while. The problem is that he doesn't know how to use it, so it's what you might call a decorative sword at present. What this hero needs is the ability to swing away at the bad guys, and that calls for some new animations!

Tip

The fully prepared sprite sheets for several character classes are available on the CD-ROM in the \artwork folder, with walking, attacking, and dying animations.

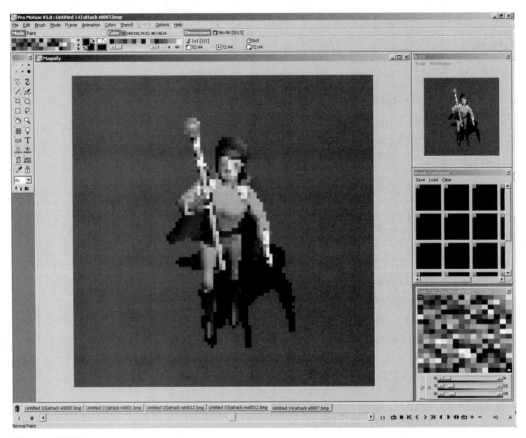

Figure 17.4
The animated Mage character is being converted to an animation strip in Pro Motion.

First, as usual, I downloaded from Reiner's Tilesets the character animations of the characters. Take a look at one of the character frames in Pro Motion, shown in Figure 17.4. You have already seen some of these sprite sheets in use in the game, because we implemented the character selection screen back in Chapter 13. But you have not, as of yet, seen how these sprite sheets were created.

Character Attack Animations

In addition to the walking animation, we need animation for attacking and dying for each character. I have also exported the animation strips for the Paladin character. Figure 17.5 shows the Wizard character sprite sheet for the attack animation. While we're looking at attack animations, let's examine the attack sprites for the Warrior (Figure 17.6), Paladin (Figure 17.7), and Scout

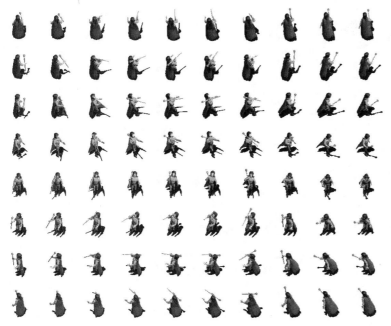

Figure 17.5
The attack animation for the Wizard character.

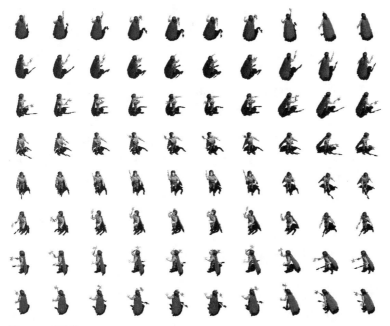

Figure 17.6
The attack animation for the Warrior character.

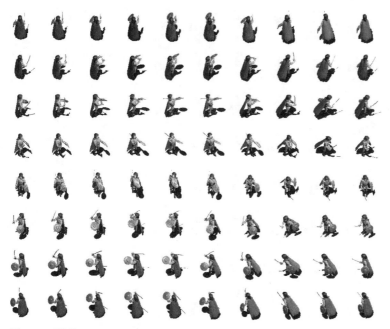

Figure 17.7
The attack animation for the Paladin character.

(Figure 17.8). Note that the archer seems to pull back his bow and fire an arrow, but we haven't included any support for projectile weapons. You will need to launch an arrow when the archer attacks; I have provided an arrow sprite in \artwork as well. Likewise, the wizard character is currently attacking with his staff, but there are fireball animations available for the wizard at Reiner's website.

While I'm on the subject of combat animations, I've got the attack frames for the Viking ready to go in this chapter as well! Figure 17.9 shows this really cool character that is sort of the main bad guy for the game; check out his huge battle axe! Although you can't tell from the figure here, this character has red hair and is a very imposing-looking figure (which is perfect for a Viking). There are so many excellent sprite sheets available from Reiner that it was hard to choose one over another. One of my favorites is the Dark Dwarf, which carries a huge battle axe and a shield! I've included artwork for about 20 more characters in \artwork; however, not all have been converted into sprite sheets. You may use Pro Motion (included in the \tools folder) to open all of those frames and save them as a single sprite sheet. It takes some patience and practice to get proficient with

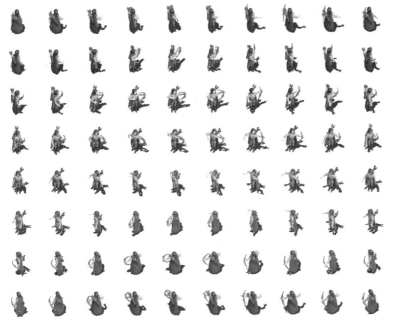

Figure 17.8
The attack animation for the Scout character.

Pro Motion, but give yourself time to master it, and you will be stunned by the results.

In addition to the attack animations for the Hero's four characters and the Viking, I have added a Skeleton to the mix to demonstrate how the game looks with different NPCs present. Figure 17.10 shows the Skeleton walking animation in Pro Motion.

Because this chapter now includes the ability to engage in combat, the Skeleton Knight needs some attack animations. Figure 17.11 shows one of the attack frames for this character.

Engaging in Combat

There are two basic things you need to do to allow the player to fight with NPCs:

- Make sure the player is close enough to an enemy to hit him.

- Make sure the player is facing an enemy while attacking.

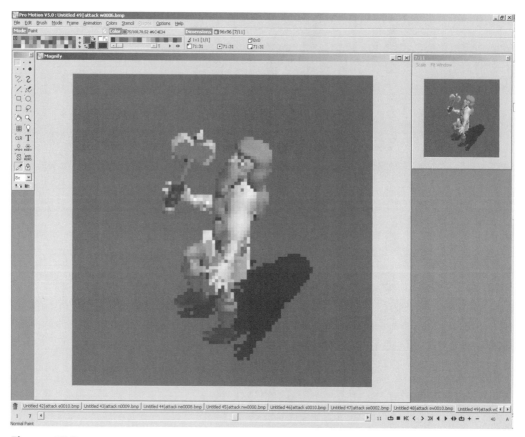

Figure 17.9
A combat animation for the Viking Warrior character.

If you can take care of these two problems, then you can create a combat system for the game. Tackle these two key problems in order. You want to be able to acknowledge that a hit has occurred when the player is in attack mode and also facing the enemy.

The first thing you need to check on before you can handle a combat strike is whether the player is close enough to an enemy character to actually hit him. That is accomplished by a subroutine called NearPerson. By passing a Person (which would be one of the enemies in the game), this subroutine will calculate whether that person is close enough to the player to allow combat to occur.

```
Private Function NearPerson(ByRef peep As Person) As Boolean
    'player located at center of screen
    Dim rect1 As New Rectangle( _
        locationPixels.X + 400 - 48, locationPixels.Y + 300 - 48, 96, 96)
```

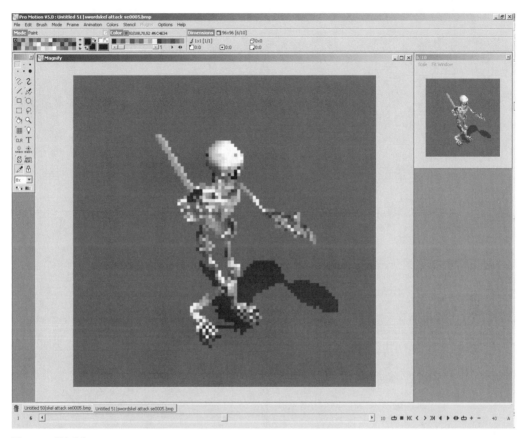

Figure 17.10
The walking animation for the Skeleton Knight character.

```
        'get other person's location
        Dim rect2 As New Rectangle(peep.curpos, New Size(96, 96))

        'collision?
        If rect1.IntersectsWith(rect2) Then
            Return True
        Else
            Return False
        End If
End Function
```

If there is no collision between the two sprites, then there definitely can't be an attack, and the swing misses! After determining whether the two sprites are close enough for an attack, see whether the attacker is at least facing the enemy. The

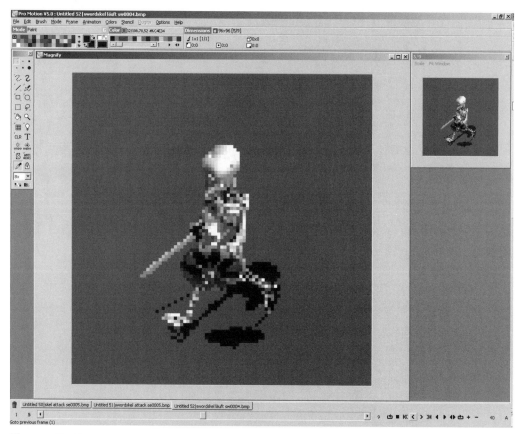

Figure 17.11
The attack animation for the Skeleton Knight character.

code that checks whether the player is facing an enemy is like the code that sets the player's animation sequence based on its direction. It is important that the player actually faces an enemy before you start to tally the attacks. Otherwise, it's possible to hit the enemy by just swinging a weapon anywhere in close proximity to him (using the earlier collision routine). The GetTargetDirection function will "point" a character from its current location toward a destination point. This is also useful for pitting NPCs against each other, not just for the player.

```
Private Function GetTargetDirection(ByVal current As Point, ByVal target As Point)
    Dim direction As Integer = 0

    If current.X < target.X Then
        'facing eastward
```

```
            If current.Y < target.Y - 8 Then
                direction = 3 'south east
            ElseIf current.Y > target.Y + 8 Then
                direction = 1 'north east
            Else
                direction = 2 'east
            End If

        ElseIf current.X > target.X Then
            'facing westward
            If current.Y < target.Y - 8 Then
                direction = 5 'south west
            ElseIf current.Y > target.Y + 8 Then
                direction = 7 'north west
            Else
                direction = 6 'west
            End If

        Else
            'facing NORTH or SOUTH
            If current.Y < target.Y - 8 Then
                direction = 0 'north
            ElseIf current.Y > target.Y + 8 Then
                direction = 4 'south
            End If
        End If

    Return direction
End Function
```

To actually cause characters to engage in melee combat, we have a new subroutine called FightWith, which accepts a single parameter representing the Person with whom the player character should fight.

```
Private Sub FightWith(ByRef peep As Person)
    Static attackDelay As Integer = 0
    Static text As String = ""
    Dim attack As Integer

    If text.Length > 0 Then
        engine.PrintLarge(200, 520, Color.Yellow, text, True)
    End If
```

```
'pause between attacks to slow down combat
If My.Computer.Clock.TickCount()> attackDelay + 1000 Then
    attackDelay = My.Computer.Clock.TickCount()

    'is player really attacking?
    If Player.state = ANIMSTATES.ATTACKING Then
        attack = Player.Attack + rand.Next(20)
        peep.health -= attack
        text = "HIT FOR " + attack.ToString + " DAMAGE!"

        If peep.health < 1 Then
            peep.state = ANIMSTATES.DYING
            text = "YOU ARE VICTORIOUS!"
        End If
    Else
        text = ""
    End If
End If
End Sub
```

Creating the PC and NPCs

After you have the combat code ready to go, there's just one little problem: The source code written in the game so far just draws the walking version of the player. With combat, the player has to swing his weapon too. The main game loop has to be modified so that you can check the player's state and then draw either the walking or the attacking animations based on what the player is doing. This is accomplished by removing the old `sprite` property from the old `PlayerType` structure. But, as it turns out, we will need the same sort of animations for all other characters as well, so it makes sense to combine the properties and merge `PlayerType` with `Person`. Here is the new merged `Person` structure.

```
Structure Person
    Dim name As String
    Dim CharClass As String
    Dim state As ANIMSTATES
    Dim alive As Boolean
    Dim Experience As Short
    Dim MaxHealth As Short
    Dim Health As Short
```

```
        Dim Level As Short
        Dim Gold As Integer
        Dim Attack As Integer
        Dim Defense As Integer
        Dim homepos As Point
        Dim curpos As Point
        Dim destpos As Point
        Dim direction As Integer
        Dim SpeedDelay As Integer
        Dim SpeedCount As Integer
        Dim attributes As Stats
        Dim animations() As CSprite
        Dim weapon As ItemType
        Dim armor As ItemType
        Dim ring As ItemType

        Public Sub New(ByVal name As String, ByVal charclass As String)
            Me.name = name
            Me.CharClass = charclass
        End Sub

End Structure
```

Likewise, the `CreatePlayer` subroutine has undergone some changes as well. Obviously, if we need three animations rather than just one, we'll have to load those sprite sheets and configure the sprite objects when the game starts up. This calls for some major additions to the `CreatePlayer` routine:

```
Public Sub CreatePlayer(ByVal classname As String)
    Const BASE As Short = 10
    Player.Name = "HERO"
    Player.CharClass = classname
    Player.MaxHealth = 100
    Player.Health = 100
    Player.Experience = 0
    Player.Level = 1
    Player.Gold = 100
    Player.Attack = (Player.weapon.attack + Player.attributes.STR)
    + Player.Level
    Player.Defense = (Player.armor.defend + Player.attributes.STA)
    + Player.Level
    Player.state = ANIMSTATES.WALKING
```

```
'init player animations
ReDim Player.animations(4)
Player.animations(ANIMSTATES.WALKING) = New CSprite(engine.Direct3D)
Player.animations(ANIMSTATES.ATTACKING) = New CSprite(engine.Direct3D)
Player.animations(ANIMSTATES.DYING) = New CSprite(engine.Direct3D)

Select Case classname
    Case "WARRIOR"
        Player.animations(ANIMSTATES.WALKING).Load("warrior_walk.png")
        Player.animations(ANIMSTATES.ATTACKING)
        .Load("warrior_attack.png")
        Player.animations(ANIMSTATES.DYING).Load("warrior_die.png")
        Player.attributes.STR = BASE + Warrior.STR
        Player.attributes.DEX = BASE + Warrior.DEX
        Player.attributes.STA = BASE + Warrior.STA
        Player.attributes.INT = BASE + Warrior.INT
        Player.attributes.CHA = BASE + Warrior.CHA
        Player.weapon = CreateItem("axe", 1)
        Player.armor = CreateItem("armor", 1)
        Player.ring = CreateItem("ring", 1)

    Case "PALADIN"
        Player.animations(ANIMSTATES.WALKING).Load("paladin_walk.png")
        Player.animations(ANIMSTATES.ATTACKING).Load("paladin_
        attack.png")
        Player.animations(ANIMSTATES.DYING).Load("paladin_die.png")
        Player.attributes.STR = BASE + Paladin.STR
        Player.attributes.DEX = BASE + Paladin.DEX
        Player.attributes.STA = BASE + Paladin.STA
        Player.attributes.INT = BASE + Paladin.INT
        Player.attributes.CHA = BASE + Paladin.CHA
        Player.weapon = CreateItem("sword", 1)
        Player.armor = CreateItem("armor", 1)
        Player.ring = CreateItem("ring", 1)

    Case "SCOUT"
        Player.animations(ANIMSTATES.WALKING).Load("scout_walk.png")
        Player.animations(ANIMSTATES.ATTACKING).Load("scout_
        attack.png")
        Player.animations(ANIMSTATES.DYING).Load("scout_die.png")
        Player.attributes.STR = BASE + Scout.STR
        Player.attributes.DEX = BASE + Scout.DEX
```

```
            Player.attributes.STA = BASE + Scout.STA
            Player.attributes.INT = BASE + Scout.INT
            Player.attributes.CHA = BASE + Scout.CHA
            Player.weapon = CreateItem("bow", 1)
            Player.armor = CreateItem("armor", 1)
            Player.ring = CreateItem("ring", 1)

        Case "WIZARD"
            Player.animations(ANIMSTATES.WALKING).Load("wizard_walk.png")
            Player.animations(ANIMSTATES.ATTACKING).Load("wizard_attack.png")
            Player.animations(ANIMSTATES.DYING).Load("wizard_die.png")
            Player.attributes.STR = BASE + Wizard.STR
            Player.attributes.DEX = BASE + Wizard.DEX
            Player.attributes.STA = BASE + Wizard.STA
            Player.attributes.INT = BASE + Wizard.INT
            Player.attributes.CHA = BASE + Wizard.CHA
            Player.weapon = CreateItem("staff", 1)
            Player.armor = CreateItem("armor", 1)
            Player.ring = CreateItem("ring", 1)
End Select

'load walk animation (64 frames)
Player.animations(ANIMSTATES.WALKING).FrameThreshold = 2
Player.animations(ANIMSTATES.WALKING).FrameWidth = 96
Player.animations(ANIMSTATES.WALKING).FrameHeight = 96
Player.animations(ANIMSTATES.WALKING).Columns = 8
Player.animations(ANIMSTATES.WALKING).StartFrame = 0
Player.animations(ANIMSTATES.WALKING).EndFrame = 7
Player.animations(ANIMSTATES.WALKING).X = (800 - 96) / 2
Player.animations(ANIMSTATES.WALKING).Y = (600 - 96) / 2

'load attack animation (80 frames)
Player.animations(ANIMSTATES.ATTACKING).FrameThreshold = 1
Player.animations(ANIMSTATES.ATTACKING).FrameWidth = 96
Player.animations(ANIMSTATES.ATTACKING).FrameHeight = 96
Player.animations(ANIMSTATES.ATTACKING).Columns = 10
Player.animations(ANIMSTATES.ATTACKING).StartFrame = 0
Player.animations(ANIMSTATES.ATTACKING).EndFrame = 9
Player.animations(ANIMSTATES.ATTACKING).X = (800 - 96) / 2
Player.animations(ANIMSTATES.ATTACKING).Y = (600 - 96) / 2

'load death animation (64 frames)
Player.animations(ANIMSTATES.DYING).FrameThreshold = 3
```

```
Player.animations(ANIMSTATES.DYING).FrameWidth = 96
Player.animations(ANIMSTATES.DYING).FrameHeight = 96
Player.animations(ANIMSTATES.DYING).Columns = 8
Player.animations(ANIMSTATES.DYING).StartFrame = 0
Player.animations(ANIMSTATES.DYING).EndFrame = 7
Player.animations(ANIMSTATES.DYING).X = (800 - 96) / 2
Player.animations(ANIMSTATES.DYING).Y = (600 - 96) / 2
End Sub
```

Likewise, we must modify the previously developed `LoadCharacters` sub-routine in order to load up the walk, attack, and die animations for NPCs. This gives us an opportunity to write custom routines for each type of character. Thus far, I've only included a single NPC into the game, the Viking warrior. Let's take a look at the `LoadCharacters` routine, followed by a helper routine, `CreateViking`.

```
Public Sub LoadCharacters()
    Dim start As Point
    Dim n As Long

    Persons = New Generic.LinkedList(Of Person)

    For n = 0 To 10
        'set starting location on world map
        start.X = engine.ScrollX + 400 + rand.Next(500)
        start.Y = engine.ScrollY + 300 + rand.Next(500)
        'create the new person
        CreateViking(start)
    Next n
End Sub


Public Sub CreateViking(ByVal start As Point)
    Dim viking As New Person("Viking", "person")
    viking.attributes = Warrior
    viking.state = ANIMSTATES.WALKING
    viking.homepos = start
    viking.curpos = start
    viking.destpos = start
    viking.direction = 0
    viking.Health = 100
    viking.alive = True

    ReDim viking.animations(4)
```

```
        'load walk sprite

        viking.animations(ANIMSTATES.WALKING) = New CSprite(engine.Direct3D)
        viking.animations(ANIMSTATES.WALKING).Load("viking_walk.png")
        viking.animations(ANIMSTATES.WALKING).Identifier = 800
        viking.animations(ANIMSTATES.WALKING).Columns = 8
        viking.animations(ANIMSTATES.WALKING).StartFrame = 0
        viking.animations(ANIMSTATES.WALKING).EndFrame = 7
        viking.animations(ANIMSTATES.WALKING).FrameThreshold = 3
        viking.animations(ANIMSTATES.WALKING).FrameSize = New Point(96, 96)

        'load attack sprite
        viking.animations(ANIMSTATES.ATTACKING) = New CSprite(engine.Direct3D)
        viking.animations(ANIMSTATES.ATTACKING).Load("viking_attack.png")
        viking.animations(ANIMSTATES.ATTACKING).Identifier = 800
        viking.animations(ANIMSTATES.ATTACKING).Columns = 10
        viking.animations(ANIMSTATES.ATTACKING).StartFrame = 0
        viking.animations(ANIMSTATES.ATTACKING).EndFrame = 9
        viking.animations(ANIMSTATES.ATTACKING).FrameThreshold = 2
        viking.animations(ANIMSTATES.ATTACKING).FrameSize = New Point(96, 96)

        'load die sprite
        viking.animations(ANIMSTATES.DYING) = New CSprite(engine.Direct3D)
        viking.animations(ANIMSTATES.DYING).Load("viking_die.png")
        viking.animations(ANIMSTATES.DYING).Identifier = 800
        viking.animations(ANIMSTATES.DYING).Columns = 10
        viking.animations(ANIMSTATES.DYING).StartFrame = 0
        viking.animations(ANIMSTATES.DYING).EndFrame = 9
        viking.animations(ANIMSTATES.DYING).FrameThreshold = 2
        viking.animations(ANIMSTATES.DYING).FrameSize = New Point(96, 96)

        Persons.AddLast(viking)
    End Sub
```

Moving the State-Based NPC

With all of these different states to handle walking, attacking, and dying, the code that moves and draws the NPCs has to be modified to take them into account. Here is the current MovePerson subroutine, which is called by the main game loop:

```
Private Sub MovePerson(ByRef peep As Person)
    'start character walking to a new location
```

```
If peep.curpos = peep.destpos Then
        peep.destpos.X = peep.homepos.X + rand.Next(1000) - 500
        peep.destpos.Y = peep.homepos.Y + rand.Next(1000) - 500
    End If

    peep.direction = GetTargetDirection(peep.curpos, peep.destpos)
    Select Case peep.direction
        Case 0
            peep.curpos.Y -= 1
        Case 1
            peep.curpos.X += 1
            peep.curpos.Y -= 1
        Case 2
            peep.curpos.X += 1
        Case 3
            peep.curpos.X += 1
            peep.curpos.Y += 1
        Case 4
            peep.curpos.Y += 1
        Case 5
            peep.curpos.X -= 1
            peep.curpos.Y += 1
        Case 6
            peep.curpos.X -= 1
        Case 7
            peep.curpos.X -= 1
            peep.curpos.Y -= 1
    End Select
End Sub
```

Drawing the State-Based NPC

In addition to moving the NPCs differently based on state, the drawing code also has to take into account the character's state. Different sequences for the walking and attacking animations have to be accounted for in the draw routine. This is where the dying sequence takes place as well. We animate NPCs with the AnimatePerson routine and draw characters with DrawCharacters.

```
Private Sub AnimatePerson(ByRef peep As Person)
    Dim columns As Integer = peep.animations(peep.state).Columns
    peep.animations(peep.state).StartFrame = peep.direction * columns
    peep.animations(peep.state).EndFrame = peep.animations(peep.state)
    .StartFrame + 7
```

```
        peep.animations(peep.state).Animate()
End Sub

Public Sub DrawCharacters(ByVal location As Point)
    Dim pos As Point
    Dim peep As Person

    Dim screenArea As New Rectangle( _
            location.X - 200, location.Y - 200, 800 + 400, 600 + 400)

    For Each peep In Persons
        If peep.alive Then
            'is this scenery object near the player?
            pos.X = peep.curpos.X + 48
            pos.Y = peep.curpos.Y + 48

            If screenArea.Contains(pos.X, pos.Y) Then
                pos.X = peep.curpos.X - location.X
                pos.Y = peep.curpos.Y - location.Y
                peep.animations(peep.state).DrawFrame(pos)
            End If
        End If
    Next
End Sub
```

Making the Game Modular

The Celtic Crusader game is now becoming rather large and complex. When you think about how far we've come and how simple the game started out, it's pretty amazing how big it is now. At this point, it is important to make the game more modular and expandable. Switching the NPCs and PC to a state-driven model rather than procedural was a big help. Otherwise, it can be daunting to maintain the complexity of many animation sequences simultaneously in memory, along with tracking what the player is doing and so on. You can now add a new animation to characters by adding a new entry to ANIMSTATES and then loading the additional sprite sheet, and the game engine will accommodate the new animation, simple as that! The project is available on the CD-ROM, and should be opened and examined, because the code presented here is not presented in its entirety—only the key routines are provided while explaining how melee combat works in the game.

Level Up

This chapter filled in the most important aspect of the game thus far. A combat system is essential to a good RPG, but your list of core techniques were not up to the challenge until this point in the book. Now that you have a rudimentary combat system available, there is no limit to what you can do with this game engine. You have come so far since the first few chapters on building the tile-based scroller! It's incredible that things have progressed so much; it feels like ancient history. You are now working with high-level concepts that brought the game to life! I've been running the game in full-screen mode, and it looks fantastic. This is entirely due to the high-quality artwork made available by Reiner's Tilesets, and I take no credit for the artwork (although properly *using* it is no simple feat, as you have seen so far).

Epilogue

This also concludes the Celtic Crusader project and the book itself. I must say, I thoroughly enjoyed working on the game while writing this book, and I sincerely hope you will enjoy continuing what I have started here. This game is *not* meant to be a complete, playable, polished game. It's a *book game,* after all! But you do have a robust and customizable RPG engine, a huge game world, and some awesome artwork with which to build *your* vision for the ultimate RPG. Feel free to give it an entirely new name and even replace the game world with one of your own design. (The Ireland map is so huge that maybe you will want to cut it down in size to speed up load times.) I am eager to see what you will come up with on your own. After you have completed your first RPG, please stop by my site for a visit and share some screenshots of your own RPG with others. My website is at www.jharbour.com, and the forum is at www.jharbour.com/forum. I look forward to hearing from you.

INDEX

You're a teen with a great imagination...

Written specifically for teens in a language you understand, on topics you're interested in! Each book in the *For Teens* series features step-by-step instructions to help you conquer the tools and techniques presented. Hands-on projects help you put your new skills into action. And the accompanying CD-ROM or web downloads provide tutorials, instructional videos, software programs, and more!

...unleash your creativity with the  series!!

Game Programming for Teens
Second Edition
ISBN: 1-59200-834-8 ■ $29.99

Digital Filmmaking for Teens
ISBN: 1-59200-603-5 ■ $24.99

3D Game Programming for Teens
ISBN: 1-59200-900-X ■ $29.99

Digital Music Making for Teens
ISBN: 1-59200-508-X ■ $24.99

**Digital Photography
for Teens**
ISBN: 1-59863-295-7 ■ $34.99

Web Design for Teens
ISBN: 1-59200-607-8 ■ $19.99

**Adobe Photoshop and
Photoshop Elements for Teens**
ISBN: 1-59863-379-1 ■ $34.99

Game Art for Teens
Second Edition
ISBN: 1-59200-959-X ■ $34.99

COMING SOON!

**Microsoft Visual Basic
Game Programming for Teens, 2E**
ISBN: 1-59863-390-2 ■ $29.99 ■ October 2007

Computer Programming for Teens
ISBN: 1-59863-446-1 ■ $29.99 ■ December 2007

Torque for Teens
ISBN: 1-59863-409-7 ■ $29.99 ■ December 2007

Web Comics for Teens
ISBN: 1-59863-467-4 ■ $29.99 ■ December 2007

THOMSON

License Agreement/Notice of Limited Warranty

By opening the sealed disc container in this book, you agree to the following terms and conditions. If, upon reading the following license agreement and notice of limited warranty, you cannot agree to the terms and conditions set forth, return the unused book with unopened disc to the place where you purchased it for a refund.

License

The enclosed software is copyrighted by the copyright holder(s) indicated on the software disc. You are licensed to copy the software onto a single computer for use by a single user and to a backup disc. You may not reproduce, make copies, or distribute copies or rent or lease the software in whole or in part, except with written permission of the copyright holder(s). You may transfer the enclosed disc only together with this license, and only if you destroy all other copies of the software and the transferee agrees to the terms of the license. You may not decompile, reverse assemble, or reverse engineer the software.

Notice of Limited Warranty

The enclosed disc is warranted by Thomson Course Technology PTR to be free of physical defects in materials and workmanship for a period of sixty (60) days from end user's purchase of the book/disc combination. During the sixty-day term of the limited warranty, Thomson Course Technology PTR will provide a replacement disc upon the return of a defective disc.

Limited Liability

THE SOLE REMEDY FOR BREACH OF THIS LIMITED WARRANTY SHALL CONSIST ENTIRELY OF REPLACEMENT OF THE DEFECTIVE DISC. IN NO EVENT SHALL THOMSON COURSE TECHNOLOGY PTR OR THE AUTHOR BE LIABLE FOR ANY OTHER DAMAGES, INCLUDING LOSS OR CORRUPTION OF DATA, CHANGES IN THE FUNCTIONAL CHARACTERISTICS OF THE HARDWARE OR OPERATING SYSTEM, DELETERIOUS INTERACTION WITH OTHER SOFTWARE, OR ANY OTHER SPECIAL, INCIDENTAL, OR CONSEQUENTIAL DAMAGES THAT MAY ARISE, EVEN IF THOMSON COURSE TECHNOLOGY PTR AND/OR THE AUTHOR HAS PREVIOUSLY BEEN NOTIFIED THAT THE POSSIBILITY OF SUCH DAMAGES EXISTS.

Disclaimer of Warranties

THOMSON COURSE TECHNOLOGY PTR AND THE AUTHOR SPECIFICALLY DISCLAIM ANY AND ALL OTHER WARRANTIES, EITHER EXPRESS OR IMPLIED, INCLUDING WARRANTIES OF MERCHANTABILITY, SUITABILITY TO A PARTICULAR TASK OR PURPOSE, OR FREEDOM FROM ERRORS. SOME STATES DO NOT ALLOW FOR EXCLUSION OF IMPLIED WARRANTIES OR LIMITATION OF INCIDENTAL OR CONSEQUENTIAL DAMAGES, SO THESE LIMITATIONS MIGHT NOT APPLY TO YOU.

Other

This Agreement is governed by the laws of the State of Massachusetts without regard to choice of law principles. The United Convention of Contracts for the International Sale of Goods is specifically disclaimed. This Agreement constitutes the entire agreement between you and Thomson Course Technology PTR regarding use of the software.